THE COMPLETE
GEOFFR]

What are the contexts of The Canterbury Tales*?*

What can we learn about texts, editing and the role of the audience through the study of Chaucer?

So many questions surround the key figures in the English literary canon, but most books focus on one aspect of an author's life or work, or limit themselves to a single critical approach. *The Complete Critical Guide to Geoffrey Chaucer* is part of a unique series of comprehensive, user-friendly introductions which:

- offer basic information on an author's life, contexts and works
- outline the major critical issues surrounding the author's works, from the time they were written to the present
- leave judgements up to you, by explaining the full range of often very different critical views and interpretations
- offer guides to further reading in each area discussed.

This series has a broad focus but one very clear aim: to equip you with *all* the knowledge you need to make your own new readings of crucial literary texts.

'This book is ideal for students beginning the study of Chaucer. It covers all the important information and offers valuable guidance, while prompting further thought and providing jumping-off points for this.'
Jocelyn Wogan-Browne, *Fordham University, USA*

'Remarkably successful as an introduction to Chaucer for new readers of any age.'
Derek Pearsall, *formerly of Harvard University, USA and York University, UK*

Gillian Rudd is a Lecturer in English at the University of Liverpool. She is the author of *Managing Language in 'Piers Plowman'* (1992) and of numerous articles on medieval literature.

THE COMPLETE CRITICAL GUIDE TO
ENGLISH LITERATURE

Series Editors
RICHARD BRADFORD AND JAN JEDRZEJEWSKI

Also available in this series:

The Complete Critical Guide to Samuel Beckett
David Pattie
The Complete Critical Guide to John Milton
Richard Bradford
The Complete Critical Guide to Alexander Pope
Paul Baines

Forthcoming:

The Complete Critical Guide to Robert Browning
The Complete Critical Guide to Charles Dickens
The Complete Critical Guide to Ben Jonson
The Complete Critical Guide to D. H. Lawrence
The Complete Critical Guide to William Wordsworth

Visit the website of *The Complete Critical Guide to English Literature*
for further information and an updated list of titles
www.literature.routledge.com/criticalguides

THE COMPLETE CRITICAL GUIDE TO
GEOFFREY CHAUCER

Gillian Rudd

London and New York

First published 2001
by Routledge
11 New Fetter Lane, London EC4P 4EE

Simultaneously published in the USA and Canada
by Routledge
29 West 35th Street, New York, NY 10001

Routledge is an imprint of the Taylor & Francis Group

Typeset in Schneidler by
HWA Text and Data Management, Tunbridge Wells
Printed and bound in Great Britain by
TJ International Ltd, Padstow, Cornwall

British Library Cataloguing in Publication Data
A catalogue record for this book is available from the British Library

Library of Congress Cataloging in Publication Data
A catalog record for this book has been applied for

ISBN 0–415–20241–8 (hbk)
ISBN 0–415–20242–6 (pbk)

CONTENTS

Series editors' preface   ix
Acknowledgements   xi
Abbreviations and referencing   xiii

Introduction   1

Part I   LIFE AND CONTEXTS   3
(a)   Chaucer's biography   5
      (i)   Establishing dates   5
      (ii)   Family background and early years   7
      (iii)   Education   8
      (iv)   The Ulster household   10
      (v)   Royal service and connections with John of Gaunt   13
      (vi)   Travels to Italy   15
      (vii)   The case of Cecily Champaign   17
      (viii) Controller of Customs and the London years   18
      (ix)   The Peasants' Revolt and the move to Kent   21
      (x)   Time in Kent   22
      (xi)   Clerk of the King's Works   23
      (xii)   The return to London: the last years   26
(b)   Social, literary and historical contexts   29
      (i)   War and chivalry   29
      (ii)   Chivalry   30
      (iii)   Courtly love and marriage   32
      (iv)   Marriage and remarriage   33
      (v)   Death, plague and revolt   34
      (vi)   Church as institution   35
      (vii)   Religion and philosophy   37
      (viii) Literary contexts   39

CONTENTS

Part II		WORK	45
(a)		Short verse	47
	(i)	Three early short poems	48
	(ii)	Other complaints	51
	(iii)	Boethian ballades and envoys	55
(b)		The dream poems	61
	(i)	*The Romaunt of the Rose*	62
	(ii)	*The Book of the Duchess*	65
	(iii)	*The House of Fame*	71
	(iv)	*The Parliament of Fowls*	77
	(v)	Prologue to *The Legend of Good Women*	81
(c)		Non-fiction prose	83
	(i)	*Boece*	83
	(ii)	*A Treatise on the Astrolabe*	86
	(iii)	*The Equatorie of Planetis*	88
(d)		*Troilus and Criseyde*	89
(e)		Collections of Tales: *The Legend of Good Women*	100
	(i)	*The Legend of Good Women*	102
	(ii)	The pretext for writing the *Legend*	102
(f)		Collections of Tales: *The Canterbury Tales*	106
	(i)	The 'whole' collection: manuscripts, texts and dates	106
	(ii)	The General Prologue	107
	(iii)	The Knight's Tale	110
	(iv)	The Miller's Tale	113
	(v)	The Reeve's Tale	115
	(vi)	The Cook's Tale	117
	(vii)	The Man of Law's Tale	118
	(viii)	The Wife of Bath's Prologue and Tale	120
	(ix)	The Friar's Tale	123
	(x)	The Summoner's Tale	125
	(xi)	The Clerk's Tale	126
	(xii)	The Merchant's Tale	128
	(xiii)	The Squire's Tale	129
	(xiv)	The Franklin's Tale	130
	(xv)	The Physician's Tale	132
	(xvi)	The Pardoner's Tale	133
	(xvii)	The Shipman's Tale	135
	(xviii)	The Prioress's Tale	136
	(xix)	The Tales of *Sir Thopas* and *Melibee*	138
	(xx)	The Monk's Tale	140
	(xxi)	The Nun's Priest's Tale	141

CONTENTS

(xxii) The Second Nun's Tale 142

(xxiii) The Canon's Yeoman's Tale 144

(xxiv) The Manciple's Tale 146

(xxv) The Parson's Tale 148

(xxvi) The Retraction 149

Part III   CRITICISM 151

(a) Biography 156

(b) Text, manuscripts, editing 157

(c) Chaucer's language 161

(d) Sources, literary background, rhetoric and poetics 162

(e) Narrators, irony and satire 165

(f) Historicism, old and new 169

(g) Politics and ideology 172

(h) Feminism and gender 174

(i) Imitation, modernisation, allusion 179

Chronology 183

Bibliography 187

Index 197

SERIES EDITORS' PREFACE

The Complete Critical Guide to English Literature is a ground-breaking collection of one-volume introductions to the work of the major writers in the English literary canon. Each volume in the series offers the reader a comprehensive account of the featured author's life, of his or her writing and of the ways in which his or her works have been interpreted by literary critics. The series is both explanatory and stimulating; it reflects the achievements of state-of-the-art literary-historical research and yet manages to be intellectually accessible for the reader who may be encountering a canonical author's work for the first time. It will be useful for students and teachers of literature at all levels, as well as for the general reader; each book can be read through, or consulted in a companion-style fashion.

The aim of *The Complete Critical Guide to English Literature* is to adopt an approach that is as factual, objective and non-partisan as possible, in order to provide the 'full picture' for readers and allow them to form their own judgements. At the same time, however, the books engage the reader in a discussion of the most demanding questions involved in each author's life and work. Did Pope's physical condition affect his treatment of matters of gender and sexuality? Does a feminist reading of *Middlemarch* enlighten us regarding the book's presentation of nineteenth-century British society? Do we deconstruct Beckett's work, or does he do so himself? Contributors to this series address such crucial questions, offer potential solutions and recommend further reading for independent study. In doing so, they equip the reader for an informed and confident examination of the life and work of key canonical figures and of the critical controversies surrounding them.

The aims of the series are reflected in the structure of the books. Part I, 'Life and Contexts', offers a compact biography of the featured author against the background of his or her epoch. In Part II, 'Work', the focus is on the author's most important works, discussed from a non-partisan, literary-historical perspective; the section provides an account of the works, reflecting a consensus of critical opinion on them, and indicating, where appropriate, areas of controversy. These and other issues are taken up again in Part III, 'Criticism', which offers an account of the critical responses generated by the author's work. Contemporaneous reviews and debates are considered, along with opinions inspired by more recent theoretical approaches, such as New Criticism, feminism, Marxism, psychoanalytic criticism, deconstruction and New Historicism.

The volumes in this series will together constitute a comprehensive reference work offering an up-to-date, user-friendly and reliable account of the heritage of English literature from the Middle Ages to the twentieth century. We hope that *The Complete Critical Guide to English Literature* will become for its readers, academic and non-academic alike, an indispensable source of information and inspiration.

RICHARD BRADFORD
JAN JEDRZEJEWSKI

ACKNOWLEDGEMENTS

I would like to thank the Houghton Mifflin Company for permission to use extracts from the following material:

Benson, Larry D. (General Editor), *The Riverside Chaucer*, Third Edition. Copyright © 1987 by Houghton Mifflin Company. Reprinted with permission.

Any work of this kind naturally owes a great debt of gratitude to all the critics and scholars mentioned in its pages and cheerfully quarried for information and debate. However I am aware of particular debt to the two excellent critical biographies of Chaucer by Derek Brewer and Derek Pearsall, which have frequently provided me with clues while writing this Guide: 'I n'am but a lewed compilator'.

Liz Thompson at Routledge and the series editors, Jan Jedrzejewski and Richard Bradford, have offered much appreciated, helpful comments. Val Gough gallantly read the complete manuscript: I am grateful for her generosity as well as her sharp eye. Needless to say, all remaining errors are my own.

To friends, family and colleagues whose patience I have tried and 'stedfastnesse' proved, I can offer only my heartfelt thanks.

ABBREVIATIONS AND REFERENCING

Throughout the text, references to Chaucer's works are from *The Riverside Chaucer*, general editor Larry Benson (Oxford: Oxford University Press 1998), abbreviated as *Riverside*. Individual works are abbreviated as follows:

Duchess: *The Book of the Duchess*
House: *The House of Fame*
Legend: *The Legend of Good Women*
Parliament: *The Parliament of Fowls*
Tales: *The Canterbury Tales*
Troilus   *Troilus and Criseyde*

References are to fragment and line numbers for *The Canterbury Tales* and line numbers for all other texts.

For all other references, the Harvard system is used; full details of items cited can be found in the bibliography.

Cross-referencing between sections is one of the features of this series. Such references are to relevant page numbers and appear in bold type and square brackets, e.g. **[37]**.

INTRODUCTION

Described by Dryden in 1700 as 'the Father of English poetry', Chaucer's position as presiding genius of English literature has remained remarkably intact throughout the six hundred years since his death in 1400. To us he is primarily the author of *The Canterbury Tales*, praised for his variety of tone, his irony, his ability to sketch character and caricature and also, as we get to know more of him, for his fascination with books, with the origins and telling of stories and for his intellectual range. Historical records present a very different figure: a page and courtier; a civil servant and collector of taxes who travelled abroad on undisclosed royal business; a man accused of rape and frequently summoned for debt, who lived in London and Kent, was buried in Westminster Abbey and later moved to become the first poet in 'Poet's Corner'. He lived in the turbulent times of the Hundred Years War with France and the beginnings of the Wars of the Roses, the Peasants' Revolt and the Black Death, yet little of this surfaces in his writing. To his contemporaries, he was an acclaimed translator, writer of lyrics and philosopher. This volume seeks to give some impression of all these aspects, while yet retaining a focus on his writings.

Part I is divided into a biography of Chaucer, with some discussion of the different Chaucers biographers have created over the years, and an overview of his literary and social contexts, which also serves as a brief introduction to late medieval England. Part II concentrates on his writing, covering every text currently believed to have been authored by Chaucer. As far as possible, they are treated chronologically, with fresh readings and suggested thematic links between texts. Some of these themes are then elaborated in Part III, which surveys Chaucer criticism, taking account of his place in linguisitic as well as literary study. Many areas which are currently commanding general attention have been debated for some time by Chaucer scholars: issues of the presentation of text, editing and the role of the audience are central to Chaucer study, and are enjoying new currency as our understanding of what constitutes a text is altered by the increasing use of electronic media in a change as radical as that from manuscript to print culture. Attitudes towards literary tradition are also pertinent, and Chaucer's standing as an icon for Englishness is touched upon. Other questions more specific to Chaucer are discussed in the light of modern criticism: are we content to praise Chaucer's presentation of women? What light does New Historicism shed on his portrayal of fourteenth-century society, or our creation of it?

In all, this volume provides a manageable and readable discussion of what we know of Chaucer and reactions to his works, offering both straightforward information and range of opinion on a many-faceted, familiar, yet strangely elusive figure. For six hundred years Chaucer has provided enjoyment, laughter, conundrum and food for thought, which all contribute to his hold on the English literary imagination. This Guide aims to be part of that continuing process.

PART I

LIFE AND CONTEXTS

(a) CHAUCER'S BIOGRAPHY

(i) Establishing dates

When beginning a biographical sketch it would be pleasant to be able to start with the simple fact of the year of birth. Alas, establishing such a date in the case of Geoffrey Chaucer is no easy matter. Writing in 1803 William Godwin begins his 'dissertation upon the Period of the Birth of Chaucer' with the statement that 'the dates assigned to the birth and death of Chaucer ... have never been questioned or disturbed' (Godwin 1803: xxi). He continues, 'it is undoubtedly pleasing, in a subject which in many particulars is involved in obscurity, to be able to seize some points which are free from the shadow of doubt.' The tone of certainty introduces what was the first suggestion that the hitherto received date for Chaucer's birth of 1328 was in fact open to question. The trouble arose from a disposition made by Chaucer on 15th October 1386 in which he is described as 'Geffray Chaucere esquier del age de xl ans et plus armeez par xxvii ans' (Crow 1966: 370). As Godwin realised, regarding 58 as forty years and more, while technically correct, nevertheless admits the possibility of a rather later date of birth. Despite this admission, and despite his own acknowledgement that the phrase 'forty years and more' was often (though not inevitably, see Pearsall 1992: 315n1) used as a formula to indicate that the witness was of respectable years and could be regarded as reliable, Godwin himself did not relinquish 'the old chronology' as he terms it (Godwin 1803: xxvii) preferring to retain the erroneous 1328 as the best guess.

That date of 1328 itself is something of an invention, having emerged, it seems, from Thomas Speght's estimation of Chaucer being born 'about the second or third yeer of Edward 3', in his 1598 'Chaucer's Life' which prefaced his edition of Chaucer's works. The vague 'about' was transmuted into the misleadingly precise date of 1328 by John Urry in his edition of Chaucer's work of 1721 (see Crow 1966: 370) and was cited with little hesitation until Godwin himself hesitated over it. However, in the end Godwin charmingly disposes of the discrepancy of some fourteen to eighteen years, implied by the disparity between being born in 1328 and being forty in 1386, through reference to common human failings:

> Chaucer, with all his wonderful endowments, was a man; and it is incident to perhaps one half of mankind, particularly of that part

of our species who are accustomed to associate with the opulent and refined, when advanced beyond the middle period of human life, to be willing to be thought younger than they are.

(Godwin 1803: xxxv)

Appealing as such an explanation is, and much as it concurs with my own impression of Chaucer as a man who did not lightly underestimate himself or his talents, nevertheless, we must exonerate him of this particular foible. Evidence not available to Godwin (legal proceedings concerning the abduction of John Chaucer, Geoffrey's father, declare John to have been unmarried in 1328. See Crow 1966: 3, 8, 370–4) results in the current, if less definite, supposition that Geoffrey Chaucer is likely to have been born in London in the early 1340s. As Derek Pearsall puts it, 'it is wise not to be too specific about matters where there can be no certainty' (Pearsall 1992: 11), however much we may desire it.

Tracing this long debate about Chaucer's birth date, with its asides on the type of person Chaucer is deemed to have been, serves to highlight the way biography is a form of criticism in itself **[156]**.

When it comes to the date of Chaucer's death, things are more certain. Thanks to records of the annuities he was drawing and his standing as an acclaimed poet, courtier and public figure, his death merits a more precise date. We know that he died towards the end of 1400 and here there is less hesitation about taking the word of tradition and accepting the date of 25 October. This precision bestows a slightly spurious degree of certainty. The source of this date is a sixteenth-century inscription on Chaucer's tomb in Westminster Abbey. The inscription itself is now illegible, and the tomb on which it was inscribed was erected in 1556 by Nicholas Brigham, who replaced the previous, original, tomb. There is thus no extant positive evidence of a precise date being inscribed on the original tomb, nor do we have any other evidence which provides the 25 October date, such as a will or contemporary record of Chaucer's death. However, it does not do to be over-suspicious; the traditional date accords with what other evidence there is: the last recorded payment to Chaucer was made on 5 June 1400 and the lease on the last house he occupied passed to a Master Paul some time between 28 September 1400 and 28 September 1401. Thus there are no obvious grounds to dispute the usually quoted date of death as 25 October 1400, giving a life-span of some 55 or 60 years, which is a fair average for someone of his status in the fourteenth century.

(ii) Family background and early years

In a time of general social mobility, Chaucer did his fair share of climbing and certainly more than his fair share of travelling. It is therefore tempting to see him as an example of someone rising by force of merit from lowly origins to a position of high regard: a symbol of the rising middle classes of which we hear so much in the later middle ages. However, this is far from the case. John Chaucer, Geoffrey's father, was a vintner and merchant of London who served in military campaigns in 1327 and 1329 and was deputy butler to John de Wesenham (the king's chief butler) from 1347–49, during which time he was also responsible for collecting the custom on cloth exported from five ports. He was a man of means having inherited several properties as a result of deaths in the family, probably due to the Black Death of 1349. He himself died in 1366, leaving a widow and, as far as we can tell, his only son, Geoffrey. It is likely that Geoffrey was the only child, despite one document of 1619 which refers to a Katherine Manning as Chaucer's sister (there are no fourteenth-century references to any siblings). Chaucer's fame over the intervening two and a half centuries may well have led to him being ascribed a sister on no other evidence than a shared surname and some known dealings with the Manning family. Chaucer's mother, Agnes, was likewise a person of means. She was the daughter of John de Copton, whose brother, Hamo, owned various properties which Agnes inherited in 1349. It is, as they say, an ill wind which blows nobody good, and the plague of 1349 seems to have been responsible for making Chaucer the son of a rather wealthy house before he was ten years old and sole recipient of the advantages the Chaucer parents had to bestow. These included connections to well-established families and an immediate background in a well-regarded, even prestigious, trade and a tradition of valued royal service. Moreover, as both parents survived until he was well into adulthood, he had the advantage of an unusually secure and settled childhood to speed him on his way to a remarkable life.

Before 1357 we have no documentary references to Geoffrey Chaucer, so our impressions of his early years must be based on surmise and the knowledge we have of what contemporary families in similar situations did. It is likely that he spent his early years in his parents' London house, 177 Upper Thames Street in the St. Martin parish of the Vintry ward of the city. As its name implies, this was an area frequented by native and foreign merchants, particularly wine merchants (vintners) and one in which many of them lived. In his boyhood Chaucer would thus have been accustomed to seeing and

7

hearing people from the many countries who traded with England at this time, and he may even have picked up some knowledge of their languages, such as Italian. The London of the fourteenth century was a comparatively small city for a European trading and banking centre, though certainly the largest in England, with a population of around 50,000. Most of these people lived within the walled city, which occupied roughly a square mile of largely unpaved streets, containing churches, religious houses, hospitals, colleges, schools, taverns and also sudden spacious gardens, large public buildings and splendid town houses, as well as the many more crowded and decidedly less splendid dwellings of the less affluent and poor. It was a thriving and busy environment and one in which Chaucer's various biographers have loved to picture him, speculating happily on the basis of very little **[156]**.

(iii) Education

A fine example of this habit of creating a background and childhood for Chaucer to fit one's own vision of the poet is provided by F. J. Furnivall, who describes Chaucer in his preface to his *Life Records of Chaucer* in 1900 as

> a natty, handy lad, but full of quiet fun – messing, I dare say, in Walbrook, ... At school – St. Paul's perchance – sharing in all the games and larks that Fitzstephen so well describes some 200 years before ... well up in his classes, I'll be bound.
>
> (Furnivall 1900: vii)

In actual fact, we have no evidence that Chaucer went to school, though various of his biographers, such as D. S. Brewer, have been keen to send him (see Brewer 1998: 14–17) and there is a reasonable likelihood that he went: the Vintry ward of London was well placed for schools, the prestigious St. Paul's, with its good library, amongst them. It is usually there that he is sent and often presumed to have been a quick pupil. Even if he did not attend a school, knowledge of what they taught and of the kinds of thing children in the fourteenth century were likely to have been taught at home, gives us a fair idea of the kind of initial education Chaucer would have received.

To begin with, not long after learning to speak he would have been taught his prayers in English and the alphabet from horn books. He may well have then learnt to read, to write, quite probably to count, and may have been introduced to Latin. Equipped with such basics, it is possible he then went to a song-school of the kind mentioned in The Prioress's Tale (*Tales*, 495–529), there was one close at hand, attached to St. Paul's, but it is equally likely that he simply received his education at home, from his parents or (unlikely, but still possible) from a tutor. Or, indeed, he may have gone to a grammar school at about the age of seven. By now he would be embarking upon acquiring a ready knowledge of Latin. Boys who went to school were not only trained in reading and writing Latin, but also in speaking it fluently. For Latin was not only the language of the church, but also of much legal work, of trade and general exchange across Europe. Texts on science, philosophy and medicine were written in Latin and to have an ease with the language and knowledge of at least extracts of its literature was still very much the sign of an educated person.

We must be careful not to over-estimate the level of knowledge of Latin texts. School books used extracts from Aesop's Fables, Ovid, Virgil and Claudian amongst others, and collections of such extracts were compiled and would have been relatively readily available for reading in libraries held by schools, if not individually owned. Therefore, the kind of reading open to someone of Chaucer's background would have relied on collections and the chance of what came his way. We must not, for example, take a reference to Ovid as an indication that an author had read, still less had constant access to, all of the *Metamorphosis*. In these days of cheap paperbacks, it is hard to imagine what it would have been like when books were copied by hand, were hence expensive and therefore scarce. A collection of twenty volumes would have counted as a sizeable library. On the other hand, the common use of books of extracts and the necessary habit of memorising lessons, meant that there was a large body of shared literature, to which writers such as Chaucer could refer with the knowledge that the authors and even extracts named would be familiar to their audience.

Latin was thus the principle subject taught at grammar schools, in a course which concentrated almost entirely on its linguistic and literary aspects. Correct spelling, syntax, pronunciation and constructions were the main goal, though one might speculate on how much the subject-matter of the texts thus studied might seep into the pupil's imagination. There is little evidence that mathematics formed any part of this curriculum; the thorough study of this subject was the province of a university education. However, here again we encounter the bias of Chaucer's biographers who rightly point out that, given his use of numerology and astronomy in his writings, he must have learnt mathematics at some point. It is also worth bearing in mind that while arithmetic was a new subject at the time, the people most likely to have a use for it were the very merchants and traders to whom Chaucer's family belonged. It is by no means ridiculous to believe that he acquired at least the basics of these subjects while still fairly young. As William Courtnay points out

> Learning was not required or enforced by the state or society but was incumbent only upon those who desired a career for which it was a pre-requisite or an advantage. By the fourteenth century most occupations apart from agriculture benefited from literacy, but few required advanced degrees. Education in the late Middle Ages was still, therefore, an opportunity, not an obligation.
>
> (Courtnay 1987: 14)

As the son of a wealthy merchant house with court connections, it is clear that in some way or another Chaucer would have been equipped with the necessary education for a life of civil and court service.

Somewhere in this education French would have figured, perhaps not formally, but certainly importantly. As well as being the language of the court, it was used for some legal and state documents and was certainly widely spoken in affluent homes. Italian was a good deal less central, but it is clear that Chaucer knew the language in the late 1370s, before he was sent to Lombardy, and it seems most likely that he acquired this knowledge while in London. How early he began to learn Italian, or how fluent he became, it is impossible to know. His writings make it clear that he was well versed in the increasingly important Italian authors of his time (Dante, Petrarch and Boccaccio were influences on and sources for his work) though it seems that, as with his Latin reading, he was happy to use a French crib when one was available. How far such cribs served for comparison or for initial comprehension is, like so much else, open to speculation.

What we do know for certain is that in 1357 he was a member of the court of Elizabeth, Countess of Ulster and wife of Lionel, son of the king, Edward III.

(iv) The Ulster household

The earliest record we have for Chaucer is contained in a fragment of household accounts for Elizabeth, Countess of Ulster, which was discovered unexpectedly in the binding for another book. Such are the chances that characterise historical research. This document deals with expenses for the period July 1356 to January 1359 and here, in 1357, we find one Galfredus Chaucer (since the accounts are in Latin, the names are Latinised) being given 4 shillings for a paltok (short cloak) and 3 shillings for a pair of black and red hose and a pair of shoes. This provided him with clothing appropriate for a page. Later in the same year expenses are incurred in ensuring he has 'garniture' for the Sunday before Pentecost and for his necessary preparations for the feast of the Nativity. From these records it is generally assumed that Chaucer was a page (though the term is not specifically applied to him in the documents) and as such was a member of Elizabeth's separate household which would have travelled with her round the country. Pages ranged in age from 10 to 17 and were in effect servants and personal assistants, sometimes given specific responsibilities. They were given board, lodging and clothing, but relied on their own family for cash. In return for their service they were educated in the ways of polite society and given the chance to establish links with the influential of the land and prove themselves useful and capable. It is possible that household clerks, who would be educated men in minor orders, were assigned to teach the pages, but even without such formal teaching there would be the opportunity to learn from the household and its visitors. Pages could improve their Latin and French, which were still the languages of polite and formal exchange at court, with English probably reserved for more relaxed moments. There would also be the chance of hearing or reading the literature of the moment: the French allegorical poems and romances, the books of religious instruction and debate, perhaps even the new works from Italy, written, remarkably, in the Italian vernacular, amongst which the name of Dante might have figured. With all this going on it is possible that a page from a good family, furnished with the basics, could acquire a wide education while in service. Inevitably the experience would also include composing verse and music: the fact that no texts that we can call Chaucer juvenilia survive does not mean he did not write any.

Regardless of exactly where Chaucer did his learning, books would have been scarce. They were expensive objects, laboriously copied by hand from copy-texts (*exempla*). Some were standards, such as Psalters, or the collections of extracts from Aesop, Ovid, Virgil and others, such as were used as school books; others were collections of texts assembled to suit the taste of the person who commissioned the manuscript and might reflect their particular interests. Often individual manuscripts were added to a library over time and only collected and bound into book form at a later date. With few actual volumes around, literature was still most often read aloud to assembled groups. Thus, most of what was learnt was acquired through listening and remembering, and while books did circulate and the wealthier households had considerable libraries, we should guard against a mental image of Chaucer the page leafing idly through texts on his own in a book-lined room. The culture was at least as much oral as literate, in which speaking well and remembering accurately were essential skills. Indeed, the function of the memory was itself a topic of interest at the time. Mary Carruthers has brought together much of the material on the medieval ideas of the memory and the ways people could train themselves to remember efficiently, in her valuable study *The Book of Memory* (Carruthers 1990).

Clearly in this kind of social arrangement, the better the household an individual joined the greater the chances available. John Chaucer did well for his son in this: Elizabeth de Burgh, Countess of Ulster was married to Lionel of Antwerp, son of King Edward III and later Duke of Clarence. The Christmas celebrations for which we see Geoffrey Chaucer being furnished with clothes in 1357 were held at the house of Edmund, younger brother to Lionel, and presided over by Queen Philippa. Another brother was also there, John of Gaunt, who was to play a large role in Chaucer's life later on. The fact that both of them were in the same place for the Christmas of 1357, and were much of an age, entices speculation on possible early meetings, despite their very different social circles. Speculation is also rife about another member of Queen Philippa's household, Philippa Pan. This name, Pan, is almost certainly an abbreviation, but no-one is clear of what. She may be the elder sister of Katherine de Roet (who became John of Gaunt's mistress and later wife) and also the Philippa who married Chaucer. Or, of course, she may not.

To return to less speculative grounds: in 1359, when Lionel came of age, his household and that of Elizabeth merged and Chaucer became one of the prince's attendants. As such, he went to France on military service in Lionel's company in September of 1359. By now he was a 'valettus' or yeoman and was bearing arms. He was also worth £16 when he was ransomed on 1 March 1360, having been captured in France. The campaign had targeted Reims, traditionally the city where kings of France had been crowned and where Edward had hoped to be crowned himself, thus making good his claims to the French throne. It is also the place where Chaucer is likely to have seen the arms displayed which were later to be the focus of the Grosvenor/Scrope dispute, which occasioned Chaucer's deposition some twenty-five years later in 1386, which in turn gives rise to our calculations for Chaucer's date of birth. All that lay ahead, however, while in 1359–60 English expectations and armies alike were defeated and the month of March saw the end of that particular episode of the Hundred Years War.

Having been ransomed, Chaucer was then back in France that autumn, being paid 9 shillings in October of 1360 for carrying letters to England for Lionel, who was then Earl of Ulster (through his marriage) and in Calais for the ratification of the Treaty of Breigny. This may have been the first instance of being sent on such a commission, which was standard employment for a valettus and is likely to have been a case of carrying personal letters, rather than state documents. We then lose sight of Chaucer for a few years. Lionel went to Dublin in 1361 as Viceroy to Ireland, but there is no evidence that Chaucer went with him. It seems more likely that he spent his time in the royal courts of England or Acquitaine, although there has been a prejudice in favour of believing he spent some time during this period at the Inns of Court or Inns of Chancery in London, acquiring the knowledge of legal affairs that is evident in his writing. Here he would have had the opportunity to learn French and Latin formulae and Chancery Hand, which was the official handwriting style, or script, for government documents and which Chaucer was to use later when he became a civil servant in the 1370s. He would have been able to combine such study with his court duties, attending sporadically, when not called to be elsewhere. The belief that Chaucer did spend some time in this way is based partly on the knowledge of legal ways which infuses his poetry, such as *The House of Fame* or the depiction of the Man of Law in the *Canterbury Tales*, and partly on the statement in Speght's 'Life' that Master Buckley (who was Keeper of records for the Inner Temple in Speght's time) records seeing an entry for a fine of 2 shillings levied on Geoffrey Chaucer for beating a Franciscan Friar in Fleet Street. The record itself has never been retrieved, and while the details tally with known fines of the time, and while it is conceivable that Chaucer spent some time gaining informal training at the Inns, it is also worth heeding Pearsall's point that by the sixteenth century it would have done an institution no harm to be able to prove some connection with Chaucer. It is tempting to assume that in this period Chaucer was composing the lyrics and songs to which he refers in his Retraction (few of which survive). Certainty eludes us, however, and the best we can do is say that it is more than likely that he was writing, experimenting with the French forms that influenced much of his poetry **[41]**.

(v) Royal service and connections with John of Gaunt

Whatever else he was doing between 1360 and 1367, Chaucer certainly suffered the death of his father in 1366. That same year seems to have been the one in which he married Philippa, who appears in records as Philippa Chaucer of the Queen's chamber and receives an annuity of 10 marks in September 1366. It also appears that Chaucer was abroad in this year, as a 'Geffroy de Chauserre' was granted safe conduct by Charles II of Navarre between February and May 1366. As there are no indications of exactly what Chaucer was doing to require such safe conduct, speculation again abounds. It is possible that he was on pilgrimage to the famous shrine of St. James of Compostela, although it would be an odd time of year to be making such a trip. Alternatively he may have been engaged on formal royal duties, but, if so, we would normally expect to find some mention of such business in the safe conduct document itself. Appealingly, this leaves open the option of a secret mission, possibly to do with Edward, Prince of Wales's dealings with Pedro of Castile, in which the at least tacit support of Charles of Navarre was also desirable. 1367 seems to have been a less hectic year, with Chaucer being granted an annuity of 20 marks and with the birth of a son, Thomas. Sometime during this year Chaucer moved up a further rung of the social ladder, as household expenses for 1368 list him as a squire (though formal Latin records do not use the equivalent term until 1372) which he was to remain until 1378.

From the late 1360s the dominant figure in Chaucer's biography was that of John of Gaunt, Duke of Lancaster. Thanks to a fortuitous and apparently, happy, marriage to Blanche in 1359 and the swiftly following deaths of her father and sister, John of Gaunt was, by 1362, Duke of Lancaster and the richest man in England. Blanche herself died young, in 1368, aged 28. Her death is significant to us because it is commemorated in Chaucer's poem *The Book of the Duchess* **[65]**. However sharp his grief at his wife's death (and there is evidence that he felt strongly), political affairs moved on apace for John of Gaunt, who was to be found once again in France engaged in military campaigns in 1369. It seems that Chaucer was with him: a reward of a 'prest' (an allowance to cover expenses) for £10 to Chaucer in this year is significant as being the earliest indication of his association with the Gaunt household, although it is highly likely that they had encountered each other well before this. Chaucer's wife, Philippa, also joins the household eventually as, following Queen Philippa's death in 1369, she moved to the court of Constance of Castile, who was to become John of Gaunt's second wife in 1372. Despite being attached broadly to the same family, their respective duties would have meant that Geoffrey and Philippa would have spent much time apart. The household would have served as a base for them, albeit one which moved around the country following the often separate movements of Gaunt and Constance. Even after Chaucer acquired a house for himself in 1374, he did not spend much time there at first as he remained on royal service, liable to be sent on various missions around the country or abroad. Such separation was usual at the time, so it is as well not to read too much into it, regardless of the many and heavy jokes fired at marriage throughout Chaucer's works.

(vi) Travels to Italy

Even before 1374 Chaucer's standing had risen again, as he is recorded among the sixty-two 'scutiferis camere regis' or esquires of the king's chamber, from 1371–73. As such, he was part of the 'secreta familia', a kind of inner household, which travelled with the king wherever he went. Chaucer was a member of this circle for only a short period, however, as he was certainly sent abroad to Genoa and Florence in 1372–73. He went to Genoa to negotiate the appointment of a special seaport for the use of the Genoese merchants, which formed part of the commercial agreements being put in place at the time, following a peace treaty between England and Genoa in February of 1371. We do not know why he went to Florence, though Edward III was negotiating for loans and ships at this time. This was probably Chaucer's first trip to Italy and it is more than likely that he was chosen for it because he could already speak Italian. While there he would have had the chance to increase what knowledge of the literature he had previously acquired; and, yet again, biographers have delighted in speculating on literary encounters he may have had. Certainly Florence was already the centre of a Dante cult (Dante died in 1321) and the writings of the elderly, but still living, Petrarch and Boccaccio would have been in circulation. All three authors were significant literary influences for Chaucer **[40]** but it is highly unlikely that he encountered either of the latter in the flesh: Petrarch died a year later in 1374, and Boccaccio in 1375.

1374 seems to have been an eventful year for Chaucer. Having returned from Italy the previous year, he was granted in April a gallon of wine a day for life. Even for those times, that is a prodigious amount of wine, albeit an appropriate grant for the son of a vintner; the grant was confirmed by Richard on his accession to the throne in 1377. In 1378 Chaucer petitioned to have this daily ration converted into hard cash, and was allowed to take it in the form of 20 marks from then on – a highly respectable income, as well as a more disposable one. May of 1374 sees him receiving a house over Aldgate in London rent-free in return for keeping it in good repair and not sub-letting it. These were common terms of lease for city officials, and indeed on June the 8th of that year Chaucer was appointed Controller of Customs for wool in the port of London at an annual salary of £10. On 13 June he was granted an annuity of £10 by John of Gaunt, 'in recognition of his services', a phrase which some have taken to indicate gratitude for the poem *The Book of the Duchess* **[65]**. Philippa also received a mention in this grant for her services to Gaunt's mother and his wife (this being Constance, his second wife, not Blanche). All in all, the Chaucers ended 1374 in more than comfortable circumstances.

The later 1370s found Chaucer engaged in quite a lot of travelling, often for unspecified reasons. The desire to regard these journeys as engagements on 'secret affairs', and thus add a touch of glamour to Chaucer's life, is aided by documents listing payments to Chaucer for just that. Although we do not know that he was going overseas in 1370 'in eisdem secretis negotiis ipsius domini regis' ('on those same secret negotiations of the lord king himself', Crow 1966: 45), he certainly was in 1377, when he engaged not only in 'secret business', but also in the open business of treating for peace and negotiating a possible marriage between the then Prince Richard and a French princess. These negotiations came to nothing, as did several other such attempts at potential unions through marriage, including one with Catherine, daughter of Bernabò Visconti, Lord of Milan.

This latter negotiation meant that in 1378 Chaucer again visited Italy, this time going to Milan. It is likely that it was at this point, not before, that he acquired more thorough knowledge of the writings of Petrarch and Boccaccio. Even if he did meet either or both of these venerable poets on his first Italian journey of 1373, their influence seems to have been less then than Dante's. Now, five years later and in a different region (Milan was ruled by Petrarch's patron, Galeazzo Visconti, Bernabò's brother), Chaucer seems to have acquired not only more knowledge of these poets, but also copies of some of their work. Chaucer's own poetry now begins to reflect the influences of Petrarch and Boccaccio (*Anelida and Arcite* **[52]** draws on Boccaccio's *Teseida*), whereas his earlier writing owes more to Dante and the Classics. While at Milan Chaucer would also have viewed at first hand the workings of a despotic, even tyrannical court ruled by a cruel man. The Viscontis were not people to cross lightly, and traces of Chaucer's reaction to visiting their court can be found in The Monk's Tale **[140]** where 'Barnabo Viscounte' is described as 'God of delit and scourge of Lumbardye' (*Tales* VII: 2400), although his murder by his son-in-law draws only the carefully neutral comment 'But why ne how noot I that thou were slawe.' (*Tales* VII: 2406). Critics have also seen the effects of this Italian visit in Chaucer's rendition of the story of Griselde which forms The Clerk's Tale: **[126]** on which readers may find David Wallace's article '"Whan She Translated Was": A Chaucerian Critique of the Petrarchan Academy' of interest (Patterson 1990: 156–215).

For us, 1378 is significant also as being the year in which John Gower is mentioned in a legal document in connection with Chaucer. He was granted powers of attorney for Chaucer in May to cover the period of Chaucer's journeys to Lombardy. While it is evident from both poets' writings that they knew and admired each other, this is the earliest documentary evidence of their friendship. Granting Gower power of attorney may have been no more than an kind of insurance policy against having law suits taken out against Chaucer in his absence. It was common for people who expected to be travelling for a while to make such arrangements and since by now Chaucer was a significant public figure, it was no more than commonly prudent of him to ask for such an attorney to be appointed. However, while it is best to regard it in such a light, it is tempting to see in this a pre-emptive strike against the charge which was probably already rumbling away in 1378 and which was finally laid to rest in 1380. This was the charge of *raptus* brought by Cecily Champaign.

(vii) The case of Cecily Champaign

As with so much else in Chaucer's life, there is a good deal of speculation and disagreement over what exactly the charge of *raptus* means in this instance. Many seek to dismiss it as being 'rape' as we understand it today, preferring to consider it inconceivable that one of our major literary figures could commit such a crime, and pointing out that the Latin term *raptus* was taken to indicate 'abduction' not sexual assault. In the 'Chaucer's Life' which prefaces the Riverside edition of Chaucer's Works, Martin Crow and Virginia Leland put the case concisely.

> It [*raptus*] could have meant physical rape; or it could have meant abduction ... The record, however, is clear; it means that Cecilia Chaumpaigne clears Chaucer of all responsibility.
>
> (*Riverside*: xvii)

We can see here the desire to clear Chaucer of the blot of any unseemly behaviour. However, while it is true that *raptus* could mean abduction, with no implication of physical or sexual assault, Pearsall points out that it takes on this meaning only when modified by the term *abductus* (Pearsall 1992: 135–7; see also Crow 1966: 343–7). Frequently such abductions aimed to force a marriage, usually in order to secure an inheritance for the abductor's family. Such was the case with Chaucer's father, John Chaucer, who was abducted by his aunt in an attempt to force a marriage between him and his cousin in 1324 (see Crow 1966: 3). The attempt came to nothing but legal wrangling, with no hint that John himself suffered more than being carried off by eager relations, but the point is that here the terminology is *rapuerunt et abduxerunt*, with exactly the use of *abducere* referred to by Pearsall. When not so moderated *rapere* seems to have carried all the significance of our modern verb 'to rape'. Necessarily it also carried all its associations and it is possible that Cecily Champaign simply used the threat of prosecution for rape as a lever to get money out of Chaucer. We even have a possible reason for her feeling she was due some recompense in the figure of 'lyte Lowys, my sone' (*Ast.* 23–4) to whom Chaucer dedicates his *Treatise on the Astrolabe* **[86]** in 1391, referring to him as being ten years old. This makes 1380 the year of Lewis's birth and allows for the chance that he is in fact the son of Cecily. Perhaps Cecily was raped and Lewis was the result, or perhaps he was the result of a happier liaison and she was simply ensuring some upkeep for the child. Or, indeed, Lewis may be a late child of Philippa's and Cecily may have been acting from other motives: Chaucer was a public figure moving in powerful circles and she may have hoped that such a man would do a lot to avoid the embarrassment and scandal of prosecution for rape, regardless of whether it was proved or not. Whatever the truth of the matter, the fact is that in 1380 Chaucer was released from the charge and any others arising from it; Cecily received £10 from John Grove, who, with Richard Goodchild, released Chaucer from any legal actions he might have against him and at the same time Chaucer called in several debts, including expenses for the Italian trip in 1378, and sold his father's house. As Pearsall suggests, this sudden eagerness to raise funds may indicate that other payments were made to Cecily (Pearsall 1966: 136–37).

(viii) Controller of Customs and the London years

Throughout this time and until 1387 Chaucer continued as Controller of Wool Custom and wool subsidy, adding to these Controller of Petty Custom in 1382. The post was perhaps more arduous than prestigious. It required the meticulous keeping of records of taxes levied on merchants, the careful monitoring of the quantities of wool, wool-skins and leather-skins being shipped out, together with the careful calculation of amounts due in tax. This last was a far from simple task: wool attracted both customs payments and subsidy payments, while a different and more general customs charge was applied to a wider, miscellaneous range of goods, which came under Chaucer's remit. Chaucer would have been dealing with around a thousand export documents ('crockets') each year and was expected to keep records in his own hand. This is when his time associated with the Inns of Court and the acquisition of Chancery Hand would have proved useful. He was probably already well acquainted with the kinds of formulae used for such documents, and indeed may well have been familiar with them from childhood because of his father's business. His familiarity with court ways and the operation of a favour system there would have stood him in good stead for a different aspect of the post: dealing with the various people who were awarded the post of Collector of customs over the years. The Collector derived direct and personal profit from taxes. Depending on how trade went, such profit could be handsome and of course each Collector would be keen to extract as much profit as possible during their time of office. Those given the post would often be merchants to whom the king owed a favour, they were granted the collectorship as a reward and as a cheap way (from the crown's point of view) of paying off debts. Chaucer would have thus been caught between the collectors and the traders, trying to see fair play, or at least fair enough not to disgruntle either party too much. It could not have been an easy task, albeit not without its own rewards.

Some of those rewards came from positions which came Chaucer's way as a result of the connections he made as Controller, rather than coming directly from the job itself. These occasional roles indicate his increasingly well-established position in the influential circles of London through the 1370s and 1380s. An example is standing mainprize or surety for other powerful men, such as John de Romsey, whom he had known when they were both squires at court and who had gone on to become the treasurer at Calais. Chaucer is cited as surety for him in 1375 (Crow 1966: 279–81), which involved being cited as a guarantor that Romsey would appear before the exchequer when required and give good account of his use of the property and money which had come under his jurisdiction as treasurer in Calais. In this case the property came from a man accused of sedition. Chaucer performed a similar role in 1378, this time on behalf of Sir William Beauchamp, who was granted the guardianship of the heir of Pembroke, who was then a minor. In this instance Chaucer was expected to ensure that Beauchamp did not abuse his position and squander the property for personal profit, thus depriving the heir of his due. Such positions remind us not only of Chaucer's public standing, but also of the smallness of the London circle: Sir William was not only a friend, but also Chamberlain to the royal household from 1378 to 1380, a witness for Chaucer in the Cecily Champaign case and also helpful in some unrecorded way in Calais in 1387.

Traces of the smallness of this London world may be seen in the motifs of enclosure and inwardness that permeate not only Chaucer's Dream Poems, which reflect court negotiations [61, 77], but also his epic *Troilus and Criseyde* [89], which was probably written in the early 1380s, the same period in which he translated Boethius's philosophical work *De Consolatione Philosophiae* [83].

As well as roles indicative of high social standing, Chaucer also took on more directly lucrative posts. One such was the wardship of Edmund Staplegate. Edmund was a ward of court, which meant he was heir to his father's property, but, being under age at his father's death (i.e. under 21) could not himself control his lands and estate. As his father was a tenant-in-chief of the king, wardship fell to the crown, with the king supposedly being his guardian. In practice such wardships were usually granted by the king to some favoured person, perhaps as reward or as a way of paying off some kind of debt. The appointed guardian received some income from the estate, and was also due any payments that would have gone to the father, such as those made on marriage. In this case Edmund came of age only a few years after becoming a ward of court, and bought back the right to his own marriage payment for £104 – a substantial sum. Edmund was perhaps fortunate in his guardian: it was not uncommon for wards to have to go to court to claim back their own lands from unscrupulous guardians.

A further indication of the high regard in which Chaucer was held as Controller of Customs was the fact that he was allowed to appoint deputies to cover the times when he was sent abroad, as was the case in 1376. Eventually he was permitted to appoint permanent deputies to both the wool and petty customs, which he did in 1385. In 1386 he gave up the lease on his Aldgate house and seems to have moved out of London and into Kent. He had sold his father's house in 1381, which was also the year of his mother's death, but had continued to live in the house in Aldgate until this time. This means he was formally resident in London at the time of the Peasants' Revolt and through the three days during which the mob of dissatisfied peasants, town workers and apprentices held sway in the capital. We do not know whether or not Chaucer was actually in London at the time, but we do know that Aldgate was one of the gates through which the insurgents streamed in June.

(ix) The Peasants' Revolt and the move to Kent

Dissatisfaction had been brewing for some time amongst the poorer classes in England. Ever since Edward III's death in 1377 and the accession of the ten-year old Richard, there had been tussles for power between various nobles, and tensions between nobles and commoners, which had been exacerbated by increasingly heavy taxation, including the introduction of the Poll Tax which was levied in 1377, 1379 and again in 1380. This last seems to have helped bring matters to a head in the form of the Peasants' Revolt of 1381. Since taxation was the focus of grievance, the principle targets of the uprising were the tax collectors, the hugely rich John of Gaunt (whose Savoy palace was burnt down during the riots) and the Flemish weavers recently brought over and regarded as foreigners depriving native English people of work. As a Controller of Customs and associate of John of Gaunt, Chaucer would have been well aware of the danger of his position, but he makes little direct reference to it in his writing. Maybe he was lucky and absent from London at the time. Whatever the truth, it is clear that he knew of events – the slaughter of the innocent Flemmings provides matter for a simile in The Nun's Priest's Tale **[141]**, where the furore following the attack of the fox on the hen run is described thus:

Certes, he Jakke Straw and his meynee
Ne made nevere shoutes half so shrille
Whan that they wolden any Flemyng kille,
As thilke day was maad upon the fox.
                                   (*Tales* VII: 3394–7)

We may speculate, then, that the move to Kent was a welcome escape from the various tensions of life in the City, reflected in the lyric *Lak of Stedfastnesse*, arguably composed at around this date **[56]**. Not that this meant moving out of the current of events. Having been part of the commission for peace in Kent in 1385, which meant he was in effect a Justice of the Peace, he was appointed a 'knight of the shire' in 1386 and as such sat as a member for Kent in the Parliament of October–November 1386. Chaucer was not a knight, but, due to the reluctance of men of influence to become knights and accept the various financial and military burdens that entailed, it had become common to appoint well-regarded and well-connected commoners to such positions. Like his Franklin, Chaucer was thus a parliamentary knight, for which he received 4s per day while Parliament sat.

The session he attended was a fairly lively one, with Parliament seeking to curb the power of the lords and magnates attacking each other: Gloucester demanded the removal of Suffolk, who was highly powerful and very much in King Richard's favour. Richard objected, left Parliament, was out-manoeuvred, and returned to find Suffolk impeached. Heady stuff. Less glamorous, but closer to home for Chaucer, was a minor petition that all life holders of public offices should be removed (on the general assumption that they were bound to be corrupt) and such posts never again be appointed for life. Nothing came of this directly, but it so happens that Chaucer resigned both his controllerships and left the customs at the end of the year. It is hard not to think that this move may have been prompted by political canniness as much as by the pressure of his increasing duties in Kent, or indeed by simple weariness with the posts.

(x) Time in Kent

1386 was also significant as the year of the Scrope/Grosvenor trial, the dispute over the right to a certain coat of arms, in which Chaucer made his deposition from which all calculations of his birth are taken. One might expect things to quieten down a little after all this and with his move to Kent, but that isn't quite the case. For one thing 1387 saw what seems to have been his last journey abroad, when he went to Calais on undetermined business, during which William Beauchamp was so helpful. Thereafter, he returned to Kent and his duties there, and also to his writing. By now he was a well-respected poet, having translated *Le Roman de la Rose* (part of which may survive in the Middle English *Romaunt of the Rose*) **[62]** in the 1360s, composed *The Book of the Duchess* in the late 1360s or 1370s, completed his dream poems, *The Parliament of Fowles* and *The House of Fame*, and also the narrative poem *Anelide and Arcite*. He had written *Troilus and Criseyde*, finished his translation of Boethius, which we know as the *Boece* and probably begun *The Legend of Good Women*. Now, in 1387, the year of his wife's death, we believe he began work on *The Canterbury Tales*.

However, life in Kent was not all writing poetry. As a Justice for the Commission of Peace, he shared with magistrates the duty of dealing with minor offences, such as assault, unfair or unlawful trading, and also for conducting preliminary hearing for cases which would be referred on to other courts. The post was a definite step up the ladder from his roles in London, as well as having the advantage of removing him from the increasingly restive capital. It must be remembered that Chaucer was very obviously associated with the king's party, albeit in a politically unimportant way. As a whole Richard's reign is not renowned for its domestic peace and harmony between the magnates: a wise man was better off out of it.

So Chaucer would have altered his circle from that of wealthy merchants and influential court officials to that of equally wealthy and differently influential lawyers and gentry, while also encountering all walks of life as they came before or appealed to the Justice of the Peace. Not that all Chaucer's dealings with the law came from the one side of the bench. He was summoned for debt on several occasions, six times, indeed, by a Henry Atwood, innkeeper, between January 1389 and January 1390. At this point it is reasonable to suppose the matter was settled out of court, since it appears Chaucer never answered the summons. Such evidence of outstanding debts should not be taken as a sign of penury, despite the fact that earlier biographies of Chaucer depict these years as times of hardship resulting from civic upheaval and possible loss of favour at court. As we have seen, the move to Kent was by no means disadvantageous, but it is the case that in 1388 Chaucer resigned his exchequer annuity (held since 1367) and the one resulting from his wine grant of 1378. Both these were transferred to John Scalby, but while this reduced Chaucer's annual income substantially, it may well have saved him from prosecution by Parliament, which had turned its attention to members of the king's household, particularly those granted annuities by Edward III. Here again we see signs of a man capable of reading a political situation wisely and acting accordingly to avoid trouble.

His reputation as a poet may have helped. Although we are now fond of regarding his poetry as a great social document, giving us insights into the life of his times, it is nevertheless carefully silent about many of the burning social issues of the day. Reading his works, one can remain as oblivious of the Peasants' Revolt and the effects of the perpetual wars with France as one can of the Napoleonic Wars when reading Jane Austen.

(xi) Clerk of the King's Works

Canny as Chaucer undoubtedly was, he did not remove himself entirely from the civil duties associated with the royal household. In 1389 he was appointed Clerk of the King's Works, a position which was conferred by Richard two months after regaining his regality in May 1389. It is possible to see in this appointment evidence of the continued favour of Richard and a recognition of reliable service from Chaucer as a loyal servant in civil duties as well as in his poetry. Certainly, following his politic resignation of his annuities two years before, this post represented a doubtless welcome increase in income, paying 2s a day: enough to keep at bay the likes of Henry Atwood. Lucrative as it was, the post was no sinecure. It involved overseeing more financial affairs than his previous post as Customs Controller and included responsibility for the maintenance of various royal properties. He was the head of all the clerical staff involved in the running of these estates, and as such chiefly responsible for the payment of wages and provision of workmen and materials for upkeep and repairs. The properties under his particular care included The Tower of London, Westminster Palace, the royal houses of Eltham, Sheen (mentioned in the Prologue to the *Legend of Good Women* **[81, 100]**) and King's Langley and, from 1390, St. George's Chapel and Windsor. Of these the two biggest enterprises were the Tower, which was having a new wharf built, and the Chapel. St. George's Chapel was in such poor repair that it was recorded as 'en poynt du ruyne et de cheirer a la terre si ele ne soit le plustost faite et emendee' that is, 'on the point of ruin and of falling to the ground unless it is speedily restored and repaired' (Crow 1966: 408). Chaucer's attempts to get work done here were futile and the Chapel did indeed fall down roughly thirty years later, despite some restoration in 1396, well after the end of Chaucer's terms of office.

Chaucer remained as Clerk of the King's Works until June of 1391, when he was commanded to give up the office to John Gedney, who was, in Pearsall's term 'much more of a professional civil servant' (Pearsall 1992: 214). This change in type of appointee may reflect the ever-increasing administration demanded by the post, and in turn Chaucer may have been glad enough to relinquish the position. Of course, it is also possible that Richard was glad enough to be rid of him. Richard's building plans were always ambitious and would have kept any Clerk of Works busy, travelling from project to project and pushing on the work. Other events might also have contributed to Chaucer's possible willingness to leave the post. He had been attacked and robbed three times in September of 1390; once on the 3rd and twice, incredibly, on the 6th. It may have been bad luck, or deliberate targeting of a man likely to be carrying substantial sums of money (as indeed he was, losing £20 6s.8d of the king's money on the 3rd and a total of £19 43d on the 6th, plus his own horse and various effects). The first robbery happened at a place appropriately termed 'le fowle ok' and was never accounted for, though Chaucer was acquitted from repaying the money stolen from him. Richard Brierley, a known highway-man, was caught and confessed to the second robbery, and implicated others of his gang in the third. Such incidents would certainly take any shine off the job of Clerk of Works, and may well have contributed, in one way or another, to Chaucer's leaving the post in June of the following year.

Chaucer was also writing busily during these years; as well as continuing with *The Canterbury Tales* and beginning his *Treatise on the Astrolabe*, he translated Pope Innocent III's *De miseria condicionis humane*, (also known as *De contemptu mundi*), to which he refers in his *The Legend of Good Women* **[81, 100]** as 'Of the Wreched Engendrynge of Mankynde' (*Legend* G: 414). While such works are not popularly interesting now (and indeed may never have been, judging from the fact that no copies survive) it is salutary to remember that a noticeable amount of the time Chaucer devoted to literary activities was spent in translating or adapting a wide range of works by other writers, from the early experiments with French lyrics and dream poems through to such major treatises. Having been thus absorbed, the influence of such works would often show up in his own fictional poetry: both the Pardoner's and the Man of Law's Tales bear witness to Chaucer's imaginative recycling of Pope Innocent's text.

When Chaucer ceased being Clerk of Works his annual income would have dropped noticeably. While in office he had incurred several debts on the crown's behalf, and it was some considerable time before he was reimbursed. The final, large, sum of £66 13s 4d, was paid in May 1393. Before this he had secured a gradual repayment of another debt due to him, but money seems to have been tight, or at least he was unwilling to part with it lightly, as we once again find him being sued for debt during these years. His pattern seems to have been to allow the summonses to build up until the last possible date and then settle out of court. It is a process not unknown today, and then, as now, the running up of debts may have been as much a sign of reasonable affluence and a certain attitude towards paying bills, as of financial difficulties. Moreover he was not totally without income, since his annuity from Gaunt seems to have continued until Gaunt's death in 1399, when a grant from Gaunt's son, by then Henry IV, seems to have been in effect a continuation of the original annuity. Similarly, from 1394 he received an annuity of £20 granted by Richard II in recognition of his good service (whether literary or civil is unspecified) and again confirmed by Henry. Gifts, too, were forthcoming in the 1390s as we see him receiving a rich gown from Henry in 1395 or 96 (while Henry was still just the Earl of Derby, and simply the son of John of Gaunt, rather than the claimant of the throne) and in 1397 a tun of wine annually from Richard. Nor was he long without employment as at some point in the 1390s he was appointed Deputy

Forester for North Petherton in Somerset. The exact duties of this post remain unclear, but it is unlikely that it involved much riding around in woods. It may have been another post which involved acting as arbitrator, this time between the family which owned the estate (the Mortimers) and that which farmed it.

For all this time Chaucer was resident in Kent, appearing in various records as a witness to contracts or transfers of property, usually involving men he would have known through his court connections. Thus, he witnesses for Sir Nicholas Sarnesfield, the king's standard-bearer, in 1393 and in 1395 for a transfer of land from the Archbishop of York to, amongst others, the Archbishop of Canterbury, and one of Chaucer's old friends, Sir Philip de le Vache. Life in Kent was thus no reclusive retirement, and indeed in 1398 he was on the move generally through England on the king's 'arduous and urgent business' (*ardua et urgencia negocia*). We have no details of what that business was, nor any clear explanation for the fact that Chaucer secured a warrant of protection in May 1398, to last for two years and cover him for any law suits brought while travelling. There was one such suit on the horizon, as the widow of Walter Buckholt was trying to collect the considerable sum of £14 1s.11d which had been due to her husband. However, if this was the reason for requesting the royal warrant, Chaucer does not seem to have used it, and the case went through the usual motions of court, being settled, it appears, some time between October 1398 and June 1399 (Crow 1966: 62–64 and 397–401). 1398 seems to have marked the end of his time in Kent, as by 1399 he is back in London, not in Aldgate but in a house in Westminster, associated with the Abbey. Rather pleasingly we know this because responsibility for collecting from him a debt for £1 payable to the crown is transferred from the Sheriff of Kent to that of London in 1399: later that same year it was declared 'desperate' or uncollectable.

(xii) Return to London: the last years

For England as a whole 1399 was a momentous year: Henry Bolingbroke, John of Gaunt's son, was so enraged by Richard's cool sequestration of the Lancaster estates on Gaunt's death, that he returned from exile in June, landed in the North of England (while Richard was engaged in Ireland) and forced Richard's abdication in September. In many ways it was a remarkably bloodless overthrow, and certainly from Chaucer's point of view the shift in power was less worrying than it might have been, since, despite his connections with the royal household of Richard, his links with John of Gaunt and Henry himself were strong. In effect it seems merely to have required going through the rigmarole of re-establishing his various annuities and grants, with the inevitable delays such negotiations always seem to entail. By now Chaucer may well have been ailing. The house in Westminster has been described as the fourteenth-century equivalent of sheltered accommodation (Pearsall 1992: 275) as it lay within the grounds of the Abbey and as such was under its general care. It was, naturally, a prestigious lease whose previous and subsequent tenants were also royal servants, so it may have been a way to confirm his own status as well as to take some steps towards an easier life. It is here that we presume Chaucer died on 25 October 1400. He was buried at the entrance to St. Benedict's chapel in Westminster Abbey, which was at this time just beginning to be used for the burial of Abbey tenants and royal servants. Later, in 1556, he was moved to his current position in what is now termed 'poets' corner' and a large commemorative tomb erected for him by Nicholas Brigham.

Chaucer was definitely survived by his son Thomas, whom we believe to be his first child, and possibly also by Lewis. We know next to nothing of Lewis, expect that the *Treatise on the Astrolabe* was written for him, and that he is mentioned, with Thomas, in a record of payment to them as men at arms in Carmarthen in 1403. Records for Thomas are fuller and reveal an astutely managed political career which included being Speaker for the House of Commons. It also included a typically advantageous marriage and continued links with the House of Lancaster. His daughter married well, becoming on her third marriage, the wife of William de la Pole, Earl and Duke of Suffolk, at one time the most influential man in England. Quite a social shift from the well-regarded but nonetheless merchant base of her grandfather. Two other children are attributed to Chaucer, both daughters and both probably spurious. An Elizabeth Chausier was nominated as a nun at St. Helen's Priory, London, in 1377 and a record exists for expenses paid by John of Gaunt covering outlay and gifts for an Elizabeth Chaucy becoming a nun at Barking Abbey. The two Elizabeths are likely to be the same person and the mention of John of Gaunt has inclined people to regard her as Geoffrey Chaucer's daughter, but no direct mention of her father exists and Chaucer was a common enough name for this to be simple coincidence. Likewise, an Agnes Chaucer is listed as in attendance at the coronation of Henry IV, but no further indications exist to tell us whether she was related to the poet in any way.

The very fact that Chaucer is given these conjectural daughters attests to his significance, both as poet and public figure. He lived through some of the most restless years of England's history, but seems to have steered a pretty safe course throughout. Given his background, it is tempting to see him as a man of his times, albeit one of the lucky ones who survived plague, civil unrest, battle, law suits, and managed a fair degree of social betterment in the process. Well before his death his reputation as a poet was firmly established; he had his admirers and his imitators, just as he had been an admirer and imitator in his turn. It is possible that he even had his portrait drawn. If so we are indebted to Hoccleve for it, who includes it his *Regiment of Princes* of 1411–12, suddenly thinking that readers may not have seen Chaucer in the flesh and might be interested in a picture of the great man. The picture is present in a copy of the text probably intended for presentation to Henry, Prince of Wales, who would have seen Chaucer and so would have been in a position to judge its accuracy. Pearsall, who devotes an appendix to the tradition of Chaucer portraiture (Pearsall 1992: 285–305), suggests that this picture may have been the template for that of Chaucer as Pilgrim in the Ellesmere manuscript. The existence of this portrait is significant not only because there is a fair chance of it being a reasonable likeness, but also because its very existence attests Chaucer's standing. It was highly unusual to attempt realistic portrayals of people at this time, when the habit was to idealise features and present the subject as a type rather than an individual. Such individual representations as did exist, whether as tomb effigies or in manuscripts, tended to be of lords and magnates. Significantly, the earliest tradition of realistic likenesses of a lay individual is the case of Dante. One cannot help feeling that Chaucer would have felt it fitting that he should receive similar treatment to that of the great Italian vernacular poet whose cult he had encountered in Florence in 1372.

Further Reading

The two best modern biographies of Chaucer are Brewer 1998 (offering detailed readings of some of Chaucer's poems as well as a literary appraisal of his life and times) and Pearsall 1992 (an accessible and highly informed critical biography). Speght 1598, Godwin 1804 and Coulton 1908 are interesting for what they tell us about the ways Chaucer biography has been treated in the past, but are factually unreliable. The brief 'Life' which forms part of the preface to *The Riverside Chaucer* is a useful, compact overview. *Chaucer Life Records* is an invaluable and very readable source for any study of Chaucer's life (Crow, M. and Olson, C. 1966).

(b) SOCIAL, LITERARY AND HISTORICAL CONTEXTS

Tracing Chaucer's life provides some idea of the personal background to his literature, but that personal background was itself set against a wider social and historical backdrop and there are elements of that which it is useful to bear in mind.

(i) War and chivalry

Throughout Chaucer's life, England and France warred intermittently and were engaged in the series of battles which is now termed The Hundred Years War and which included the campaigns and peace treaties in which Chaucer was involved **[12–17]**. Edward III laid claim to the French throne in 1337, thus starting the conflict which passed through stages of war and uneasy peace until it was eventually resolved in 1453. Over the years methods of waging war changed markedly, but the notion of a Knight and of Chivalry remained current. Even in the twentieth century the concept of the chivalric knight is familiar, as he rides through films and fiction, although one would be hard pushed to say when one last existed in the flesh. During the mid-fourteenth century, though, the figure of the knight was dominant both on the field and in the imagination. Skilled and respected, he engaged in one-to-one conflict in battles, was a member, or leader, of a company based on a lord's household and its expectations of service. There were infantrymen, but they tended to be regarded as of little importance and were rarely marshalled with the same forethought as cavalry (although yeomen and tenants of all degrees were required to render military service when called upon, and sometimes to provide companies of foot soldiers, depending on their own social standing). The expertise and the reputation rested with the knight: basically, horses bestowed kudos.

The battle of Crécy (1346) changed that. Here Edward used both bowmen and infantry to deadly effect. The range of a longbow, the ability to send over repeated showers of arrows and the skill of the archers undermined the concept of a brief shower of javelins followed by close engagement. Additionally, Edward's use of footsoldiers armed with long knives made the infantry a force to be reckoned with. Of course there were still knights, and while the bowmen won acclaim, the figure of the knight still reigned supreme, especially in the popular imagination. This was greatly aided by the person of Edward, Prince of Wales, eldest son of Edward III (popularly known since the sixteenth century as the Black Prince). He seemed to embody all the qualities of perfect knighthood: indisputably of noble blood; a renowned soldier and commander; capable of acting in the most chivalrous manner, as when, having captured King John II of France at Poitiers, he insisted on acting as his squire. All this must have helped to maintain the ideal of knighthood. The fact that Edward was also capable of coldly watching the slaughter of defeated French men, women and children, while rewarding his supporters with prodigal gifts, all fits with the chivalric concept. Add to this that, like all English nobles, he was fluent in French (his mother, Queen Philippa, was French and half the French royal family were living as prisoners in the English court at the time) and that he was married to Joan of Kent, whose beauty led her to be called The Fair Maid of Kent, and we have a perfect picture of knighthood. Finally, by dying at the relatively young age of 46 in 1376, and thus never becoming king, his popular appeal was left untarnished. Richard, his son, who became Richard II, had a hard act to follow in some ways. He, too, used the idea of chivalry, even commanding lists to be built for a tournament at Smithfield in 1390, when Chaucer was Clerk of the King's Works. The lists were a poor show, but the idea still retained a certain romantic appeal and Richard may well have been using them as a political ploy.

Two sets of associations with war thus co-existed in fourteenth-century England: the relatively new, but clearly efficient, version which involved greater use of commanders, increased use of conscription and frequent levying of taxes to pay for it all, and the older version centred on the figure of the knight with the idea of household companies under the command of nobles who were obliged to raise, equip and pay a given number of men whenever required. While the newer version had its social effects as it revived the concept of every adult male being obliged to possess arms appropriate to his station and know how to use them too, the established concept of the knight-at-arms continued to hold sway in the literature.

(ii) Chivalry

The idea of chivalry has an enduring appeal, associated as it is with the rarefied life of court culture, and summoning up a world of brave and elegant knights often in love with beautiful ladies, who might be loving or cruel in return. All in this world are musical, compose verses with ease in English, French and probably also Latin, and are of noble, or 'gentle' blood. While the concept had its representatives in life, its influence is most evident in the literature. The figures of the Knight and Squire among the Canterbury Pilgrims are obvious examples, as are the Man in Black of *The Book of the Duchess* **[66]** and Troilus in *Troilus and Criseyde* **[89]**, while the discussion of what it means to be 'gentil' or 'fre' in the Wife of Bath's and Franklin's tales **[122, 131]** bear witness to the wider scope of the concept. Beyond Chaucer, the knightly ideal is central to the anonymous poem *Sir Gawain and the Green Knight*, which, in the only surviving manuscript, is ended with the motto of the Order of the Garter. This order was founded by Edward III in 1348 in a move which demonstrated not only his own enthusiasm for the courtly ideal, but also his shrewd political sense, as the ideas of honour and companionship could do much to unite the noble and powerful families of the time, thus reducing their inclination to fight amongst themselves or with the king. This concept of what is essentially a brotherhood was most completely brought together in English by Malory when he undertook his Arthurian tales around 1400, in what we now tend to term Malory's *Morte D'Arthur*. Malory reinvigorated the tales of Arthur and his knights, presenting them as the flower of knighthood, but also, significantly, setting the tales in a distant and undetermined bygone age, while lamenting the loss of such ideals in his own time. Like all Golden Ages, that of Chivalry is always past.

In what was once a standard work on Chaucer, *Chaucer and his England* (1908) George Coulton eulogises the role of the theory of chivalry:

> Essentially exclusive and jealous of its privileges, the chivalric ideal was yet the highest possible in a society whose very foundations rested on caste distinctions, and where bondmen were more numerous than freemen. The world will always be the richer for it; but we must not forget that ... it postulated a servile class; the many must needs toil and groan and bleed in order that the few might have grace and freedom to grow to their individual perfection.
>
> (Coulton 1908: 188)

Coulton is right to remind us of the underbelly of this idealised world, as it is important to retain the distinction between what was an increasingly literary concept and real life. By the fourteenth century men actually sought to avoid becoming knights due to the burdens of tax and obligations of military service the position entailed, hence the dearth of knights which made it possible for Chaucer to be elected as a parliamentary knight in 1386. Nevertheless, the idea still commanded respect and the qualities associated with knightly behaviour, such as 'gentilesse' (on which Chaucer composed a lyric **[58]**) were still highly regarded. Those who wish to explore the concept of chivalry further, will find Maurice Keen's book *Chivalry* most helpful.

(iii) Courtly love and marriage

Matching the code of chivalry and in part contributing to it, was the concept of courtly love. There is some debate over how much this was a purely literary code and how much it actually affected the behaviour of courtiers or those who aspired to polite living. What is not in doubt is its standing as a recognised convention underpinning much of the writing of Chaucer and his contemporaries. The first part of the French allegory, *Le Roman de la Rose*, written by Guillaume de Lorris (d. 1237) and translated by Chaucer, epitomises that code **[62]**. In this dream poem the lover (male) enters the Garden of Love, which is open only to those who are beautiful, wealthy and leisured. In it he finds the Rose (female), whose beauty enslaves him and which he desires to gain. The Rose is, however, guarded and not just by thorns. Dangers of various kinds confront the Lover, which he must overcome by bravery or trickery in order to reach his goal. In Lorris' text, the allegory is intricate and largely concerned with courtly love, but he never finished the work. In around 1277 Jean de Meun picked up the text and provided an ending in a rather different tone, expanding the allegory's frame of reference to include ideas on the faculty of reason, social satire and snide attacks on his contemporaries. Chaucer clearly read and was influenced by de Meun's text, but it is de Lorris who provides the most courtly element. For twentieth-century students of the convention, C.S. Lewis's study *The Allegory of Love* (1936) remains the best starting point.

In brief, courtly love posited a Lady, always beautiful, often married or apparently unobtainable, who was the object of love for a knight. This knight was handsome and accomplished and expected to prove his worth through the eloquence of his speech and readiness to undergo any trials set by his lady with unerring loyalty. The lady's role was to test her suitor's devotion by expressing lack of interest, setting tasks and in general putting objects in his way. All of this came under the general heading of 'luf-daunger' which might also include the oppositions of relatives or a perceived mis-match in social station. The true lover-knight overcomes all obstacles and remains devoted. His reward is becoming the recognised lover of his lady (which might or might not include marriage and/or physical consummation of the affair, depending on the text). It is probably a mistake to assume that much of this was actually enacted by members of the various courts of the fourteenth century, but it was certainly an available fiction which informed the cultural climate, much as the wider and associated conventions of chivalry did. Among families with inheritances to protect, early marriages were not uncommon, nor was the practice of contracting engagements between children, or marriages between partners of widely differing ages. The higher up the social scale, the more likely such matches; Richard II provides a case in point as he married Anne of Bohemia when he was 15 and she 16. After her death he married Isabella of France, who was then only seven years old. Richard was 30; it was a political marriage. Although this is the extreme, it is worth remembering that merchants, too, had lands and investments to protect and wise marriages to contract. Where such disparity in ages exists and marriage more openly regarded as a business matter than it is now, and not necessarily a personal affair, the imaginative appeal of courtly love is readily understood.

(iv) Marriage and remarriage

Where marriages could be contracted between partners of such different ages, it is to be expected that widowhood for both men and women was fairly common. As well as simple age difference, disease, war and dangers of childbirth all had their effects, making second and third marriages fairly common; even fourth marriages were not unduly out of the way. John of Gaunt married three times, as did Alice, Chaucer's grand-daughter. Divorce was, of course, all but unheard of and annulments rare: each was shameful and expensive, requiring dispensations from the Pope as well as legal palaver, making such things the preserve of the rich. Remarriage could follow pretty soon after the death of the previous partner without attracting undue comment. Chaucer's mother, for instance, married Bartholomew Chappell in 1366, the year of John Chaucer's death. On the other hand, some men made their widow's inheritance conditional upon not remarrying in order to prevent some unrelated person benefiting from their hard work. Jenny Kermode cites one sixteenth-century London merchant who neatly sums up the attitude:

> She will marrie and enrich some other with the fruites of my travaille. Wherefore I think it necessarie to abridge her of that liberty which the custom doth extende.
>
> (Kermode 1999: 8)

It is against this background of common practice that we must read Chaucer's portrayals of marriage, and in particular the Wife of Bath's prologue **[120]**.

(v) Death, plague and revolt

The Black Death of 1348 seems more striking in our retrospective view of the late medieval period than it did to those who lived through it. The general level of infant mortality was around four in five (that is one in five infants surviving) and every summer brought increased level of disease and the threat of epidemics, while winter had its own hardships. The bubonic plague (Black Death) was one such disease: arriving in Europe in 1347, it spread rapidly and arrived in England in 1348, where it raged for the best part of a year. This was not the only occurrence of the disease (it struck again, severely in 1361, and then again in 1368–69, 1371, 1375, 1390 and 1405) but it was its most virulent. Of the estimated 4–5 million people in England 1.5–2 million died. For those who saw it close at hand, it must have been an horrific disease. Those infected suffered boils, acute pain and gave off an appalling stench. Very few survived, most dying within three days. Given this, it is perhaps surprising that Chaucer's writing hardly refers to it. However, living through a time of disease is not the same as surviving the disease itself. The vast majority of those who came through the epidemic of 1348 (and its later recurrences) did so because they were never infected, which may well lead to a different attitude to the disease. Besides, even the most severe outbreak brought some benefits: for labourers it further loosened the ties to land-owners and increased the chances of higher wages, while for the middle classes there was property to inherit. Life simply went on.

Likewise, the Peasants' Revolt of 1381 goes oddly unremarked by Chaucer, although it presumably had an impact. It is hard to pin-point exactly why the revolt occurred when it did, as the various contributing factors (e.g. high taxation, labour laws, the obvious power of magnates apart from the king) had existed for some time (see Dobson 1982: 20; Dyer 1994: 221–39). What is clear is that charismatic leaders were to hand and much of the energy of the uprising comes through the writings of the rebels at the time. Some of these have been collected by Professor Barry Dobson in his book *The Peasants' Revolt of 1381* (Dobson, 1983) and make interesting reading. Chaucer's near silence on the matter (with the exception of the line in The Nun's Priest's Tale **[21]**) is remarkable not only because the mob entered London through 'his' gate of Aldgate, but also because Kent, where he had associations, was one of the centres of the first uprisings. His comparative silence may be a mark of caution, given Chaucer's links with several of the groups targeted by the mob, or a sign of a lack of sympathy with the grievances of the rural poor or town apprentices. Such a lack would not be surprising in a wealthy townsman and civil servant. Whatever his personal convictions, Chaucer was not a political or social poet in the way his contemporary William Langland was. While most classes are represented in Chaucer's writing, all his characters are literary creations. As Coulton pointed out, 'we believe in them conventionally, but know on reflection that they are there only to point an artistic contrast', while Chaucer's imagination was evidently caught by individuals and their quirks, 'the multitude interested him comparatively little' (Coulton 1908: 268).

(vi) Church as institution

For our purposes it is probably easier to think of Church as institution as separate from the concept of religion. Such a division is not entirely inaccurate. England, like the rest of Western Europe, was predominantly Christian, which at this time meant Catholic, with the titular Head of the Church being the Pope, and monarchs of individual countries ruling by Divine Right. This is not to say that everyone held precisely the same beliefs, or even followed exactly the same practices, but the Church provided the framework for thought, just as the Christian calendar, with its rituals and festivals provided a structure for the year. But having one structure, however dominant, does not exclude others: as the opening of *The Canterbury Tales* reminds us, April means not only the start of the pilgrimage season, but also the season of spring and general lifting of the spirits. The seasonal year was at least as noticeable as the ritual one. It would be a mistake to think that people in general were necessarily more pious simply because pervasively held Christian belief created common terms of reference.

Conversely, the day to day contact with the institution of the Church in all its various forms would have been so common as to be unremarkable. As well as attending mass when required (at least once a week, and usually more), one would have encountered some officer or associate of the Church with a frequency which would astound us now. The Church was a huge employer, forming almost a mini-state within a state. It had its own courts, with attendant officers, such as summoners; it had parishes and churches, with the attendant parsons, priests, bishops, and archbishops, as well as the many religious houses – the monasteries and convents, inhabited by monks, nuns, friars or canons, each again, with its individual hierarchy. There were also roles more tangentially attached to the Church, such as those of itinerant mass-priest, who made his living saying masses for the dead, but was not licensed to conduct all the offices of a priest, or that of pardoner, who might be licensed to preach, hear confession and give pardon, but, again, could not perform the other offices, such as marriages or baptisms. Moreover, most formal education came under the province of one aspect of the Church or another, be it the church schools, or the universities, and thus many people we would now think of as civil servants or secretaries were technically members of the Church, albeit only in lower orders, and may never have performed any religious service. It was not always the case; although he was Clerk of the King's Works, Chaucer never held a religious qualification, but a 'clerk' could be both clerk, as we use the term, and cleric.

As well as providing all these possible posts or roles, and thus offering a complete career structure for both men and women (to be the head of a convent would be no mean post, especially if one managed to join one of the wealthier and so better provided ones), the Church was also a major landowner. A peasant would be as likely to be working on church land as that owned by a lay lord or yeoman, and tenant farmers might be renting their land from an Abbey. The richer abbeys and monasteries (and some, such as Bury St. Edmunds which more or less became the town, or Fountains in Yorkshire, were extremely rich) would also employ builders, carpenters and other tradesmen as and when required and would often have a kind of satellite community made up of lay-brothers who were not fully ordained, but were closely attached to the monastery.

All this activity did not ensure respect, of course. Rather the opposite. We can sub-divide the Church into secular clergy, (concerned with parish churches and ordained as members of the general Christian church) and the religious (monks, friars, canons or nuns who were members of particular religious orders and followed their rules). Monks were criticised for being too rich, too keen on good living and too willing to travel the country, away from their monastery or abbey, which was where they were supposed to be enclosed. However, at least they were established (the term used for those attached to a particular house) and so, theoretically, they contributed to their local communities in terms of employment and were to some degree self-sufficient. Friars were criticised for not being thus established, and while this meant they were not so often associated with rich houses, they were instead dependent on charity, which might take the form of money or food given to the friar in return for confession. Canons came in for less formal criticism, perhaps because, as communities made up of secular and religious members and usually attached to substantial town churches, they seemed more part of the community. One of the largest groups followed the rule of St. Augustine, and were referred to as Canons Regular, or Black Canons (from the colour of their cloaks); the Canon of Chaucer's *Canterbury Tales* is one of these.

At the head of all these various forms of Christian life was the Pope, who at least nominally was the head of the whole Christian church. However, that position was somewhat compromised by the Great Schism, which occurred in 1378 and resulted in two popes co-existing: one, Urban IV, in Rome, the other, Clement VII, in Avignon. The split was not resolved until 1417 with the election of Martin V. Gower and Langland express deep concern over this split: characteristically, Chaucer remains silent on the matter, though, as England sided with the Italians (and against France), it may have been a reason for his journey to Italy at that time.

(vii) Religion and philosophy

So much for the structure of the Church. Its influence on the philosophy of the time was even more far-reaching, but that is not to say it was stultifying. The most complex systems of thought at the time had been established by intellectuals within the Church, where there was better access to libraries and possibly more time to devote to study. Entering a religious order allowed people with intellectual ambition to pursue their studies, often learning from an established philosopher. Two orders of Friars, both founded in the thirteenth century, dominated the intellectual landscape at the time: the Dominicans, with Albertus Magnus (d.1280) and St. Thomas Aquinas (d. 1274), and the Franciscans, with Duns Scotus (d. 1308) and William Ockham (d.1349). The ideas advanced by these people, their followers and their critics covered not only theological matters, but also the function of reason, discussions of how memory worked, ideas on teaching, the role of mankind in the world, principles of science; in short all aspects of philosophy. It was taxing intellectual stuff, and it was also fascinating and pertinent. For those wishing to enter the area now, the best starting place is probably still Gordon Leff's *Medieval Thought: St. Augustine to Ockham*, in which the first half of the fourteenth century is characterised as 'scepticism versus authority' (Leff 1958: 262).

Part of that scepticism was evident in the growing number of increasingly educated lay people who were becoming involved in theological enquiry. Probably the most readily identifiable group were the Lollards (a term derived from the Dutch for 'mumbler') who advocated a return to a simpler way of Christian life and rejected the over-rich and corrupt state of the Church. Needless to say, they were eventually regarded as heretics and were persecuted in the fifteenth century, but in the fourteenth century the movement was still young and provided a common ground for many who were both critical of prevailing ideas and hierarchies and seriously interested in finding alternatives. The Lollards drew support from the ideas of John Wyclif (although Wyclif himself was not actually a Lollard) and those ideas included the call for having the Bible translated into the vernacular, to ensure a more direct access to it for the majority of people who did not understand Latin easily, if at all, and also criticism of any liturgical practice not obviously supported by Biblical example. In particular, discussions of the questions surrounding the concept of free will figured in Lollardry, questions which Chaucer also explores in The Knight's Tale **[110]** and *Troilus and Criseyde* **[89]**. It is unlikely that Chaucer himself was a Lollard, but his name is linked frequently with the group of Lollard knights (including John Clanvowe, a diplomat and writer, and Simon Burley, Richard II's tutor) who clearly formed a significant part of his audience (see for example, Crow 1966: 343; 347; 360).

There is one final, more amorphous, group to add to this welter of intellectual activity, that of the mystics and recluses. There was a significant number of these people, whose existence bears testimony not only to a fervent religious strand, but also to the strength of individualism at the time. Some of them became well-known and respected figures, who were sought out and consulted by others. One such was Dame Julian of Norwich, who became something of a cult figure after writing her account of her experiences during a severe illness in 1373 and her interpretation of them (known as *The Revelations of Divine Love* or *The Shewings of Divine Love*). Others would have had more local reputations. They tended to live simple, devotional lives and some, often called anchorites, chose to withdraw from direct contact with the world, sometimes even to the extent of being literally walled up in a small cell at the side of a church with one angled window, through which they could see the altar and partake in services, without themselves being seen. Versions of mysticism and debates about the best kind of life to live were also popular, with different views being held by the author of *The Cloud of Unknowing* and Walter Hilton, who wrote the *Scale of Perfection* and *The Mixed Life*. All of these authors were Chaucer's direct contemporaries and their writing offers a wider context for The Parson's Tale, his depiction of female religious characters and his debates on the operation of individual will. At the same time, the ancient world still exerted its influence, as people continued to draw on Plato and Aristotle, and still attempted to reconcile the classical and Christian philosophies, as Boethius had in the sixth century.

On a more popular level, Saints' Lives were widely read and also promulgated Church morals and doctrine. As a form such Lives fall somewhere between adventure story and romance and indeed drew on the language of each. They provided entertainment in an irreproachable form, so much so that reading or hearing one counted as an act of devotion. A good summary of this now largely extinct genre can be found in Wogan-Browne and Burgess (1996).

In all these ways the church and religion played a part in social, economic, political and intellectual life, but not all of Chaucer's influences, and certainly not all of his context, were religious.

(viii) Literary contexts

English

One of the most significant changes during Chaucer's lifetime was the increased use of the vernacular as a medium for all writing, regardless of its function. Although legal and formal documents were still written primarily in Latin or French, Parliament opened for the first time in English in 1362 and philosophical or religious treatises were appearing in English. *The Cloud of Unknowing* is a case in point, while Wyclif and the Lollards were pressing for the Bible to be translated into English. John Gower, Chaucer's contemporary and friend, whom he calls 'moral Gower' at the end of *Troilus and Criseyde* (V: 1856), wrote in English (albeit with the Latin title *Confessio Amantis*) as well as French and Latin, which perhaps demonstrates that he considered English just as prestigious as the other two languages. There was also the flourishing alternative tradition of alliterative verse, which retained links with the older Anglo-Saxon verse forms and which Langland used for *Piers Plowman*, while the Gawain poet combined it with a rhyming structure for *Sir Gawain and the Green Knight* and *Pearl*. Chaucer does not seem to have had much time for this form: his Parson dismisses it as northern, asserting 'I am a Southren man;/I kan nat geeste "rum, ram, ruf", by lettre' (*Tales*, X: 42–3). It is hardly a fair comment, nor an accurate one, since Langland was based in the Malvern Hills and in London, but it does reveal the prejudice in favour of the more French-influenced version of English which prevailed in London and which Chaucer helped to become standard.

Other literature in English also permeated the times. Secular, political and religious lyrics abounded, as did ballads and romances. In general romances told stories of love or adventure about high-born people in distant places and enshrined noble ideals and courtly behaviour. They might also retell Classical legends and a sub-group, the lai, tended to include magic. They are often contrasted with fabliaux, also a thriving genre, which, like the romance, had French roots. Fabliaux were bawdy tales about low-born people in contemporary settings, whose plots revolve around sex and trickery and tend to be amoral if not immoral. Both were popular genres which made use of stereotypes and narrative conventions and, importantly, shared much the same audiences. In addition there was the drama. Best known to us are the cycles of plays (mystery plays) performed by Guildsmen, often on wagons working their way round the streets of cities, but there were also plays about saints lives (miracle plays) and allegories, such as *Everyman*.

An important manuscript, the Auchinleck Manuscript, epitomises much of the range of English writing available to Chaucer and his contemporaries. It is a miscellany of things, the majority in English, including romances, saints' lives and various satirical, didactic or religious pieces. A modern facsimile (Pearsall and Cunningham 1977) offers the chance of browsing through the kind of material and presentation Chaucer would have encountered. Moreoever, there is some evidence that this manuscript may have been owned by the Chaucer family at some stage (see Pearsall and Cunningham 1977: ix).

Italian

Although surrounded by this welter of English, Chaucer was also a man of his times and class in being aware of Italian and French literature. During the 1290s Dante had asserted the claims of Italian to be regarded as a worthy vehicle for high literature in his *Vita Nuova*, driving the point home in the *Divina Commedia* (Divine Comedy) and arguing that Italian should replace Latin in *De Vulgari Eloquentia* (On the Eloquence of the Vernacular). Chaucer makes direct reference to Dante (even parodying his eagle in the bird of *The House of Fame*), as he does also to Petrarch (for instance in The Clerk's Tale *Tales*, IV: 31–5), but although Petrarch wrote his long sonnet sequence in Italian, he used Latin for much of his work, and indeed did much to revive the study of Greek and Latin. Boccaccio, the third influential Italian, is oddly not mentioned directly by Chaucer, although he was clearly a source for many of his texts, in particular *Il Filostrato* (The Love-Struck) for *Troilus and Criseyde* and the *Teseida* for The Knight's Tale. Boccaccio and Chaucer seem to have shared some of the same interests in types of writing. Boccaccio's *Decameron* is a collection of tales, told over ten days by nobles escaping the Black Death. Influenced by Petrarch, he also studied the classical humanists – perhaps he was a little too close to Chaucer for him to name him overtly in his works. Detailed studies have been made of Chaucer in relation to his Italian sources and contemporaries, such as Boitani's book *Chaucer and Boccaccio* (1977) and his collection of essays on general Italian influences (Boitani 1985) or Nick Havely's work on Chaucer and Boccaccio (Havely: 1980), which will be of interest to those wishing to explore thoroughly this aspect of Chaucer's work.

French

As well as the Italians there were the French. Some mention has already been made of courtly lyrics, the French romance form and above all of *Le Roman de la Rose*, but there were also broader forms, just as there were in English, consisting of the comic tales (fabliaux) and *chansons de geste*. During his early career, Chaucer was surrounded by and imitated the many styles of literature in French which flourished in the English court, with its French queen and the court in exile of king John II of France. Guillaume de Machaut (*c.*1300–77) is a particularly significant figure: a musician and poet, he was one of the most influential writers of his time and many of Chaucer's works are indebted to him either directly (e.g. *The Book of the Duchess*) or in more general terms of style. Chaucer's relation with another Frenchman, Oton de Granson, seems to have been more reciprocal, as each imitated or adapted the poems of the other. They were exact contemporaries moving in the same circles: Granson was in the households of Edward III, then Gaunt and finally Richard II. Deschamps, meanwhile, not only imitated Chaucer, but also sent him some of his own ballads in the 1380s, prefaced with a dedicatory poem, praising Chaucer as 'le grand translateur' of *Le Roman de la Rose*. Those wishing to trace Chaucer's French influences will find Charles Muscatine's *Chaucer and the French Tradition* a good place to start (Muscatine 1957), while James Wimsatt provides more detailed discussion of Chaucer's relation to French contemporaries and the love poets (Wimsatt 1968 and 1991). One of the most significant French figures for us was the poet and chronicler, Jean Froissart. Froissart and Chaucer clearly knew each other well by the 1360s: their poetry shows mutual influence and Froissart mentions Chaucer several times in his *Chroniques*. As well as providing source material for some of Chaucer's earlier poetry, the tone of voice adopted by the chronicler, which is one of disinterested close observation rather than moral judgement, is similar to that used in *The Canterbury Tales*. Far from signalling lack of engagement, or of interest, this tone allows for a sharp description of character which Pearsall terms 'a kind of connoisseurship' (Pearsall 1992: 69). In addition to such literary input, Froissart's accounts furnish us with a vivid (albeit idiosyncratic) impression of court life and provide us with some insights into the political intrigues of the day, as well as descriptions of the culture and hospitality that went with them. Then, as now, corporate entertaining was an expensive and significant business.

When it comes to Chaucer's influence on English poetry and language, it is this adaptation of French and Italian habits of rhyme and the use of lightly anglicised French or Italian words which tends to strike us a paramount, and led Lydgate to term him the father of English poetry, a title which seems to have stuck. It was not all gain, of course. The northern English and Anglo-Saxon traditions had their own vocabulary and verse forms, which created a different kind of richness, but one which did not suit Chaucer's purposes so well. The loose-limbed alliterative verse form was based on two alliterating words in the first part of the line, a pause (caesura) and at least one further alliterating word in the second half line. This allowed for a varying number of syllables and stresses in each line, which makes it a good vehicle for long narrative poems, but was of little interest to Chaucer. His preference was for a more marked rhythm and he clearly loved rhyme, developing the rhyming couplet as his favoured form for narrative. It is this we can hear echoing down the years through his many followers and imitators: Henryson, Dunbar, Hoccleve and Lydgate all continue where Chaucer broke off, and help form the wider literary context and history in which we read him now.

The more one explores this context, the more fascinating it becomes, revealing the fourteenth century as a rich and fertile time for literature. Nonetheless, one of the most significant contexts in which to read Chaucer's works is that created by the texts themselves, so it is to those works this volume now turns.

Further Reading

The specific topics of chivalry, religion and courtly love are covered by Keen (1984), Leff (1958) and Lewis (1936), respectively. Boitani (1977 and 1985) and Havely (1980) cover Chaucer's Italian influences. Muscatine (1957) and Wimsatt (1968 and 1991) explore the French connection generally, and examples of contemporary fabliaux (not all

French) can be found in Benson and Andersson (1971). Rigby (1996) offers a straightforward presentation of Chaucer in his social context, while Dyer (1994) is an approachable account of life in general in Medieval England. Brewer (1998) and Pearsall (1992) naturally focus more precisely on Chaucer, and are invaluable. Burrow (1982) is an accessible and reliable introduction to Chaucer's general literary context and *Ricardian Poetry* (Burrow 1971, 1992) draws the connections between Chaucer and three of his great English contemporaries: Gower, Langland and the *Gawain* poet.

PART II
WORK

(a) SHORT VERSE

In his Retraction **[149]**, commonly printed at the end of *The Canterbury Tales*, Chaucer refers to 'many a song and many a leccherous lay' which he has written over the years. While the impression of prolific output created by this phrase fits with similar phrases used for Chaucer by Gower and Lydgate, it is hardly borne out by the relatively few short poems (twenty-two, not all strictly songs or lecherous) which have survived and are generally agreed to be Chaucer's. The answer may lie in part with the very similarity of phrase – it seems to have been common to refer to a poet as having written many such short pieces and indeed Chaucer makes use of this habit when referring to the 'manye layes,/Songes, compleintes, roundels, virelays' Aurelius composes in The Franklin's Tale, as Scattergood points out (Minnis 1995: 455). This appears to be an entirely positive reference, in contrast to the much-mocked Absolon of The Miller's Tale, who merely sings the songs, he does not write them. It may also be that such short pieces were regarded as enjoyable, but essentially ephemeral and so not worth recording.

When writing these poems Chaucer may have had a specific audience in mind: a group made up of court and civil servants like himself. Patricia Kean put forward this view in 1972 and is supported by Scattergood, who refers to them as 'coterie poems' with in jokes and references (Minnis 1995: 457). They are relatively overlooked by critics, although Laila Z. Gross points out that, after prolonged neglect, some of them are beginning to receive attention (*Riverside*: 631–3). Much of the neglect is attributed to the fact that several of them (notably 'A Complaint to his Lady' and 'An ABC') are clearly exercises in verse form and adaptation or close translation. Robinson termed them 'exercises in conventional styles of composition', a view Gross endorses, but without therefore dismissing them, while David's reading of 'An ABC', prevents us regarding it as primarily translation, however adept (David 1982). Indeed, as Ruud (Ruud 1992) and Scattergood (Minnis 1995: 455–512) illustrate, these poems reward attention. Moreover, they provide a good introduction to a Chaucer beyond that associated with the *Canterbury Tales* by illustrating his interest in the dominant poetic forms of his time, which he both copied and adapted, and by providing succinct examples of some of the major traditions, such as the courtly love vocabulary and devotional verse, which surface again embedded in his major works.

'Womanly Noblesse' might be taken as an instance of such exploration of a popular theme. Although the *Riverside Chaucer* places it among

Chaucer's lyrics, this attribution has been challenged, and is questioned by Pace and David (Pace and David 1982: 179–86). The title, invented by Skeat in the 1890s, is rather misleading as the poem does not focus on womanly 'noblesse', nor, indeed, on any other single quality but is an expression of love service in general terms. Its main interest lies in the technical feat of writing 32 lines rhyming only on '-aunce', '-esse' or '-hede', thus epitomising Robinson's description of the lyrics as poetic experiments.

It is impossible to date these poems precisely. While some of the shorter poems are undoubtedly early, with 'An ABC' being probably the earliest complete text surviving, Chaucer continued to write lyrics throughout his life, some in comic vein, some still as experiments in form and style. Although there are some aspects which suggest the influence of contemporary Italian authors (such as Dante and Boccaccio **[40]**), which are generally agreed to indicate a later date of composition, many of even the later lyrics show an abiding French influence, and remind us that ballades, roundelays, complaints and other French forms, as well as the topic of love, throve throughout the fourteenth century. The most informative edition to date is Pace and David for the Variorum Chaucer (Pace and David 1982).

(i) Three early short poems: 'To Rosemounde', 'An ABC', 'The Complaint Unto Pity'

Chaucer was the first to adapt the French ballade form to English verse. This ballade is distinct from the English minstrel ballad form (as exemplified in *The Tale of Sir Topas*) being a poem of three eight-line stanzas, each rhyming ababbcbc, where the last line forms a common refrain for each stanza. The poem might then be rounded off with a separate 'envoy' addressed to a lady or to a prince.

'To Rosemounde'

The simplest, and possibly earliest, example of this form is 'To Rosemounde'. It consists of three stanzas, but has no envoy. Despite the name in its title, it is possible that it was not written specifically for a woman called Rosemond, as the name was to some degree typical for a love poem, much as Celia and Sylvia were to become in later centuries. Literally, Rosemond means either 'rose of the world' or 'rosy mouthed' and as such could be taken to signify the beauty of any woman. There is a theory that this ballade was in fact written for Isabelle de Valois, Richard II's seven-year old bride who came to London in 1396. The fact that the poem begins with the word 'Madame' can support this theory, as 'madame' was the formal title given to the eldest daughter of the house of Valois. However, it was also a common enough form of polite address, and other scholars believe this ballade belongs to an earlier period of Chaucer's writing, mainly because of its simplicity.

That simplicity is an integral part of its charm. The language is typical of conventional love poetry as the woman's eyes are compared to crystal and her cheeks to rubies. The idea of love as a form of sickness, for which only the beloved has the cure, is hinted at in line seven, where seeing Rosamounde dance 'is an oynement unto my wounde'. However, the refrain of this particular ballade refers to the commonly bewailed heartlessness of women. 'Though ye to me ne do no daliaunce' asserts that she ignores the poet, 'daliaunce' implying the friendly encouragement of attentions that the poet says he desires, but which he will continue to do without, regardless. In thus ignoring him, Rosamounde is acting in a perfectly conventional manner, one which we will see again in Criseyde's initial response to Troilus **[98]**, and indeed the poet seems not particularly disheartened by the state of affairs. A suggestion of comedy even enters into the similes invoked in the final stanza which begins 'Nat never pyk walwed in galauntyne/ As I in love am walwed and ywounde'. The image of a fish smothered in aspic to be served cold may be an accurate representation of how it feels to be devoted to one who overlooks you, but it is not without humour. Perhaps such overstatement is appropriate for a verse composed for a grand but nonetheless young girl. A more serious note returns in the comparison to Tristram, the legendary knight famed for his love of Isolde. Such brief allusion is typical of courtly verse, and could be simply a reference to lovers renowned for their mutual devotion, but here, too, there is an appropriate element if the verse was indeed composed for Isabelle, in that these two lovers met when Tristram was escorting Isolde to her wedding to King Mark.

The poem ends with a typical assertion of continued devotion, regardless of the lady's behaviour, as the poet declares himself Rosamounde's 'thral', her slave, thus ending the ballade in the same conventional tones as it began.

'An ABC'

While 'To Rosamounde' is a ballade of courtly love, 'An ABC' is a devotional poem which uses the same rhyme scheme (though without the refrain) and ten-syllable (decasyllabic) line with five stresses or accents.

This line pattern (iambic pentameter) adapts the eight syllable (octo-syllabic) line of the French ballade form. It had rarely been used in English before, but was to become a favourite with Chaucer. 'An ABC' itself is a close translation of a prayer to Mary which appears in the long allegorical poem, *Pèlerinage de la Vie Humaine* (first brought out 1331) by Guillaume de Deguilleville. Each verse begins with a different letter of the alphabet (j, u, and w are omitted, probably because the capital forms of these letters would be identical to I and V or VV respectively) and contains a different image or allegory appropriate to the Virgin as the poet petitions Mary for help. It is likely that this poem belongs to an early point in Chaucer's writing career, when he was experimenting with poetic forms. On this basis Pearsall places it in the 1370s (Pearsall 1992: 83) but Thomas Speght (reprinted in Brewer 1969) records a tradition that Chaucer composed it at the request of John of Gaunt's first wife, Blanche, for her to use as a prayer. There is no support for this tradition, and it may well reflect Speght's desire to strengthen Chaucer's links with the Lancastrians.

'Unto Pity'

'An ABC' is usefully read in conjunction with 'The Complaint Unto Pity', which is also allegorical, but is entirely secular. Both texts draw on the same two lexical areas, law and courtly love, in a way which illustrates how much overlap there was between terms used for secular and religious spheres of life. Thus in 'An ABC' the 'cruel adversaire' of the first stanza is not only sin, the enemy, but also, it becomes apparent, a legal adversary, while in 'Unto Pity' 'crueltee' becomes personified and is not only Pity's opposite ('contraire', 64), but also her opposition. In each text a further allegorical level is also in play. The cruel adversary of 'ABC' is Sin in the abstract, who brings the legal action (accioun, 20) and is also the poet's own 'perilous langour' (7) which has prevented him fulfilling his religious duties and allowed him to fall into a state of sin. In 'Unto Pity' Pity, whose death is being lamented, is not just the general, abstract quality of pity, but the pity in a particular lady's character. As her mercy and pity to the poet die, her cruelty (also personified) takes over, condemning the poet to bewail his fate, while yet allowing the lady to retain her

> Beauty, Lust, Jolyte,
> Assured Manner, Youth and Honeste,
> Wisdom, Estaat, Drede, and Governaunce
> (39–41)

which, with 'Bounte', surround Pity's hearse and have taken on the aspect of conspirators with the word 'Confedred' (42). All of these qualities are expected elements in the character of the courtly lady, so we need not feel the text relates any actual or personal experience on the part of Chaucer.

The conventional aspect of this vocabulary is reinforced through comparison with 'An ABC' where the Virgin is also described in terms appropriate for ladies in court poetry. Thus Mary is 'Ladi bryghte' (181) and 'ful of merci' (173) whose 'grace' and 'socour' (156) are sought, just as Pity's mercy is implored ('Unto Pity' 92). It might also be added that in each text the poet is hoping to influence the lady's actions by invoking what she is – if she is a true lady, or the Lady of Heaven, she is bound to act with mercy and charity. Both Mary and Pity are intercessionary figures to whom the afflicted poet flees, seeking help in adversity while simultaneously promising undying service. The theme of continued service is similar to the end of 'To Rosamounde', with one major difference: there the poet is unconcerned about getting any actual response – he merely needs an excuse for the poem. In contrast, reciting 'An ABC' is itself an act of unending devotion: the move from Z to A (Zachariah to Adam) in the final stanza completes the circle of the poem by returning us to the beginning of the prayer and thus continuing the process of asking for Mary's benign inter-vention. In 'Unto Pity', however, things are less sanguine as the poet is left with the somewhat poorer consolation of his unending service to a lady whose death he has just lamented.

(ii) Other complaints: of Venus, *Anelida and Arcite*, of Mars, to his Purse

---

The rather down-beat ending of 'Unto Pity' is exactly what one would expect of a Complaint, which was more a tone than a form. Chaucer was the first to use the term in English, using it to cover a variety of lyrics which expressed emotion, without expecting any redress. The complaint is thus a peculiarly self-contained genre, which refers to a sequence of events without fully describing them. Two of the shorter poems conform to this pattern: 'A Complaint Unto his Lady' (some-times called 'A Ballade of Pity') which may be a collection of fragments rather than a complete poem, and 'The Complaint of Venus'. This is a free-standing love complaint with an envoy which reveals it to be a close adaptation of some ballades by Granson [41].

'The Complaint to Venus'

The structure of 'Venus' is a triple ballade with envoy; that is, three sections of three eight-line stanzas and a final, ten-line, stanza. The verse form is fairly tight, the stanzas of each section are closely linked through their common rhymes, patterned ababbccb, and shared final line. This requires a lot of rhyming words, a trick easier in French than English, as the envoy remarks: 'rym in Englissh hath such skarsete' (80). However, the self-referential effect of this rhyme-scheme suits the tone of complaint – Venus has no wish to change her situation, merely to express it. The discontents of love are acknowledged, but contained in the central section of the poem, where its topsy-turvy effects are described only to be dismissed in the third section, where Venus returns to thinking of her lover and his perfection. Although this inversion theme is a commonplace of love poetry, it is particularly appropriate here, since Chaucer has changed the speaker from the male of Granson's ballades to female, while yet retaining a close rendition of Granson's text. The fact that he could do this without changing too much illustrates the conventional nature of lovers' praise, but also raises the question of why he bothered. Some critics have found an answer in the manuscript rubric which records the belief that the poem was a riposte to 'The Complaint of Mars' for 'my lady of York' (*Riverside*: 1079) and that the two poems refer to a scandalous liaison between John Holland and one of Gaunt's daughters (possibly Isabella of York). However, this view has been challenged, as has the idea that the two complaints are linked, leaving 'Venus' to be read as a self-contained text.

While such self-containedness is fitting for the complaint genre, Chaucer rarely used it in this pure form. More often he prefaced the complaint with a narrative poem relating the events which gave rise to it (e.g. 'The Complaint of Mars' and *Anelida and Arcite*) or embedded it in a longer poem (e.g. Troilus's complaint in *Troilus*, I: 400–34).

Anelida and Arcite

Anelida and Arcite is an early and possibly incomplete experiment with this combination and is assumed to be Chaucer's first use of Boccaccio's *Teseida* **[40]**, from which is drawn much of the invocation and background, involving Theseus' return to Athens and the subsequent war between Athens and Thebes. Chaucer returned to this material later for The Knight's Tale, a fact which has contributed to *Anelida and Arcite* being largely regarded as a failure, redeemed only by the impressive poetic experimentation of the complaint itself. Scattergood, however, after dismissing the attempts to link it with some court scandal (also dismissed by DiMarco, the *Riverside* editor) defends the whole poem, asserting that it lives up to its grand opening in presenting the kind of love story found in classical epic (Minnis 1997: 469–73). Certainly it has its interest, particularly when read next to *The Legend of Good Women* **[100]** and *Troilus and Criseyde* **[89]**. In this tale it is the man who is deceitful and unequivocally so. Arcite is introduced as 'double in love' (87) and out to deceive Anelida. She is deceived, but despite trusting him utterly, still acts as a lady ought: 'But nevertheles ful mykel besynesse/Had he er that he myghte his lady wynne' (99–100). She is thus a contrast to Dido, whose quick (but reciprocated) love is told in both *The House of Fame* (239–387) **[73]** and *The Legend of Good Women* (924–1367) **[104]**. Arcite has no affection for Anelida but enjoys his power over her until his urge for change ('newfanglenesse') takes over and he courts another, far less receptive, woman. Here the narrative is interrupted by Anelida's metrically complex complaint. The pattern of the complaint is detailed in the Riverside edition (*Riverside*: 993 n211–350) as Chaucer ranges across a variety of rhyme schemes and stanza lengths, while yet retaining a broadly symmetrical shape and offering some fine poetry. Three lines of elusive imagery in the fourth stanza describing Arcite's fickleness stand out in particular:

> For though I hadde yow to-morrowe ageyn,
> I myghte as wel holde Aperill fro reyn
> As holde yow, to make you be stidfast.
> (308–10)

Although one stanza of resumed narrative exits after the complaint, there is no more than that and the authenticity of this one stanza has been questioned. It is possible that Chaucer intended to end the poem with the complaint, thus following the same pattern as 'Unto Pity' and 'The Complaint of Mars'. Lee Patterson prefers this view, adding that by ending with Anelida's complaint Chaucer leaves his protagonist held within her historical story (Patterson 1991: 78).

'The Complaint of Mars'

Like *Anelide and Arcite*, 'The Complaint of Mars' assumes we know something of the tale that provides the poem's context. That is the love affair between Venus and Mars, which is discovered by Phoebus, who tells Vulcan (Venus's husband). In the Ovid original, Vulcan sets an elaborate trap for the two, which results in them being trapped in a net, caught in the act. Chaucer omits this aspect, but the reference to the two being eager to avoid Phoebus reminds his audience of it. As well as retelling Ovid, the poem also describes fairly accurately the conjunction of the planets Venus and Mars of April 1385, thus providing a likely year of composition. In the poem Mars gives the date of 12 April (139), while the proem declares the story and complaint to have been sung by birds on St. Valentine's day (probably the Genoese celebration, held in May [77]). Whether it was actually written then or soon after, it attests Chaucer's interest in astronomy, an interest which the audience is expected to share: Mars won Venus 'As wel by hevenysh revolucioun/ As by desert,' (29–30) and Venus is seen to move 'as faste in her weye/ Almost in oo day as he dyde in tweye' (69–70) while the fact that the lovers must part as Phoebus (the sun) appears dramatises the fading of the planets at dawn as well as the passing of the planetary conjunction. The complaint proper makes no reference to astronomy, being instead a lament about the misfortunes of love in five parts, each with a particular theme. It is prefaced with a single stanza which sums up the essence of the complaint form:

> The ordre of compleynt requireth skyfully
> That yf a wight shal pleyne pitously,
> Ther mot be cause wherfore that men pleyne;
> Or men may deme he pleyneth folily
> And causeles; alas, that am not I.
> Wherfore the ground and cause of al my peyne,
> So as my troubled wit may hit atteyne,
> I wol reherse; not for to have redresse,
> But to declare my ground of hevynesse
>
> (155–63)

It is a nice touch that this is an occasion on which one might wish to be regarded as having no grounds for complaint. Instead, not coming in for that kind of criticism becomes a further matter for regret and leads into the description of Mars' distress. The complaint and the poem ends with an appeal to the gathered audience in which knights and scholars are asked to sympathise with him, while ladies empathise with Venus and lovers with the situation as a whole.

'The Complaint of Chaucer to his Purse'

The turning outward of the poem towards its audience seen in 'Mars' is used again in this last complaint definitely attributed to Chaucer which was written late in his life. Usually dated 1399 this complaint is presumed to be addressed to Henry IV, recently crowned and here reminded of Chaucer's need for payment. It is a true complaint in that it has no preceeding narrative and, while making the reasons for the complaint clear, does not explicitly ask for redress. That is the job of the envoy, which some believe may have been added later, presumably when Chaucer sent the poem to the new king. The poem is wryly humorous, with the purse taking the place of his lady and Chaucer mourning its lightness. The refrain line, 'Beth hevy ageyn, or elles mot I dye', exploits the literal meaning of words frequently used metaphorically in love poetry: 'hevy' would be an undesirable aspect in a lover, where it would mean 'sad', but is a most welcome sign in a purse, and without money Chaucer will literally die.

The envoy reveals the politic side of Chaucer: to describe Henry as a conqueror is no more than accurate, as is his right to the throne through blood-line. To add 'free eleccioun' is rather pushing the point, but is undoubtedly flattering. In all, the poem, with its graceful rhymes and clever exploitation of the language of both money and love, displays the skill of the mature poet returning to a favoured verse form.

(iii) Boethian ballades and envoys

'The Former Age', 'Fortune', 'Truth', 'Gentilesse' and 'Lak of Steadfastnesse' form a group of poems usually termed 'Boethian' because their themes are similar to those found in Boethius, whose *Consolation of Philosophy* Chaucer clearly read with interest and translated probably in the early 1380s **[83]**. The ballades themselves may have been written over quite a period of years (probably between the late 1380s and mid 1390s) and the influences present in them are not solely Boethian, as Chaucer also blended in elements from Virgil, Ovid and *The Romance of the Rose*, amongst others. Nonetheless, there is a certain common tone to these lyrics, perhaps because in them Chaucer is at his most straightforwardly reflective and socially critical.

'The Former Age'

This ballade describes the mythical golden age before hardships of any kind entered the world. It was a common topic which influenced the Garden of Love motif in courtly love poetry, although in the latter the lack of work is due to affluence rather than contentment with one's lot. Inevitably the 'former age' was a time of simpler values, which is the aspect Chaucer develops through the poem as he embarks on a list of all the things people then did without. As Scattergood points out, many of these are the 'questionable benefits' of fourteenth-century living (Minnis 1995: 487) including wine, dyed wool, and spices ground into wines or sauce galantyne, the very sauce which covers the fish of 'To Rosamonde' **[49]**. The playful tone of that earlier lyric is hardly heard here as Chaucer expands the tradition of the central trope, that in simpler times there were no riches to give rise to greed and in turn to strife, in particular the strife which breeds in the halls of the affluent and the corridors of power. Jupiter is here mentioned as a symbol of wilful indulgence in lust, while Nimrod represents ambitious rulers. Such descriptions have led the poem to be read as harsh political satire directed at Richard, specifically between the years 1397–99, when he was particularly despotic, although his court was criticised at earlier dates too. However, the last three lines paint a bleak picture of actual life which reaches beyond specific historical referents:

> For in oure dayes nis but covetyse
> Doublenesse, and tresoun, and envye,
> Poyson, manslawhtre, and morder in sondry wyse.

It is this tone which has led Scattergood to describe Chaucer's attitude here as 'pessimistic' (Minnis 1995: 489).

'Lak of Stedfastnesse'

The general pessimism of 'The Former Age' becomes particular in 'Lak of Stedfastnesse' which focuses on how unreliable everyone has becomes in word and deed. It begins with referring back to a time when things were secure and a man's word his bond. All that has been overthrown through greed and desire for power to such an extent that men are judged by their ability to oppress others. The third stanza expands the topic into a list of inversions, illustrating how the whole world has 'mad a permutacioun' (19), which is not only a change but also a revolution, shifting, the poem says, from right to wrong, from truth to falsehood. The final stanza is an envoy addressed to Richard II, which might have been added at a later date, imploring him to reassert right rule. It is ironic that the terms in which this is couched hint at the very oppression criticised in the second verse: 'Shew forth thy swerd of castigacioun' (26). The difference being that Richard is by right the one in the position to scold, though the envoy goes on to warn him to 'Dred God, do law, love trouthe and worthinesse' (27).

Debates over royal prerogative and objections to its abuse characterised the later part of Richard's reign, especially the Parliament of 1386, which Chaucer attended as a representative for Kent. To a civil servant and one heavily reliant on royal grants and positions, the issues would have had a personal application which perhaps accounts for the earnestness of this poem.

'Fortune'

'Fortune' likewise relates wider movements to the individual, but that may as easily result from the form of the poem as from any particular events in Chaucer's life. It is written as a debate between a plaintiff and Fortune, and thus draws somewhat on complaint conventions. Its subtitle, 'Balades de Visage sanz Peinture' (ballads of a face without paint), has given rise to some discussion. It could refer to the description of Fortune in Boethius as covered up to other people but revealed to the poet (*Consolatio*, II: pr. i), thus the poem reveals the picture of one who has never been portrayed, or it could suggest that the verse provides a naked picture of Fortune, without her benign side, here equivalent to make-up. It has also been suggested that the subtitle should in fact read 'deux visages', thus linking it to the kind of dialogue poem written by Machaut **[41]** and termed 'balades a deux visages' – between two people.

To rail against Fortune for bringing adversity, as the plaintiff does here, is a lost cause, since Fortune is by her nature unreliable. Frequently pictured with a wheel which she constantly revolves, the idea of fortune was one of change and instability: if you were up one day it was likely you would be down the next. This is the aspect of her referred to in The Knight's Tale (*Tales*, I: 925 and 1235–43) **[111]** and in *The House of Fame*, where she is mentioned as Fame's sister, and just as cavalier in doling out good or bad circumstances to people in general as Fame is in bestowing good or bad reputations on individuals (*House*: 1547) **[74]**. In this ballade, however, we are reminded of the benefits that even ill-fortune can bestow – primarily that of discovering who our true friends are. The image of Fortune holding up a mirror of truth is an unusual one which harks back to the notion of portraiture in the sub-title. However, the complainant asserts that it is his reason which allows him to distinguish the reflection of the true from the false, rather than it being simply a property of the mirror itself.

Throughout the poem, the plaintiff persists in defining Fortune only as bad luck, declaring that his self-sufficiency will see him through without her. In response she points out that in that case he has nothing to complain about (he who has sufficent, has enough), but also reminds him that she is as much the embodiment of good fortune as of bad. She is by definition changeable, and treats all people impartially in her unreliability. Although she has the last word, it is clear that the plaintiff remains unconvinced and in the envoy it seems that Fortune is aware of this as she seeks to stop his constant complaints by asking 'princes' to 'releve him of his peyne'. This envoy makes the poem into an oblique begging letter, in which the 'three of you or tweyne' may refer to the dukes of Lancaster, York and Gloucester, at least two of whom had to agree to any royal grant, after the ordinance of 1390. This allusion has been used to date the poem and to identify the 'beste frend' of the second section as Richard II.

The theme of sufficiency which 'Fortune' wields in defiance is offered as a more stoical consolation in 'Truth'. The envoy to this poem clearly refers to Philip de le Vache, a close friend of Chaucer who suffered badly in the upheavals of power of 1386–89, falling out of favour and losing his position and income. This envoy appears in only one manuscript, however, and may well have been added at a later date to add particular relevance to a pre-existing poem whose theme was already one of being content with one's lot and the advantages of obscurity. The good counsel ('bon conseyl') of the subtitle is not only philosophical but also Christian. The truth that will deliver him thus gradually becomes the truth of faith, as the reader of the poem is reminded that this life is like a journey through a potentially hostile land ('wildernesse') to our true home in the next world. The metaphors of pilgrim and driven beast reflect the somewhat ambiguous feelings that accompany such an image.

'Gentillesse'

'Gentilesse' is altogether less dour. It succinctly expresses the tenet of true gentility being a quality of character, not an attribute of wealth or family inheritance, which is also presented by the crone of the Wife of Bath's Tale (*Tales*, III: 1109–64) **[123]**. The idea is by no means original to Chaucer, being found in both Boethius **[83]** and Jean de Meun's section of *Le Roman de la Rose* **[62]**, but readers fond of making biographical connections like to see this as a particularly apt theme for an up-and-coming poet from the merchant classes. It is important to note that in putting the case for virtue to bestow nobility the poem not only assumes that such nobility is worth striving for, but also addresses itself entirely to an audience for whom such social standing was at least potentially within reach. It is more a reminder that the gentry should live up to their title, than a call for meritocracy, and is a long way from the egalitarian, not to say revolutionary cry of John Bull and the peasants of 1381, who used the ditty 'Whan Adam delf and Eve span,/Who was thanne the gentleman?' Scattergood suggests that the use of 'stok'could indicate a reference to the image of a tree trunk (stock) used by the royal house (Minnis 1995: 486) though other critics have interpreted 'stok' as referring to Adam, as first father of mankind. Henry Scogan (the addressee of Chaucer's 'Envoy') quoted the whole of 'Gentilesse' in his *Moral Balade* addressed to Henry IV's sons and took 'stok' to mean God as the source of all noble qualities.

'Lenvoy de Chaucer a Scogan'

Addressed to the Henry Scogan mentioned above, this may be a poem asking his friend who has influence at court (all manuscripts gloss 'the stremes hed' as Windsor) to use it to Chaucer's advantage, or at very least not to forget those who live further down the Thames (i.e. Greenwich). The poem is humorous in its use of exaggeration, accusing Scogan of being the cause of the downpours which accompanied an outbreak of plague in 1391, which here become the tears of Venus, weeping excessively because Scogan has ditched his mistress. It appears that Scogan has given up love, and while Chaucer cautions him that to do so is traditionally dangerous (Troilus pays for a similar offence) he simultaneously urges that to give up love is not to give up friendship. He also implies that one so important as Scogan giving up love could lead to Cupid ignoring all the other grey and fat people who might not have taken such a drastic step: though at least they will know whom to blame for being unlucky in love. Chaucer then excludes himself from this group, declaring he, too, has given up such things, ending the body of the poem with the thought that there is a time for such things and implying that both he and Scogan have had their turn, 'Take every man hys turn, as for his tyme'. Yet the envoy seems to contradict this thought as Chaucer encourages Scogan to remember his old friend Chaucer, stuck out in the wilderness, and warn him not to defy Love again. This is best accounted for by reading this last love as the love between friends, which should lead Scogan to act like the mythical king Tullius, renowned for his kindness to the poor.

'Lenvoy de Chaucer a Bukton'

Both 'envoy's to Scogan and Bukton owe much to the tradition of verse letters. Norton-Smith argues that Chaucer is particularly indebted to Horace here, and certainly the image of the pen rusting in its sheath and the exiled position of the poet in 'Scogan' echo Horace closely (Norton-Smith 1974: 213–35) as does the more general tone of 'Lenvoy a Bukton'. Attempts to indentify Bukton have arrived at two candidates: Sir Peter Bukton of Holderness and Sir Robert Bukton of Goosewold, with Peter Bukton being the more favoured candidate (see *Riverside*: 1087 and Scattergood 1987). While it would satisfy our curiosity to know exactly who Bukton was, there is nothing in the poem which demands a specific recipient. Rather it is a mock-serious warning against remarriage, working round stock responses, but presented in a manner described as 'the gently jesting style of Horace' (Norton-Smith 1974: 221). Certainly the poem is a rhetorical flourish as Chaucer balances what he dare say against what he dare not, Biblical authority against personal experience and finally actual experience against that of the fictional Wife of Bath. Buried within all this is a rare allusion to contemporary events. In 1376 there was an expedition against the Frisians, which may well have given rise to 'That the were lever to be take in Frise/Than eft to falle of weddynge in the trappe'. This is saying a great deal: the Frisians were renowned for killing their prisoners rather than putting them up for ransom. This comedy carries serious undertones; how far they reflect Chaucer's actual views on marriage must be a matter of personal conviction.

'Chaucer's Wordes unto Adam, his owne Scriveyn'

What is unambiguously clear from 'Lenvoy a Bukton' is Chaucer's awareness of the standing of his work. To refer to the Wife of Bath, however ironically, is to admit her importance. Such awareness gave rise to this short but decidely sharp poem. Here again there is a surface of humour as Chaucer calls down a curse of itchy scalp should his scribe be negligent, but under that surface is the voice of a man who not only knows that *Boece* and *Troilus* are in demand but is also well aware of the ease with which errors are made and become enshrined within texts. It is easy to think that this preoccupation is peculiar to the days before printed books, when the author was the creative one who did the 'makyng' while the scribe's job was to 'wryte', but there are twentieth century parallels: James Joyce allowed several printing errors in the proofs of *Ulysses* to stand, thus incorporating them into the final version. Chaucer's attitude to his standing as author seems to have been less relaxed as his interest in the vagaries of literary transmission that gave rise to *The House of Fame* **[71]** develops into the anxious prayer that 'non myswrite the' of *Troilus*, V: 1795. It has been suggested that 'Adam' refers to the Biblical Adam (Peck 1975: 467 and Kaske 1979), the archytypal spoiler of a good creation, but on the whole this seems unlikely, though efforts to identify Adam securely have simply given rise to a list of possibilities (Pace and David 1982: 133–4).

Further Reading

Minnis's Oxford *Guide* (Minnis 1995) is a good, informative starting place for exploring Chaucer's shorter poems. More detail can be found in a still accessible form in the *Variorum Chaucer* (Pace and David 1982). Norton-Smith (1974) offers interesting readings in the context of Chaucer's life generally, while Ruud (1992) is particularly useful on the lyrics and Scattergood (1981) offers historically informed engagement with the envoys.

(b) THE DREAM POEMS

Chaucer's major dream poems (*The Book of the Duchess, The House of Fame, The Parliament of Fowls,* the Prologue to *The Legend of Good Women*) tend to be grouped together and regarded as products of the earlier part of his writing career, that is between the 1370s and late 1380s. However, there is some support for a date of 1369 for *The Book of the Duchess* and some debate over the date of the Prologue to *The Legend of Good Women,* which exists in two versions: the earlier F text being probably composed in around 1386 while many believe the later G version to have been written in around 1397 (but see Delany 1994: 34–43). In addition and indeed prior to these texts, Chaucer translated the popular French love vision *Le Roman de la Rose.* This text is frequently overlooked for the simple reason that, although we know Chaucer translated it, we do not know for sure that the fragment of text attributed to him is in fact his. Despite this, the French original was influential enough for Chaucer and the Middle English fragment close enough to his style to merit attention. It also provides an excellent introduction to the traditions of medieval dream poetry: having read *The Romaunt of the Rose,* even only Fragment A **[62–4]**, the many elements which Chaucer borrowed and adapted from courtly poetry, in particular the love vision, become familiar, as they would have been to a contemporary audience. Chief among these are: the use of the double framework of narrator and dream; the descriptions of the natural world; the reference to other books, especially *The Dream of Scipio* or Ovid's *Metamorphoses*; the topic of love. However these poems are not

61

just variations on the theme of love and love vision. Chaucer makes good use of the tradition of the dream as a genre which could include debate of the full range of intellectual and philosophical topics and also allowed for easy movement between different forms of writing, from narrative to lyric, into debate or even song. Thus, it may be misleading to describe love as the central theme of all Chaucer's dream poems (Phillips and Havely 1997: 3) as, while love is indeed mentioned in each of them, the texts themselves seem to be more interested in other topics. *The Book of the Duchess* clearly explores grief and melancholy and touches on memory. This last is developed in *The House of Fame* to encompass ideas of how fame (living on in other people's memory) is achieved and to include thoughts on the writing of literature. *The Parliament of Fowls* blends social satire and simple fun with its debate on love, while the Prologue to *The Legend of Good Women* must serve as an introduction to a series of stories about women who died for love.

(i) *The Romaunt of the Rose*

The French allegorical poem, *Le Romaunt de la Rose* begun by Guillaume de Lorris in 1237 and continued by Jean de Meun in around 1280 was arguably the single text most influential on Chaucer. It was widely known in the thirteenth and fourteenth centuries and thus provided not only a pattern for style and poetic matter, but also a rich source of allusion. The earlier section of the text encapsulates the love vision genre, indeed Guillaume de Lorris is credited with having written the definitive love vision in his *Roman* and Chaucer was clearly impressed by it enough to not only translate it but also to use and adapt the form in his own dream poems. We know that Chaucer translated it, as he refers to his version in the Prologue to *The Legend of Good Women* where the god of Love accuses him of having translated it into plain English (*Legend*, F: 327–31; G: 253–7), we are less certain that we still have his translation. Certainly not all of it has survived, assuming he did indeed translate both de Lorris' section and de Meun's. Of the three fragments of Middle English versions which have survived two are certainly not by Chaucer, despite having been attributed to him at various stages. The other, 'Fragment A', consists of about 1705 lines, translating the beginning of de Lorris' text, but breaks off mid-sentence. The *Riverside Chaucer* prints all three fragments, but as only the first is agreed to be possibly by Chaucer, that is only one to receive attention here. However, it is clear from other texts that Chaucer was well acquainted with both parts of the poem, as he draws on elements from de Meun's section as well as de Lorris'. Study of this translation thus provides not only an idea of the kinds of writing that influenced Chaucer and an introduction to his habit of close translation as a method of absorbing texts, but also offers a good basic knowledge of dream poetry. From this it is possible to see how Chaucer went on to develop the form in his own dream poems before moving into other forms to explore narrative techniques. He never fully abandoned dream poetry; elements of it can be seen even in his latest works as he drew on theories of the significance (or otherwise) of dreams either to provide an excuse for later action (as happens in *Troilus*, II: 925–31; V: 1233–41, 1442–1540 and the Prologue to *The Legend of Good Women* **[81, 100]**) or for more simple comic effect as in the Nun's Priest's Tale **[141]**.

The poem opens with the narrator addressing the audience directly with a few thoughts on the validity of dreams and a fleeting reference to Macrobius, known for his commentary on Cicero's *Dream of Scipio (Somnium Scipionis)*. This forms the last part of Cicero's *Republic* and tells how Scipio the Younger dreamt that his grandfather, Scipio Africanus, visited him and engaged him in a long philosophical discussion. The *Republic* was not known to the Middle Ages, but the Dream of Scipio had been preserved through the long commentary that Macrobius made on it, which led to the Dream itself being mistakenly attributed to Macrobius. The commentary takes various sections of the dream as illustrations of subjects as diverse as arithmetic, the music of the spheres and the immortality of the soul and was a popular text in the Middle Ages. Above all, Macrobius' text became a source for views on the origins and value of dreams. As such it provided a secular companion for the divine authority of dreams as attested by the Bible. Other causes of dreams were also acknowledged, such as preoccupation with a particular idea or worry, a reflection of an aspect of the dreamer's personality or simple indigestion. Chaucer makes reference to these notions of dreams in several texts, summing up most of the views The Nun's Priest's Tale (*Tales*, VII: 2922–3171).

The *Romaunt*'s simple two line defence of the value of dreams is also an appropriate description of allegorical writing; each contain 'Ful many thynges covertly/That fallen after al openly' (19–20) and so the audience is primed to interpret as well as listen. As it goes on the narrator reveals that he is twenty years old, a significant detail as the brief preambles of love visions tend to contain elements which resurface in the main part of the text and here youth is revealed as an essential quality for those engaged in the pursuit of love. The poet/narrator then describes falling asleep and waking into a dream. The May setting of the dream landscape prepares us for both a love vision and the following allegory of the walled garden (associated with earthly paradise and idealised love) and the characters who populate the dream are likewise personifications or allegories. As the poem moves into its narrative, further elements of romance are introduced. The larks and parrots (81) are taken as signs of the season, although while larks are simply symbols of spring, famous for the beauty of their song, parrots have more complex associations. Their bright plumage fits with the colours of this landscape and their reputation for loving luxury and wine perhaps add to the rich overtones of the dream, but it could also introduce an unwelcome note as their voice was considered ugly. When Chaucer uses the birds again in *The Parliament of Fowls* they are 'ful of delicasye' (359) and grouped with lower order birds who are known for destructive habits and by the time he uses them in The Merchant's and Shipman's tales (*Tales*, IV: 2321–2; VII: 369), and in 'Sir Topas' (*Tales*, VII: 767) the disparaging undercurrents have become deliberate overtones, used for comic effect. It may be then, that their appearance here is not only true to the French original, but also introduces a first hint of satire into the poem.

However in the *Romaunt* the themes of unconcerned beauty are dominant, as the dreamer prepares himself for a walk in this idealised landscape by sewing up his sleeves in a suitably fashionable manner, using a silver needle, which not only indicates affluence in itself, but also gives a clue to the fineness of the fabric: a silver needle will not catch on delicate threads (97–9). Suitably attired, the dreamer wanders by a stream until he comes to a walled garden (136). On the outside are painted the figures of Hate, Felony, Villainy, Covetousness, Avarice, Envy, Sorrow, Age, Pope-Holiness (hypocrisy, particularly that expressed by pretending to be morally superior) and Poverty. Initially it seems we have a representation of human sins or failings, but the inclusion of sorrow and poverty make it clear that these figures represent characteristics which prevent entry into the garden of courtly love. One cannot afford to be sad or poor. On the other hand it is essential to have leisure: the gatekeeper of this idyllic spot is Idleness.

The garden is governed by Sir Mirth and all the company are fair, young and engaged in the refined pursuits, including dancing a formal 'karole', which is here accompanied by a song, sung by Gladness. This dance offers the opportunity to name those present in the garden, in balance to those excluded. Here are Courtesy, the God of Love, Sweet-Looking, Beauty, Riches, Largess (generosity), Franchise (nobility/ generosity of spirit) and Youth. As with the previous list of personifications, most of these figures are female, but that reflects the gender of the nouns in French, rather than being a specific choice on the part of the translator. The dreamer is invited to join the dance and when it comes to an end, he wanders off to explore the rest of the garden, unaware that the God of Love is stalking him like a hunter (1450–4). This inverts the motif of the love hunt in which the lady is often the quarry, but other elements of the motif are present in the description of the grassy area full of flowers, deer, squirrels and rabbits, which recalls the 'millefleurs' background of medieval tapestries. The dreamer rests under a tree next to a well which he recognises as the Well of Love into which Narcissus looked when he fell in love with his own reflection. The story of Narcissus is retold, thus introducing a further element of the romance genre, that of the classical tale or fable. Significantly, though, the moral drawn is not the warning against male vanity which the story most obviously offers, but a warning to ladies not to mistreat their lovers. Upon looking into the well himself the dreamer sees the reflection of a gorgeous rose-bush, which he promptly seeks and easily finds, commenting that he prefers buds to open roses, as they last longer. On this bush is one rosebud, fairer than all the others, which he describes.

At this point Fragment A ends. In the rest of the French poem the dreamer falls in love with the rosebud and strives to possess it. In de Lorris' hands the allegory remains allusive, though it is clear the rose symbolises a lady, who, after granting a kiss, is swept away and guarded by Jealousy, amongst others. The poem relates the dreamer's attempts to win the rose against all the odds, clearly with the intention that the attempt will be successful. In de Meun's continuation the allegory becomes more acerbic and he widens its sphere of reference to include social satire and philosophical debate, both of which are within the remit of the love vision genre, but only lightly present in de Lorris' text. His use of the rose symbol is also more explicit as the depiction of the final possession is a thinly disguised description of the sexual act. The mixture of elegant romance, highly suggestive symbolism and social satire, gradually surfaces in Chaucer's own writings. At this early period it seems to be the combination of courtly convention and philosophical debate which drew his attention.

(ii) *The Book of the Duchess*

This, Chaucer's most courtly poem, is generally agreed to be a commemorative text written for the death of Blanche, John of Gaunt's first wife. She died in 1368/69, and the poem may have been written shortly afterwards, or for one of the commemorative services that were held for her each year (see Hardman 1994). It is generally believed to have been written before 1371, however, as the title of Earl of

Richmond, which is punned on in the 'ryche hille' of line 1319, was restored to John de Montfort in 1372, having been John of Gaunt's title before that.

Broadly speaking, the poem is divided into three parts: the first (1–289) introduces the narrator, who retells the story of Seys and Alcione, which he has read in a book in an attempt to get to sleep. The second (290–442) comprises the dream, as the narrator is 'woken' by the sound of a hunt, which he joins, but which loses its quarry. The dreamer then follows a puppy who appears at his feet and comes across a man in black sitting under a tree reciting a lament. This leads into the third section (443–1310) which consists of the dreamer asking the knight why he is so melancholy (he has lost his lady) and of the knight's replies, which describe his lady and their mutual love and ends with the statement of her death. This signals the end of the poem (1311–34) as the hunt is heard again in the distance and the dreamer sees the hunting party enter a castle whose ringing bell wakes the narrator from his dream to find himself still holding the book he had been reading before falling asleep. He declares he will record the dream he has just had; which is, of course, the poem we have just read.

The three parts of the text are linked not only by the simple linear narrative of the dream, but also by recurrent use of the theme of bereavement, of the colours black and white and by an underlying play with the connotations of the word 'reflection'. We know little about the narrator figure of this poem, except that he is unable to sleep and has been in that state for some considerable time, due, he believes, to a sickness he has suffered for eight years. Some critics have taken this to be an indication that the poem was written eight years after Blanche's death, giving a date of composition of 1376, though some French tales, such as those by Machaut, use such phrases to provided a sense of a stretch of time (see *Riverside*: 967n30–43.) He describes this as an affliction so unnatural and severe that he fears he will die from it:

> And I ne may, ne nyght ne morwe,
> Slepe; and thus melancolye
> And drede I have for to dye.
>
> (22–4)

It is unclear whether the sorrow results in lack of sleep or whether the inability to sleep gives rise to the melancholy, but the picture is that of a man in distress. Moreover, such protracted sorrow is termed unnatural 'nature wolde nat suffyse' (16) thereby introducing the first hint that prolonged grief may be excessive and undesirable, even unhealthy, as it could result in melancholia, a state of life-denying sadness, which we might describe now as acute depression. At the time it was believed to be caused by an excess of black things in the body and one of its effects was dreams of black things (Minnis 1995: 154–5). It has been suggested that the one physician who the dreamer asserts is the only one who could cure him is his loved one and that the sickness he suffers is the love-sickness suffered also by Troilus, but it is also possible that the affliction is grief and the anticipated cure, death. The action of the poem, the reading and the dream, thus become not only variations on the theme of expressing sorrow, but also a process of cure or consolation as well.

At first it would seem that the example of Seys and Alcione is hardly an encouraging one. Seys has died at sea, but all that Alcione knows is that he has not returned from a voyage. Driven by sorrow, she prays for certain knowledge about her husband, and receives it via a dream in which the dead Seys stands at the foot of her bed and tells her both that he is dead and to cease her grieving:

> Awake! Let be your sorwful lyf,
> For in your sorwe, ther lyth no rede;
> For, certes, swete, I am but ded.
> (202–4)

The call to 'awake' links the states of sleep, grief and even death, as Seys urges his wife to rise up and continue living. Ironically, however, when Alcione does awake, she dies of grief within three days, hardly a good example of consolation. However, the original does not end there, but with the transformation of the two into seabirds, thus providing the metamorphosis of the story, and reuniting and literally reviving the two as a testament of the power of their love. Chaucer, or perhaps his narrator, deliberately omits this, thus denying the figure of consolation in that story and effectively deferring it into the rest of the poem. It is a change which would probably have been noted by the contemporary audience, also familiar with Ovid and Machaut, who would thus have been amused by the consolation the narrator does draw from the story, i.e. that there is a god of sleep who may be petitioned in the hope of being granted rest.

The sleep that he is granted gives rise to the dream, which is the bulk of the poem and in which we encounter several elements drawn from this first section of the text. First of all the May landscape, complete with birdsong and hunt, all create the atmosphere of courtly love vision, familiar to us from *The Romaunt of the Rose* **[62]**. The bright morning and wide outdoors contrast with the inside and evening setting of the first section of the text, as does the dreamer's sudden liveliness, compared to his previous lethargy. It seems he has followed Seys' advice where Alcione did not and has paradoxically come awake in his dream and indeed left behind his sorrowful life. Now full of energy he eagerly joins in the hunting of the hart, though as an onlooker rather than a main hunter. When the quarry is lost he wanders off, but is prevented from resting for too long and perhaps becoming once again too intro-spective by the puppy, which he follows until it leads him to the Man in Black, a Knight singing a lament under a tree.

The identity of this figure is one of the mysteries of the poem: as Minnis says, 'to equate the Man in Black with John of Gaunt is absurd, while to deny the connection would be perverse' (Minnis 1995: 154). The fact that this figure is lamenting the loss of a lady called 'White', a translation of Blanche's name, invites us to link the Man in Black with the presumably grieving Gaunt. The deference with which the dreamer addresses him (using the polite 'you' while the Man in Black uses 'thou') supports this reading for those who see the dreamer as figure of Chaucer. While clearly operating on one level of the text, this is not the only interpretation open to us. It is also possible to read this figure as a representation of the dreamer's melancholy self, thereby making the dream a kind of self-analysis. Such a reading is within the bounds of medieval dream theory, as both an *insomnium* (resulting from physical causes such as mental distress) or a *visium* or *phantasma* (the result of images occupying the mind on the borders of sleep). Neither form of dream is prophetic, but although they were not necessarily significant, they could be seen to reveal deep-seated pre-occupations. Certainly all the elements combine to encourage us to regard the Man in Black as an allegorical figure and indeed he himself presents himself as an icon of grief asserting 'For y am sorwe, and sorwe ys y' (597). The symmetrical balance of the sentence defies further explanation and serves to make the figure not only self-contained but also static. It is as if there is nowhere to go from that statement, just as for Alcione there was no way forward from the certainty of her loss. More than that, each half of the sentence answers the other, encapsulating a chiasmic exchange of: 'who are you?' 'I am sorrow.' 'What is sorrow?' 'I am'. The figure is thus caught in a constantly echoing pattern which leads nowhere and works like two mirrors set up opposite each other, eternally reflecting themselves. This reflection motif is continued as the Man in Black goes on to explain why he is in this state. Every thing in his world has become its opposite, as reflection becomes inversion:

My song ys turned to pleynynge,
And al my laughtre to wepynge,
My glade thoghtes to hevynesse,
In travayle ys myn ydelnesse
                    (599–602)

This is not an explanation of cause, however, but a description of being grief. We are no further on.

By now a link is established between the Man in Black of the dream and the grieving Queen of the story. This link is also a reflection, as the positions of the pairs are reversed – in the story it is the man who has died and the woman who is bereaved: in the dream it is the man who is bereft, while the lady has been lost. In each case the griever summons up the image of their lost one: Alcione through her prayer to Juno, the Man in Black first in his song – which the dreamer overhears (475–86) – and then in the series of narrative and allegory with which he answers the dreamer's questions. Reflection thus develops from mirroring into considering as the Man in Black presents his memory of his lady in a variety of literary forms and simultaneously establishes his own role as her knightly lover. The self-contained genre of lyric complaint gives way to lament as he describes his current situation (561–617) which flows into the allegory of the chess game (618–709). Chess, with its black/white contrast and mirror-image board is the ideal allegory here. It is also a pastime which the narrator rejected in favour of reading at the beginning of the text (51) when he also rejected games of chance. The Black Knight has been playing chess with Fortune, a game which proverbially he cannot win. As his 'fers' White is both his most valuable piece and also, originally, his advisor rather than his queen (see *Riverside*: 972 n652–71 and Phillips and Havely 1997: 80 n651). The use of the chess image itself alludes to *Le Roman de la Rose* (6622–5) and moves us into the romance genre, which is then continued as the Knight relates the story of his courtship of White, in which she is very clearly the typical lady of courtly literature. Significantly he describes her as a 'chef myrour of al the feste' (974), 'myrour' here taking on the meaning of 'best example', as if White is the fair copy text which all others seek to emulate. Diane Ross (1984) points out that the poem's movement through different genres offers a wide variety of ways a court lady could be presented, each of which emphasises different aspects either of the lady or of the lover's relation to her.

However, while all this variety may present many aspects of White, all are the result of remembering her and are thus in effect commemorative. She is held within these recollections, but so is the Black Knight.

The nature of such memories may keep her or her memory alive in one way, but it militates against nature in its desire to hold things as a given point. While such remembrance allows for the recreation of White and Black's love of her, it does so through literary creation, through allegory, story and song. All of these are essentially ways of presenting the past and fending off the present. Thus when the dreamer asks where she is now (1298) the Black Knight tries to avoid that 'now' by referring back to the past:

> "Now?" quod he, and stynte anoon.
> Therwith he wax as ded as stoon
> And seyde, "Allas, that I was bore!
> That was the los that here-before
> I tolde the that I hadde lorn.
> Bethenke how I seyde here-beforn,
> 'Thow wost ful lytel what thow menest;
> I have lost more than thow wenest.'
> God wot, allas! Ryght that was she!"
> (1299–307)

The animation the Knight drew from telling the dreamer his recollections drains away the moment he is drawn back into the present. His wish to return is evident in the repeated 'here-before', 'here-beforn' as he attempts to redirect the dreamer into the past, but the attempt is thwarted and the whole imaginative world of the dream collapses as the Knight is finally forced into a bald statement of White's death.

After such an unequivocal sentence, there is nowhere left to go. All the elements of the dream reappear as the hunt returns and enters the castle, leaving the Man in Black still, presumably, under his tree, but taking the dreamer back to the waking world, where the tale of Seys and Alcione is found lying on the bed. 'Al was doon,/For that tyme, the hert-huntyng' (1313–14) we are told, and the 'hert' may be not only the deer of the hunt, but also the lady of courtly love-vision poetry or even the dreamer's own heart, or melancholy. The process is only over 'for that tyme' however; it is possible that it will happen again, as would indeed be the case for an annual act of commemoration, but in the meantime we have been released from the constant reflection which prevents action and are able to shut the book and go on to something else, consoled, perhaps, by the knowledge that we can relive the process at any stage by simply re-reading the poem. It is an elegant way of presenting a process which may be cathartic but may also become stultifying, or even fatal as it was for Alcione, if one does not break out of the cycle of reflection.

The Book of the Duchess is thus a consummate occasional poem, written as an exploration of grief and the desire to remember the loved one. As such it draws on many aspects of medieval theories of memory, which are most accessibly found in Mary Carruthers' study (Carruthers 1990). The mind is much like a book in which memory writes the material which is later recalled. The book is indexed, thus allowing for one memory to trigger another, or for recollection through association, much as the dreamer in *Duchess* is led from one aspect of his dream to another. What is produced from the memory is not, however, an exact copy of the original, but a re-creation resulting from the original material and rememberer's reaction to it. It is a literal re-collection of the various parts which make the new, but remembered, whole. Jesse Gellrich made use of a similar idea some years before Carruthers' book when writing about the use of books as a concept in medieval literature. Discussing Dante's invocation of the muse of memory in Inferno book 2 Gellrich says:

> Instead of reproducing them [literary authorities] in their full presence, Dante is suggesting that writing cannot avoid becoming an interpretation of them and initiating change in the process. The "original" text cannot be recreated, only supplemented. Or, to put the matter another way, writing distances or alienates its sources even as is tries to retrieve them.
>
> (Gellrich 1985: 148–9)

The process of remembering White, or Blanche, has indeed recalled her, but also altered her, while resulting in a Book which thus becomes her memory, allowing the reader to recreate her whenever *The Book of the Duchess* is read.

This is not the only kind of memory Chaucer explores in his dream poetry, however. *The House of Fame* considers the topic too, as fame necessarily involves being remembered. Here the memory is cultural rather than personal and the effects more obviously linked to what it is like to be a poet.

(iii) *The House of Fame*

Probably begun in the late 1370s, when Chaucer was Controller of Customs (alluded to in the 'rekenynges' of line 653), the version of *The House Fame* that has survived is incomplete. Whether this is because is was never finished, as most scholars believe, or because pages of manuscript have been lost, is a matter for debate. Fyler provides a précis of the various arguments (*Riverside*: 990 n2158). It is highly unlikely that Chaucer meant it to end as it does now, with its unfulfilled promise of finally meeting the 'man of grete auctorite', who will, it is implied, have all the answers, although late twentieth-century criticism rather likes the idea that the text should be thus deliberately curtailed at the very point where an answer is promised, but before it is delivered. The ironic view of authority and the status of the author of a text created by the sudden halt works as a very consciously literary or perhaps historical joke, but on the whole seems unlikely. The text is indeed humorous, even ironic, about how authors achieve their revered status, but it is more credible that Chaucer had simply written himself into a corner than that he was inspired to end his poem on a cliff-hanger. This is to start at the end, however. We should turn to the beginning of the poem and decide what it is all about.

Certainly authority is one of its themes, but authority in its medieval sense, which included not only power, but also, specifically, a text which could be cited to prove an argument. These 'authorities' were the works of classical philosophers such as Plato, Aristotle or Cato, or writers such as Homer or Ovid, or of Christian philosophers such as Augustine. The text itself was the repository of knowledge that could be trusted and regarded as true, with the prime authority being, naturally, the Bible. An author, then, becomes one who writes such a text and is esteemed as a result. This is a more specific use of the word than our current 'author' which simply means the writer of a text. Minnis (1981) provides a full study of the various medieval concepts of authority; for a more succinct overview see G. Rudd (1994). In a time when all documents were written by hand, often by scribes who had not composed the original, there was a greater awareness of the distinction between creating and writing. The word also had connotations of leadership and the ability to increase things, through an etymological link to *augeo* to increase. Thus God may be termed the chief *auctor*, as leader and enlarger of creation as well as the true author of the Bible, with the individual writers of it being in effect scribes under divine instruction. When it came to secular texts there was still a similar division. Chaucer's references to his 'auctor' indicates the composer of the text or story he is following, half suggesting that he is a mere scribe, recording what he is told. How, though, does one choose a source to follow and how do the famous writers, characters and events achieve their status? These, in large part, are the questions *The House of Fame* poses.

Like *The Book of the Duchess*, *The House of Fame* is a dream poem, but while *Duchess* suggests that the dream results primarily from the narrator's state of mind, *House* gives no such hint, the dream is simply presented as one the narrator experienced one 10 December and retells here because it was so remarkable (59–65). The poem is divided into parts, each of which has a short proem or invocation (Book 1 has both) before moving into the main narrative. Book 1 opens the dream in a temple of glass, on the walls of which the whole story of Troy is depicted. The dreamer dwells particularly on the tale of Dido, Queen of Carthage, who loved Aeneas, and who commits suicide when he departs for Italy at Mercury's command (239–467). After marvelling at the pictures, the dreamer wonders where he is and runs out of the temple into a desert in search of someone who could tell him. The book ends with him praying for deliverance from 'fantome and illusion' (493) and seeing an eagle flying down out of the sun. In Book 2 the dreamer is swept up by the eagle, who complains he is a troublesome burden (574) and then goes on to explain that he is Jove's eagle, sent by the god to take the narrator away from his books and show him the House of Fame. There, it is implied, the narrator will hear at first hand all the tidings of love. It transpires that the narrator is a writer who spends all his time with books, either reading them or writing love poetry, but never experiencing anything beyond his doorstep, nor, it is hinted, gaining any personal experience of love.

This trip is a gift from Jove in recognition of his diligence and perhaps to give him further material for his writings. The eagle explains that the House of Fame is at the mid point between earth, sea and sky and is the place where all sounds come, rippling out from their source until they arrive there (711–822). He further offers to teach the narrator (called 'Geffrey' in line 729) about the stars, but, after the length of the explanation of sound and Fame, which has taken up the best part of the book, Geffrey speedily declines. The eagle sets him down close to the House of Fame, a very noisy place, where every sentence uttered can be seen entering the house, taking on the appearance of the person who said them as they do so. Book 3 then takes over, as the dreamer walks towards the House of Fame, which is situated on top of a high rock whose slopes are made of ice. Carved into the ice are the names and deeds of famous people, some of which are impossible to read because they have almost thawed away by the sun. Those written on the northern side are still clear, preserved by the shade of a castle and tower on the hill. Geffrey continues towards this castle, every wall of which is covered with carvings and full of windows. Every niche is filled with a minstrel or storyteller telling their tales (1194–200) among whom he sees makers of popular ballads, Latin shepherd-poets, Dutch musicians and those who told stories of famous battles. There are musicians of every kind as well as jugglers, witches and scholars: in short anyone and everyone who has some connection with words and sounds. From this noisy place the dreamer moves on to another ornately carved building, which turns out to be Fame's hall (1357). Here the goddess Fame or Renown presides, while people come to petition that they might be remembered. The hall is full of statues of famous writers, mainly writers of histories and epics such as Homer, Statius (who wrote the stories of the fall of Thebes and of Achilles in the first century AD, which were much read in the later middle ages), Josephus (who wrote the history of the Jews also in the first century and whose work was known through Latin translations in the medieval period) and Virgil. Each author carries on his shoulders the fame of the people who figure in his work. As Geffrey puts it, the hall is full of those who had written old tales (1514–15).

His contemplation of these precursors is interrupted by a mass of people noisily entering the hall like a huge swarm of bees (1522–3). Each one desires fame; some have done good works, some not, but Fame's decision about whether or not they receive a good reputation, a slanderous one, or simply sink into oblivion is dictated not by their worth but by her caprice (1559–66). In total, nine groups approach Fame:

- the virtuous seeking deserved fame, who are consigned to oblivion
- the virtuous seeking deserved fame, who receive infamy instead
- the virtuous seeking deserved fame, who receive it
- the virtuous seeking oblivion, despite their good deeds, who receive it
- the virtuous seeking oblivion, despite their good deeds, who instead receive fame
- idlers desiring fame, despite having done nothing to merit it, who receive it
- idlers desiring fame, having done nothing to merit it, who receive infamy
- workers of ill deeds, who seek deserved infamy, but receive oblivion
- workers of ill deeds, who seek deserved infamy and receive it.

The point being made is that any kind of reputation can be inaccurate and is dictated by chance more than merit. Moreover, as the poem goes on to illustrate, any kind of fame relies upon there being people to tell the story. This means not only the illustrious authors on pedestals in the hall, but also those humble minstrels and ballad-singers in the castle.

Despite the impressive array of people and deeds, Geffrey remains unimpressed, as he tells the stranger who accosts him in line 1870 asking if he has come to seek fame. Geffrey replies he indeed has not, rather he was promised he would hear something new him, some 'thynges glade' (1889). However, nothing he has seen so far is the kind of 'thynge' he meant. On hearing this, the stranger directs him toward a twiggy house, constantly spinning round, which is full of entrances, holes and echoes with rumours and gossip. Amazed at the sight, Geffrey suddenly sees the eagle perched near by, who tells him he is there to drop Geffrey into this whirling house, as otherwise he would be incapable of getting in. True to its word, the bird delivers him through a window, landing the poet in the thick of it, surrounded by people swapping news and retelling it, elaborating as they pass it on. This house is full of seafarers, pilgrims, pardoners and messengers: in short of all those whose occupations involve travel, the one thing, we may remember, that this narrator has not done. Then in a corner he hears a group talking about love and hurries up to join. It is at this point he sees a man who seems to be 'A man of gret auctorite' – and there the text ends.

Even this précis shows how packed full of detail the poem is, but also how little there is by way of plot. The text is clearly interested in the welter of material there is for narrative poetry, as the subjects of history, epic and even saints' lives (represented by those who did good deeds, not for personal glory, but for God) are brought on stage, but all are found wanting. There is no shortage of books or stories, but how is one to know which text will make a good authority, or which author to follow? This line of questioning leads into reflection on the nature of Fame, moving on from the ideas of memory and recollection of the *Book of the Duchess* **[68–71]** into a more abstract exploration of the arbitrary way reputations are decided. In this Chaucer is unusual, as Fame was a less popular subject for such reflections on the arbitrary nature of fate than the figure of Fortune. Fortune is in fact mentioned in Book 3 (1547–8), where the close relation of the two concepts is signalled by describing her as Fame's sister, but no more is made of it than that, as Chaucer goes on to develop the concept of Fame as compounded of both reputation and rumour. Despite the apparent richness of this topic, the narrator-poet of the text still seems to be having difficulty finding material for writing which suits him.

The eagle which comes down at the end of Book 1 may be an allusion to Dante's eagle, who appears in both the Purgatorio and the Paradiso sections of Dante's *Divine Comedy*. If so it seems that Chaucer is simultaneously acknowledging the greatness of Dante's achievement, and signalling that he will not be writing similar stuff. Even as a symbol of contemplation, the eagle is dismissed as inappropriate as the Geffrey of the poem declares himself too old to learn about the stars: Chaucer is by no means a contemplative writer and here clearly signals this fact. It has been suggested that the poem is best read as a kind of demonstration of the ways of writing poetry, chock full of rhetorical devices and examples (Spearing 1985: 24–7; Minnis 1995: 172–82). While there are certainly many such devices to note – the apostrophes, particularly the invocations at the beginning of each book; the exclamations (*exclamatio*); the extensive and detailed descriptions (*descriptio*); the anaphora (lines 1961–76 being a veritable *tour de force* here); the eagle's wry comments on matching form to content (854–64) – this is clearly not organised as a book of instruction. Its structure has itself provoked considerable interest, as critics seek to defend it from the accusation of simply being a text that got out of hand. Havely, following Billington, suggests that the laughter and folly, which characterise the final section of the text, support the idea that the whole poem is a bit of 'winter foolery', but also recalls the links with other literary journeys, including Dante, Boethius and The Book of Revelation (Phillips and Havely 1997: 122 and n51, also *Riverside*: 977). A connection has also been made between the somewhat confusing structure of the text and the labyrinth, or maze, which is mentioned in the description of the house of twigs (1920–1). Minnis summarises most of these arguments and indeed other readings of the poem in terms of its structure (Minnis 1995, 216–27), while Doob offers a thorough study of mazes (Doob 1990). Meanwhile Delany regards the poem as enacting the conflicts between the different kinds of truth found in literature, philosophy and religion (Delany 1972). While all these approaches offer fruitful ways of reading the text, it remains true that the poem is weak on narrative impetus. The only place the poem seems to be carried by plot is in the first book, where the story of Dido is retold.

Chaucer returns to this tale in *Legend* (924–1364) **[104]**, so it clearly interested him and of course it is a love story, which fits with the figure of the dreamer as a writer of love poetry. However it is also a story with two main sources and thus two 'auctors' – Virgil's *Aeneid* (which Chaucer probably knew, as well as being likely to be acquainted with the popular French romance version, the *Roman d'Enéas)* and Ovid's *Heroides* where the story is told from Dido's viewpoint (the *Heroides* being a collection of stories of wronged women, presented in the form of letters which they write before they die). Chaucer here blends elements from each, which results in a richer version in which the audience is not immediately sure whether Aeneas is being accused of being a deceitful absconder (as in lines 267 and 294), or a hero driven by his fate against his will (427–32). Dido, on the other hand, may be held up to be pitied, but she is scarcely admired here. We are invited to understand her folly: 'Loo, how a woman doth amys/To love hym that unknowen ys' (269–70), but the upshot is that she joins the ranks of women whose complaints and lamentations (their only weapons) fail, leaving suicide as the only recourse. Interestingly, she, like Criseyde after her, bewails the fact that her story will be known throughout the world and her reputation is thus fixed:

> O wikke Fame! – for ther nys
> No thinge so swifte, lo as she is.
> O, sothe ys, every thinge ys wyste,
> Though hit be kevered with the myste.
> Eke, though I myght dure ever,
> That I have do rekever I never,
> That I ne shal be seyde, allas,
> Yshamed be thourgh Eneas –
>
> (*House*: 349–56)

Even if she lived forever, whatever she did would not alter the fact that she would be remembered as the woman Aeneas betrayed. This is perhaps the inevitable fate of those who star in someone else's story.

As a whole, *The House of Fame* is an experiment in discussing the matter of fiction. Chaucer takes us on a journey through various kinds of narrative material and treatments of Fame providing several complicated images en route, but in the end he seems to have become trapped in the labyrinth of his own text and never found a way out.

(iv) *The Parliament of Fowls*

This is the only dream poem written in rhyme royal, which Chaucer had used for the narrative poem *Anelide and Arcite* **[52]** and used again for *Troilus and Criseyde* as well as for some of the Canterbury Tales. The change to a stanzaic verse-form with a more complex rhyme pattern seems to have allowed for a greater range of registers and more natural speech rhythms than the eight syllable rhyming couplets of *Duchess* and *House*. In *Parliament* Chaucer ranges across formal but straightforward diction of general narration, to elaborate lofty rhetoric, to low-brow informal chatter of cuckoos and geese. For the content of the poem he makes use of several traditions connected with St.

Valentine's Day. As well as being associated with love generally it is also, supposedly, the day the birds choose their mates for the year. This provides the central motif of the poem as Nature presides over the court of birds who, having selected their mates, have gathered to hear the formel eagle decide between the three male eagles who court her. The court is also a debate, hence the 'parliament' of the title and the topic under discussion is, appropriately, love. The debate form is another literary tradition Chaucer draws on here, and it has been suggested that a court reading of the poem would have been followed by a general debate in which case the lack of conclusion within the text may have been designed to feed elegantly into the live debate to come. The connection of birds with love was an established one, and even the idea of a debate about love conducted by birds is not original to Chaucer, though Chaucer's use of it here seems to have influenced the *Songe Saint Valentin* by his French contemporary and friend, Oton de Granson. The various sources and analogues for the poem are usefully collected in Windeatt's edition (Windeatt 1982).

While we can be certain of the St. Valentine's Day associations, quite which day it was is less certain. Matters are complicated by the existence of a popular feast of a Genoese St. Valentine (one form of Italian influence on the poem) which was celebrated in May. It is possible that this feast and the universally established date of 14 February for the other St. Valentine became conflated. Some have gone so far as to claim that Chaucer himself inaugurated the tradition of Valentine celebrations with this poem, but, although this is the implication of the *Riverside* introduction, others find it a little far-fetched (see Minnis 1995: 256–61).

Another claim made for *Parliament* is that it is an occasional poem, reflecting various marriage negotiations for Richard II. If this is the case it gives a composition date of between 1377, when such negotiations began, and 1382, when Richard married Anne of Bohemia (Chaucer himself was involved in some of these negotiations [16]). In 1890 John Koch first suggested that the poem refers to negotiations surrounding Anne and Richard, giving a possible composition date of 1381, allowing a year's space between the 'courting' of Anne and the marriage in 1382. Supporting this theory, and assuming Richard to be the first eagle, various people have been identified by Benson as likely candidates for the other two suitors (Benson 1982). A particularly neat detail is that the marriage treaty was ratified on 2 May 1381: the feast day of St. Valentine of Genoa. Minnis points out that 3 May seems to have been a significant date for both Richard II and Chaucer, inferring that *Parliament* was written to celebrate the first anniversary of the treaty in 1382. All of which is, as Minnis admits, 'pure speculation' (Minnis 1995: 260).

There are several elements which *Parliament* has in common with Chaucer's other dream poems: once again we have a shadowy narrator persona who, like that of *House*, seems to be a love poet, though one without first-hand knowledge of love whose 'I knowe nat Love in dede' (8) links him to the narrator of *Troilus and Criseyde* 'that God of Loves servantz serve' (*Troilus*, I: 15). Books also figure largely; generally as the source of all the narrator's knowledge and specifically in *The Dream of Scipio*, the book he reads for a full day in search of 'a certeyn thing' (20), though we never discover what. As with *Duchess* and *House*, *Parliament* moves from book to dream in which the narrator is guided by Africanus to a walled park whose gates present both the promises and pitfalls of love. He is rudely shoved through these gates by a mocking Africanus, with the promise of being shown something to write about (168). This promise is reminiscent of *House*, while the garden we enter recalls the idyllic landscapes of both *Duchess* and *The Romaunce of the Rose*. Several of the figures within the garden also recall *Romaunce*: Cupid is there, beside a well, as are Beauty, Delight, Gentilesse and Youth among many others (211–28). Venus is also here, ensconced in her temple, surrounded by servants and pictures of love in all its guises.

It is Nature, however, who presides over this garden. Before her are gathered all the birds, ranged according to their status, determined by their diet. The carnivorous 'foules of ravyne' (323) are highest, the worm-eaters next, with water fowl after that and seed-eaters last. The social distinctions are easily mapped onto human social groups, with the birds of prey associated with the richer and courtly classes, down to the peasants at the bottom of the heap. It is this classification in which all have their place and appropriate use (which may also be seen reflected in the earlier list of trees, 176–82) which lends the text to the kind of reading offered by David Aers, whereby the 'lower' birds' views function as serious criticisms of the privileged and impractical ways of the noble stock (Aers 1986: 14–17). This is one of the few readings to link the poem with the Peasants' Revolt of 1381 **[21]**.

Chaucer has a field-day with the list of birds and succinct descriptions, displaying his skill at this kind of listing (*ennumeratio*) which was clearly much enjoyed at the time, and which can still draw applause, but eventually the poem moves on to debate as the central figures are introduced. These are the formel (female) eagle and her three suitors, ('tercel' reflecting the belief that every third eagle hatched was male). Nature's plan is that the birds will select their mates in turn according to their species' social standing. The roles of courtship operate: males propose, females accept or refuse, with the clear expectation that they will accept some mate or other. Certainly this seems to be the presumption for the chief of birds, the royal eagle who speaks first to choose the formel who sits on Nature's hand. His terms are suitably elaborate: the formel will be his 'sovereign lady' not merely his mate or equal 'fere' (416); his devotion is such that he will die without her and if he is found unfaithful, may he be torn to pieces by the assembled birds. It is the typically excessive vocabulary of courtly love, which informs the speeches of the Black Knight in *Duchess* **[65]** and is parodied in the figure of Absolon in The Miller's Tale **[113]**. It may be that *Parliament* marks the beginning of Chaucer's irony about this form of speech, as the two other eagles (who butt in after the royal eagle) put forward their claims just as hyperbolically, and the verbal contest goes on till sunset. This is too much for the other birds, who must wait for the royal eagle to be matched before they can get on with the mating game themselves. Their cry 'Whan shal youre cursed pletynge have an ende?' (495) elicits a smile from the audience and leads Nature to invite each order of birds to depute a spokesman to give their verdict on which eagle deserves the formel.

Inevitably opinions differ, and the discussion is taken off into an exchange over the virtues or folly of fidelity even where love is unrequited. It is this which allows the poem to be read as a social satire or as a critique of courtly love values, implying that they may be all very well for those with leisure, but they are ridiculous and impractical in the eyes of common folk. The precise question of which eagle should win the formel is thus lost, as the birds exchange insults until Nature turns to the bird herself, saying she should choose her mate of her own free will (though quite how free a choice it is when Nature also says that were it her choice she would select the royal eagle, is another matter). The formel then defies all expectation by asking for a year's deferral. In so doing she is perhaps acting as a lady should, but her request effectively prevents the debate reaching a conclusion. Instead the poem shifts register into a song as the other birds pair off and depart. The song is a triple roundel – a circular form in which the first lines of the song become the refrain, thus bringing it round on itself in a way which partly reflects the pattern of *Parliament* as a whole. For the narrator the song is less a harmony than a cacophony which wakes him from his dream and leaves him determined to go back to his books.

Taken together, these three dream poems reveal not only common themes, but also the development of Chaucer's particular interests. He moves steadily away from the more ornate, artificial, traditions of the French style towards a more flexible narrative form. He becomes increasingly interested in the figure of the narrator and begins to develop it from a simple persona who relates a story, into a character who affects the tale he tells. By the time he reaches *Parliament* Chaucer is experimenting with moving between different speakers to a far greater extent and makes them more distinct from each other than has been the case before. Although he continues to write lyrics throughout his life **[47]** (as well as fulfilling his posts and finding the time to translate Boethius **[83]** and compose the *Treatise on the Astrolabe* **[86]**), he now leaves behind the dream vision form and embarks on larger fiction projects which involve not only telling more complicated stories, but also using a variety of narrators. He still refers to dreams and even includes them in his plots as for instance in Criseyde and Troilus's dreams, (*Troilus*, II: 925–31; V: 1233–41), or Chanticleer's (*Tales*, VII: 2898–907) but when he returns to the dream vision form it is to use it only as a Prologue to the collection of tales which form *The Legend*.

(v) Prologue to *The Legend of Good Women*

The Prologue exists in two versions, now called F and G after the manuscripts in which they were found. Twelve manuscripts survive, of these eleven contain the version of the Prologue now termed the F Prologue (after the best of these manuscripts: Bodley Fairfax 16) with the G version appearing in just a single manuscript, University Library Cambridge Gg 4.27 (hence its name). There is some debate over which of the two is the earlier. The alphabetical order of our modern titles F and G is a coincidence, which makes it harder to bear in mind that, as Sheila Delany points out, there is no certainty about the order of composition (Delany 1994: 34–43). Debate continues both over this and over the relative merits of the two versions. Brewer (1998: 246–7; 249–52) assumes F to be the earlier and G the better text, whereas Delaney takes issue with both these views. In terms of dating, the question revolves around the reference to the Royal palace at Shene which exists in F but not in G: '...whan this book ys maad, yive it the quene,/On my byhalf, at Eltham or at Shene' (F: 496–7). Shene was Queen Anne's palace. After her death in 1394 Richard was (apparently) so distraught that he ordered the destruction of Shene, an act which may account for the deletion of these lines in the G Prologue. It also suggests dates for the two versions of the Prologue: F can be assumed to have been written in the late 1380s. If G is later, Chaucer must have returned to the poem and revised at least the Prologue sometime after June 1394. If G is taken as earlier, the lines in F consitute a memorial allusion to Anne, which is further developed through the association of Anne and Alceste (who figures as the God of Love's consort, see below). Despite this, it is not necessarily the case that the *Legend* was written at royal command, indeed Pearsall points out that it is highly unlikely that Anne either commissioned or received the work (Pearsall 1992: 191). The two versions of the Prologue are distinct and Phillips believes they should be taken as individual texts (Phillips and Havely 1997: 281), but they contain much of the same material and are similar enough to be treated together here.

Chaucer's use of dream vision for the Prologue is a deliberate return to a form he had abandoned for a work which takes as its pretext a general review of his poetry to date. This overview takes exception to his portrayal of love and of women in love in particular; to couch such criticism in a poetic form associated with courtly love is itself a wry joke. All the elements we have come to expect of Chaucerian dream poetry are here: the use of the typical landscape (a grassy bank strewn with daisies); the fair lady (Alceste, who, as a figure from antiquity is also a bookish reference); the narrator figure (a mere poet, buried in his books except when he goes out in May to lose himself in adoration of the daisy – so Chaucer here portrays himself); the books which give rise to the dream (and here are Chaucer's own writings, another witty twist). Alceste may be a figure of Anne of Bohemia, who, according to Lydgate in his *Fall of Princes*, commissioned the *Legend* (*Riverside*: 1059; Phillips and Havely 1997: 283). She is certainly very much the ideal lady and also an intercessor with her consort, here the God of Love, which may be intended to recall Anne's intervention with Richard II as well as roles associated with Mary (Phillips and Havely 1997: 283–6). For some this is Chaucer's best dream text, with F being praised for its warmth and G for its better structure. A good analysis of the G prologue is to be found in R. Payne's *The Key of Remembrance*, but in the main the Prologue is treated as part of the *Legend* as a whole, so further consideration will be deferred to later in this volume.

Further Reading

Phillips and Havely (1997) is a useful edition of the Dream Poems and a reasonable starting place for critical reading. Windeatt's collection of sources and analogues is a fund of information (Windeatt (ed.) 1982). Delany offers a challenging and now influential reading of *House* (Delany 1972). Chaucer's relation to previous representations of fame have been fully explored by Piero Boitani (Boitani 1984) while Niall Rudd discusses his use of Latin sources with particular reference to

Dido (Rudd 1994: 1–31). Two articles on *Duchess* are particularly useful: 'Understanding the Man in Black' (Morse 1981) and 'The Play of Genres' (Ross 1984). A full study of the medieval ideas of authority can be found in Minnis (1988), a more succinct one in G. Rudd (1994: 29–31). The best work on the Prologue to *Legend* remains *The Key of Rememberance*, which is also relevant for *Parliament* (Payne 1963).

(c) NON-FICTION PROSE

(i) *Boece*

Boethius (*c*.480–524) was a Roman patrician who rose to high office in the state, but was put to death for treason. He was a Christian, who was also deeply interested in the philosophy of Aristotle and Plato, whose works he translated into Latin to allow more people access to them. While in prison he composed *De Consolatione Philosophiae* (*Consolation of Philosophy*) in which he presents himself bewailing his fate, but then visited by Lady Philosophy, who points out that it is useless to upbraid Fortune, since by her nature Fortune is changeable. Instead he should draw consolation from considering the true value of things. Over the course of five books Philosophy demonstrates that material goods (riches, social status, fame, beauty) are unimportant when compared to true happiness, which is to be found by uniting with the one Good from which we came. This Good may be identified with God, who orders all things. This leads to a discussion of how human free will and divine foreknowledge can co-exist, on which note the text ends.

Although the doctrine Philosophy presents is largely reconcilable with Christian belief, Philosophy herself is more of a Neoplatonic figure, drawing on the classical and late-classical traditions that Boethius had studied for most of his life. Readers in later centuries tended to make the work more explicitly Christian, mainly by emphasising the link between the concepts of Good and God, and often adding commentaries and glosses to the text which enhanced the more Christian aspects of the work. Despite occasional patches of relative obscurity, by the fourteenth century Boethius' *Consolation* was well-known in educated circles and very influential. However, since it was written in late-classical Latin, only those with a fair degree of Latinity could read it. In some ways Boethius had thus become a figure like Aristotle and Plato in his own day – a respected philosopher rendered obscure through difficulty of language. Translations had been made at various points over the centuries (including one into Old English by Alfred the Great), as had later Latin versions, and there was also a strong tradition of interpretative commentaries. Of these two of the most influential were by William of Conches (*c*.1080–1154) and by Nicolas Trevet, published in 1307.

Chaucer first encountered Boethius through Jean de Meun, who drew on it for *Le Roman de la Rose* and translated it into French prose as *Li Livres de confort*, which Chaucer may have known. In the 1380s Chaucer embarked on his own translation, *Boece*, and must have completed it by 1387, when Thomas Usk used it for his *Testament of Love*. Although Boethius' original alternates between prose and verse sections, both de Meun and Chaucer translate into prose only, thus enabling a more literal translation, intended to make the text more directly comprehensible to vernacular readers. In so doing they were taking the same decision as had Boethius himself when translating Aristotle and Plato. Chaucer clearly had access to a glossed Latin text of the *Consolation*, and also to Trevet's commentary, as well as to de Meun's French translation. His *Boece* thus reflects the interpretative tradition of Conches, as well as Trevet and de Meun.

Most of the critical work on *Boece* concentrates on the accuracy of Chaucer's translation, an area which is fraught with pit-falls. Simple comparison with the texts of the original now available to us can give the misleading impression that Chaucer was inaccurate, when in fact he might have been either closely translating the version of the text before him, or arriving at a phrase which incorporated the later Latin glosses and commentaries as well as de Meun's French (see Machan 1985 and Minnis 1981). Also, of course, he could have made mistakes. Nonetheless, in compiling his translation, Chaucer not only rendered into English some of Boethius' memorable images, such as that of the man searching for the 'sovereyne good ... ryght as a dronke man not nat by whiche path he may retourne hom to his hous' (III: pr2.84–5) but also composed some striking English phrases, such as 'slydynge Fortune' (I: m5.34) who in her dealing with Boethius has kept 'hir propre stablenesse in the chaungynge of hirself' (II: pr1.54) or the rhetorical question 'what pestilence is more myghty for to anoye a wyght than a familier enemy?' (III: pr 6.69–70).

For general students of Chaucer, however, the main interest of *Boece* lies in finding here the initial source of many ideas which Chaucer reworked imaginatively in his fictional works. Thus the 'Boethian ballades' **[55]** explore further some of the themes and images found in the *Consolation*, not least the concept of 'steadfastness', which is paradoxically linked in Fortune's case to perpetual change, but in human terms comes to mean integrity. Fortune herself is shown to be most useful to men when she is adverse, thereby revealing their true friends, a theme which leads to the second section refrain in Chaucer's lyric 'Fortune' [57]: 'And eek thou hast thy beste frend alyve'. The lyric is almost an abbreviated *Boece*, while Fortune and her wheel crop up in *Troilus* (I: 138) and The Knight's Tale (*Tales*, I: 925) [111], which Chaucer was writing while working on the *Boece*. Here, too, we find Arcite using the image of the drunkard, sure he has a home, but not sure how to get there (*Tales*, I: 1251–74), which has its roots in the *Boece*, as do the speeches on free will, predestination and the greater order of things which permeate *Troilus* as well as The Knight's Tale. Indeed the Troilus who looks down on all human affairs from the eighth sphere (*Troilus*, V: 1807–13) can be read as a figure who has achieved the unity which Philosophy tells Boethius is the ultimate aim of mankind.

The form of *Boece* is of interest in itself. When we first meet the author persona he is lamenting in verse and invoking the Muses of poetry. Philosophy seems to send these Muses packing, asserting that intellectual consolation is more effective than poetic lament. We might reasonably expect no further space to be allowed for poetry in his text, but Boethius continued to use both verse and prose in the text, merely reversing the order, so that whereas previously verse sections preceded prose, they now follow them, acting partly as summations of the important points. While Chaucer's all prose translation necessarily loses this verse/prose structure, it retains traces of the original's form in the section titles – metrum (verse), prosa (prose). The language of the verse sections is more poetic and the general tone of the piece links it to 'compleynte', a favourite genre for his lyrics[51], as well as being evident in *Duchess*. *Duchess* also makes use of another important element which Chaucer took over from Boethius: the use of oneself, the author, poet or narrator, as a character within the text. As Brewer points out this 'duality of the author/*persona* creates an attractive blend of realism, and fiction: a blurring, or fluidity, of limits' (Brewer 1998: 147). It was a blend Chaucer was to exploit to the full, not only in his dream poems but increasingly in his narrative verse.

Further Reading

Walsh's new edition of Boethius provides an informative introduction covering Boethius' life and the tradition of the Consolation, as well as an accessible modern English translation of the original (Walsh 1999).

A collection of essays looks at Boethius' influence generally (Gibson 1981) in which Minnis looks at the issues of translation in particular. Another collection focuses on Chaucer's *Boece* and the medieval context of Boethius (Minnis ed. 1993).

(ii) *A Treatise on the Astrolabe*

In his introduction to this work Chaucer addresses 'lyte Lowys', saying he has written the treatise in response to Lewis' 'besy praier' to learn about the astrolabe (*Riverside* 662). It was probably written in 1391, as this is the year referred to in the text when Chaucer is providing examples of how to use the instrument. Lewis' identity has been discussed above [17]; the important facts here are that he is a ten-year old child, to whom Chaucer has given an astrolabe, for which this treatise is a kind of instruction manual. The astrolabe was an instrument for measuring the height and position of stars, which then allowed for other calculations to be made, such as latitude, time and astrological information. Astrolabes came in varying degrees of intricacy; the one given to Lewis seems to have been a comparatively basic one, as one would expect for a child, although it nonetheless contained some pretty detailed and complicated information. Apparently, the treatise was likewise written in a basic manner, with some repetition in order to make it easier to follow. For a modern reader without an astrolabe to hand, however, it is not an easy read, though not without interest. It is also unfinished – Chaucer promises five books, but only got as far as two, though it may be that a third was started and the somewhat fragmentary character of the end of the treatise results from bits of that third being added to the end of the manuscripts. Later hands have also added sections explaining other aspects of the astrolabe.

Apart from the intrinsic interest of the astrolabe as a gadget and continued fascination with astronomy, there are two literary aspects of the text which lend it interest for the student of Chaucer. The first is that it illustrates how closely astronomy and astrology were intertwined. The information required to use the astrolabe and the information calculated from it include both factual data on the positions of stars and planetary orbits, and such astrological knowledge as the signs of the zodiac and their influence on the passing planets. The prevailing model of the universe in the late fourteenth century was still the Ptolemaic one, with the earth central and the moon, sun, planets and stars revolving around it in a series of eight concentric spheres. The planets occupied a sphere each, while the stars, apparently fixed, took up the eighth, on which the pattern of the band of the zodiac was easily observable. Outside these was the ninth sphere, the *Primum Mobile*, whose function was to transform the Love of God into the force which moved the other spheres. As they move the spheres make a sound, not audible to the human ear, which is the music of the spheres. This movement also sends the planets through the zodiac, thus creating the shifting relations between planets and constellations which could then be interpreted and their presumed effect on events on earth calculated. Hence the interweaving of astronomy and astrology, of observation and interpretation.

This mixture is evident in the *Astrolabe*, in medieval literature in general, and in several of Chaucer's fictional texts in particular. So when Troilus dies and ascends to the eighth sphere, he arrives at a point beyond the influence of planetary motion and can look down on earthly events from the perspective of heavenly harmony (*Troilus*, V: 1811–13). However, Troilus inhabits a pre-Christian world, and Chaucer goes on to exhort his Christian readers to trust not in the stars but in the God whose love controls the heavens. There is a line to be drawn between the superstition of astrology and the certainty of astronomy. Thus, the magician/clerk of The Franklin's Tale is perhaps less magician than accurate astronomer, and in the *Astrolabe* itself Chaucer pulls back from his detailed exposition of the powers and influences of the ascendant to reassert his more scientific views in the face of horoscopes: 'Natheles these ben observaunces of judicial mattere and rytes of payens, in whiche my spirit hath no feith, ne knowing of her *horoscopum*.' (II: 4).

This disclaimer reminds us of the fine lines to be drawn between the effects of planetary motion on terrestial events and superstitious belief. Wood reminds us that it is only in this treatise that we can be sure that the views expressed on astrology in all its forms are Chaucer's own, as opposed to those he ascribed to fictional creations as part of their characters (Wood 1970: 12–21). The astronomical elements in Chaucer's fiction should not be dismissed lightly; as North points out, astronomy had high standing as a natural science and a complicated one at that. He praises the Astrolabe as 'the first competent work in English on such a subject' immediately adding 'it was in no sense original' (North, 1988: 38), but of course, that was not the point. As a guide to knowledge of the stars, in its widest terms, the *Astrolabe* is a remarkable text and acknowledging this goes some way to prevent us from reading references to astronomical detail or astrological belief in the rest of Chaucer's texts too glibly.

Which leads to the second feature for which the text is significant: its literary style. Its patient pedagogical tone creates what the *Riverside* editor, J. Reidy, terms 'a sustained, delicate rapport achieved by means of a mode of address in which the magistral and the familiar are happily blended' (*Riverside* 661). This tone is echoed in The Parson's Tale **[148]** and may even be heard put to different use in the ostensibly measured views of *Troilus*'s narrator **[91, 166]**. It is the tone of a writer who makes it clear that he knows exactly what he is doing. Thus in his preface Chaucer highlights his use of repetition throughout the text, defending it as a useful tool of instruction. The wit with which he offers two, closely related, reasons, for repetition should not be overlooked, nor the beautifully balanced prose in which the first reason is couched: 'for that curious endityng and hard sentence is ful hevy at onys for such a child to lerne' (Prl.44). Throughout the text such relatively simple sentence structure allows Chaucer to move easily between intricate explanation and informal address. Moreover, while this rhythmical prose is comparatively free of the French and Latin influences of his early poetry, the tropes of elegant writing are still in evidence. The modesty topos, 'I n'am but a lewd compilator of the labour of olde astrologiens, and have translatid in myn Englissh oonly for thy doctrine. And with this swerd shal I sleen envie', is a masterly example of a well-established tradition. Chaucer simultaneously reminds us of the scholarship and translation skills required to be able to compile the treatise and makes us aware that we would not like to attempt such a thing ourselves. That short second sentence displays his rhetorical skill, while also, notice, slaying envy, not preventing it from occurring.

Further Reading

Chauncey Wood provides a succinct introduction to medieval astrology in his first chapter, before going on to discuss the *Astrolabe* in some detail (Wood 1970). Julian North readably explores the astronomy in Chaucer's fiction texts (North 1988).

(iii) *The Equatorie of Planetis*

In part it is such linguistic elements which have led some scholars to assert Chaucer's authorship of the *Equatorie*. Like the *Astrolabe*, it is a manual for using an astronomical instrument, and it seems to have been written around 1393 (judging from calendar references made in the text), which makes it contemporary with the *Astrolabe*, and its manuscript is accompanied by a set of tables, one bearing the phrase 'Radix Chaucer', which inevitably led to much excitement. Several scholars find the topic as a whole fascinating, but Rand-Schmidt's book (1993) serves to remind us that Chaucer was writing in a context of broad intellectual enquiry, not as a lone genius.

Further Reading

The most recent reconsideration of Chaucer's possible authorship is by Kari Rand-Schmidt (1993) in which the *Equatorie* is compared not only to the *Astrolabe*, but also to other Middle English astronomical prose texts, on the grounds that a writer's style may be affected by the genre of the work in question.

(d) *TROILUS AND CRISEYDE*

Written between 1381 and 1386, *Troilus* is regarded by some as Chaucer's finest work; Pearsall implies that Chaucer himself treated it as such, 'quite self consciously and deliberately' (Pearsall 1992: 170) and indeed Chaucer makes large claims for it in the final section of the text (*Troilus*, V: 1786–92) where he envisages the poem paying its respects to Homer, Virgil, Ovid, Lucan and Statius, all of whom wrote epics and among whose illustrious number Chaucer thus places himself. Lucan (39–65 AD) was the author of the *Pharsalia*, which deals with the war between Caesar and Pompey. Statius (*c*.45–96 AD) wrote the *Thebiad*, which recounts the rather bloody lives of Oedipus' sons. Ovid was not only responsible for the *Metamorphoses*, but also for the *Heroides*, in which female characters from Classical myths and epic, give their own sides of their stories, usually bewailing their fates in letter form (Chaucer goes on to imitate this in his *Legend* **[102]**). Homer, of course, is the putative author of the Greek epics, the *Iliad* and the *Odyssey*, whom Virgil imitated in writing his own epic, the *Aeneid*, which deals with events for the surviving Trojans after the end of the Trojan War, thus taking up where Homer left off. Chaucer's boast is thus quite high, but his pride may have been justified: *Troilus* is Chaucer's longest single poem (the only large endeavour he actually finished) and is remarkable for its complexity of character and interweaving of plot, narration and historical background, which lend it a quality now frequently associated with novels. 'Astonishingly' so, according to Brewer (Brewer 1998: 180) although Stephen Barney, the *Riverside* editor, more coolly refers to the wider genre as historical romance, reminding us that not only Boccaccio, but also Chrétien de Troyes and Benoît (in whose mid-twelfth-century *Roman de Troie* the story of Troilus and Criseyde first appeared) wrote in similar vein. Similar, but not identical: while the story itself was well-known, and indeed Chaucer is in many ways translating Boccaccio's *Il Filostrato*, it is a translation informed by Chaucer's interest in Boethius which he was translating at roughly the same time **[83]**), in narrative and in developing his own poetic repertoire. The result is a richer text, which rewards study more than light reading.

Set towards the end of the Trojan War and divided into five books, the plot is as follows. In Book One the scene is set and the protagonists introduced. Criseyde is a young widow, alone in Troy since her father, the prophet Calchas, defected to the Greek camp, having foreseen the downfall of Troy. Criseyde is aware of her vulnerable position as daughter of a traitor, and has sought protection from Hector, hero of Troy and eldest son of the king. Troilus is one of Hector's brothers who is earning himself a reputation as a brave warrior and scoffer at love. Inevitably, the result of the latter is that he is smitten by Criseyde, whom he sees at a religious ceremony, whereupon he becomes the epitome of the love-lorn knight. Troilus' confidant is Pandarus, who, conveniently, is also Criseyde's uncle. Upon discovering Troilus' plight Pandarus takes it upon himself to do something about it. Book Two sees Pandarus presenting Criseyde with Troilus' love in extreme terms: his life is in her hands, as is that of Pandarus, for if she refuses Troilus she will lose Pandarus too. Criseyde agrees to a limited degree of contact with Troilus ('myn honour sauf', *Troilus*, II: 480) but begins to fall in love with him when she later sees him riding in from battle. Pandarus first sets about establishing a correspondence between the two and then brings them together in Deiphebus's house (another of Troilus' brothers). At this point we are reminded again of Criseyde's vulnerable position in Troy, which makes it too risky for her relation with Troilus to be acknowledged openly. However, in Book Three the two are physically united and a happy three-year love affair begins. It is ruined in Book Four by the capture of Antenor by the Greeks. The Greeks offer an exchange: Antenor for Criseyde and a Greek captive. The majority of the Trojans agree, despite Hector's objections, leaving Troilus distraught. Pandarus suggests he simply elope with Criseyde, but he refuses to act without her agreement and she demurs, setting her hopes on subterfuge and the chance that she will be able to escape from the Greek camp. In Book Five the exchange takes place and Criseyde finds herself reunited with her father, but surrounded by potentially hostile Greeks. Enter Diomede, Greek hero and more than interested in seducing Criseyde, particularly because he guesses at her affair with Troilus. Unable to escape and beset by Diomede, Criseyde gives up trying to return to Troy and accepts Diomede. Troilus, meanwhile, continues to pine for Criseyde, despite Pandarus' best advice, until one day he recognises a brooch he gave Criseyde on Diomede's cloak. Overcome, Troilus enters ever more wildly into battle, eventually finding death at the hands of Achilles. The tale ends with Troilus ascending to the eighth sphere, whence he looks down on the earth and laughs, seeing all things, including his own life, in cosmic proportion. In a final coda, the narrator sends his poem out into the world and urges his audience to value the love of Christ over worldly vanity.

As might be expected for a work of this stature, there are a variety of ways critics have approached the text. Usefully, there are some broad categories, although that is not to say there is consensus within these categories. One is source study: even the most cursory glance brings home how much Chaucer developed and expanded his source, while a simple reading of any two stanzas in the Italian and then in English makes one aware of the difference in rhythm and pacing which arises not simply from the difference in language but also from Boccaccio's eight-line stanza compared to Chaucer's seven lines. But source study is not just about how writers adapt or change their material, it also addresses why they do so and the effects of such changes. Boccaccio says that his reason for telling Troilus' story is because he has just suffered in love himself and so the tale struck a chord. This may be actually true or may be a fictional ploy, but the idea is clearly to create a close and informal relation between teller and audience. Chaucer goes about it rather differently. We are quickly aware of a narrator of the kind familiar from his Dream Poems **[61, 165]**: not just unlucky but indeed inexperienced in love, a bibliophile who is not adverse to disclaiming reponsibility for some aspects of his story by placing the blame firmly on his author's (source's) shoulders: 'if they on hire [Criseyde] lye,/Iwis, hemself sholde han the vilanye' (*Troilus*, IV: 20–1). This narrator comments on the action and motives of his characters as well as recounting them and thus makes himself felt in the poem. Yet there is some dispute over how far this figure can be equated with Chaucer (albeit a fictionalised version of himself) and how much it is in effect a distinct character, created by Chaucer to add a further layer to the text. The notion of the Narrator as a character on much the same level as Troilus, Criseyde and in particular Pandarus, was first put forward by E. T. Donaldson (1970: 68–83) for whom the Narrator was a bumbling fool. Others since then have had different opinions, but many have retained the idea of the Narrator as an individual whose character is epitomised in his early words: '... I, that God of Loves servantz serve' (*Troilus*, I: 15).

Certainly, there is a long way we can go with this kind of reading. The Narrator becomes a conscious manipulator of his text; now ironically disclaiming responsibility; now cunningly making us think thoughts that would not have crossed our minds had he not urged us to ignore them. The best example of this is probably his unexpected defence of Criseyde's sudden love for Troilus:

> Now myghte some envious jangle thus:
> "This was a sodeyn love; how myght it be
> That she so lightly loved Troilus
> Right for the firste sighte, ye parde⸮"
> (Troilus, II: 666–79)

Would we have accused her of 'sudden love'⸮ We are, after all, reading a love story in which such things are likely to happen. Following Donaldson, we detect here a clever and convoluted slur on Criseyde, which combines with phrases used of her elsewhere (not least in the summarising opening where she unequivocally 'forsook' Troilus) to create a portrait of a fickle, even manipulative, woman. Brewer, however, has no truck with this view.

The critical flaw, according to Brewer, is that this kind of interpretation 'assumes that no text is written in good faith' (Brewer 1998: 191). Moreover, it raises questions of when we refer to the Narrator and when to Chaucer. The knottiness of this problem has already been touched upon when dealing with the Dream Poems **[67, 73]**, and the case is not dissimilar here. However, there is one crucial difference between the narrators of the dream poems and the voice which recounts *Troilus*: the degree of participation in the action of the text. In the Dream poems the narrator is directly involved in the action. He goes into the gardens, quizzes the people he finds there, demands information, eavesdrops on debates – he is a participant. Here, in *Troilus*, he is not. Yet it would be critically naive to equate the narrative voice with Chaucer entirely. As much as anything, even given the little we know about Chaucer's personal life, it seems disingenuous to regard him as a non-participant in affairs of love, which is the image this narrator seems keen to project.

The question becomes particularly intricate when the end of the poem is under discussion, because here the poet addresses his audience directly, amongst whom are numbered Gower and Strode, both contemporaries of Chaucer, whom he invites almost to proof-read the text:

> O moral Gower, this book I directe
> To the and to the, philosophical Strode,
> To vouchen sauf, ther nede is, to correcte,
> Of youre benignites and zeles goode.
>
> (*Troilus*, V: 1856–9)

If we believe that the narrator is indeed a separate character, how do we account for this? Some critics take advantage of the multiple endings of the poem to imply that in these final sections, the codas as it were, Chaucer casts off his persona and addresses us directly through the text. However, if we establish the notion of a narrative stance for the duration of the tale it is possible to see here the same trick of self-presentation being used to slightly different ends. Chaucer may indeed no longer be using the persona of an anxious narrator, but the humility of the request for correction is perhaps just as much a stance. One could question how much Chaucer was inclined to believe there was 'need' for correction beyond the scribal errors which he was all too aware could creep in easily:

> And for ther is so gret diversitee
> In Englissh and in writyng of oure tonge,
> So prey I God that non myswrite the,
> Ne the mysmetre for defaute of tonge:
>
> (*Troilus*, V: 1793–7)

Here we can detect the tone which dictates 'Chaucers Wordes Unto Adam, His Owne Scriveyn' **[60]** in which *Troilus* is specifically mentioned, as the dire consequences of severe scalp disease are wished on Adam, should he miswrite Chaucer's texts.

It does not do, however, to concentrate so much on who is doing the telling as to overlook what is being told. As has been mentioned, Chaucer was re-telling an already familiar story. In this tradition Troilus is central – it is his story, as it is for Chaucer, who refers to the text as 'Troylus' in 'Unto Adam' and as 'the book of Troilus' in his 'Retraction' **[149]**. The manuscripts which give the text a title divide roughly equally between *The Book of Troilus* and *Troilus and Criseyde* (*Riverside* 1020) and indeed the opening line declares the focus of attention: 'The double sorwe of Troilus to tellen'. So what kind of figure is this central character: a hero? a knight? a lover? a philosopher? Critics have made him all four.

The opening lines firmly place him in his epic setting: he is Troilus, son of King Priam of Troy. Later we are further told that he is considered second only to Hector on the battlefield and the connection between his name and that of his city (Troilus means 'little Troy') runs throughout the text, allowing us to draw comparisons and further increasing Troilus' standing. Initially, too, he is entirely the young warrior making a name for himself on the field and having no time for love. Once he sees Criseyde all that changes and he becomes the epitome of the love-struck knight of medieval romance. He takes to his bed (when he is not on the battlefield), sickens, tells no-one, composes songs and never considers making direct contact with his love object, preferring instead to simply conjure her up in his thoughts. Interestingly, this is described thus:

> Thus gan he make a mirour of his mynde
> In which he sough al holly hire figure,
> And that he wel koude in his herte fynde.
> (*Troilus*, I: 365–7)

There are shades of *Duchess* here with its recognition of the power of memory as Troilus finds himself in a state not far from that of the Black Knight **[69]**. We have moved out of epic and into romance and Troilus adopts different attitudes accordingly.

There is a temptation to describe this Troilus as passive, reluctant as he is to make any direct move towards Criseyde, even when Pandarus has engineered a meeting between the two. However, this view of him must be tempered by the fact that throughout the affair Troilus continues to accrue credit as a fighter. He does not become inert, he simply refuses to assert control in his relations with Criseyde, a tactic which underpins The Franklin's Tale **[130]** and is recommended by the Wife of Bath **[120]**. Some regard this lack of assertion as in keeping with his role as courtly lover. According to the convention, it is the lady who calls the shots, who decides when or indeed whether the two lovers will meet and who decides exactly how things progress from there. Of course it is also possible to see Troilus as manipulating the convention to his benefit – by apparently dying from love he evokes the 'pity' from his lady which is a normal precursor to love. Certainly it is with this in mind that Pandarus goes into such detail when describing Troilus' plight to Criseyde (*Troilus*, II: 316–85) even adding the threat of his own death to that of Troilus should she refuse (*Troilus*, II: 439–46). Again, when Pandarus engineers the covert meetings of the two, first at Deiphebus's house and later at his own in order to give them opportunity to consummate their passion, Troilus is apparently incapable of independent action to the extent that rather than capitalising on

Pandarus' plan he swoons and has to be tipped on to the bed by Pandarus. Hardly the most commanding performance, but for some critics that is the point: Kittredge (1915) and Lewis (1936), each regard this as an example of Chaucer's use of the courtly love tradition. Aers (1986) takes this a step further, pointing out how Troilus, Pandarus and Diomede all exploit the language of male courtly 'service'. For each of these critics in very different ways, Troilus' inaction is thus proof of the power of love.

Caught between the role models of his two brothers, warrior Hector, the hero of Troy, and Paris the lover, whose seizure of Helen caused all the trouble to start with, Troilus follows neither fully. Having been content to go along with Pandarus' deceptions of Criseyde up to the point of this rather bizarre seduction, Troilus subsequently renounces such dominant action in favour of deferring to Criseyde. Aers sees this conversion as the triumph of the personal relationship between the lovers over the social conventions of love. However, this private concord can exist only in a 'secret oasis' (Aers 1986: 95–98) which cannot survive in the external social world, let alone when this world is one of war. Troilus' apparently fatal decision to reject Pandarus' advice (*Troilus*, IV: 529–32) to simply abduct Criseyde rather than allow her be traded to the Greeks is thus the result of his conversion to private individual from his previous social role as Trojan defender. Rather than simply 'ravysshe' Criseyde, which might echo Paris' action with Helen before the text, and rather than stoutly defending her as Hector does, Troilus consults with her, deferring to her decision to put hope in strategem over action.

Strategem fails, or perhaps Criseyde does, and Troilus is left bereft. His despair takes the form of seeking death in battle with a determination made all the stronger when he sees his own brooch on Diomede's cloak. Here it is possible to see him moving out of the romance genre and the individual role he took on after seeing Criseyde, back towards a more social one as warrior. In a way he is granted a magnificent death, at the hands of Achilles, greatest of Greek warriors, but while Troilus' 'wrath' (*Troilus*, V: 1800) may recall the wrath of Achilles which introduces the *Iliad*, the single line which describes their encounter is hardly what we expect for an epic hero: 'Despitously hym slough the fierse Achille' (*Troilus*, V: 1806). More disconcertingly, this is not the end of Troilus, let alone the end of *Troilus*. He slips up to the eighth sphere, whence he looks down on those grieving below and laughs, and then moves again to come to rest 'ther as Mercurye sorted hym to dwelle' (*Troilus*, V: 1827): we are never told exactly where that is.

It is fitting that Mercury, most elusive of gods, should thus preside over Troilus' end as the end of the poem is likewise elusive. Or rather we are given too many endings. Claudia Papka (1998: 267) describes the ending of *Troilus* as:

> ...a critically divisive textual moment: as redemption for the Robertsonian, a cop-out for the narratologist, and a self-defence for the new historicist. For many, there is the sense that there must be some mistake.

That 'sense of mistake' may arise from the fact that from the start we have been told that the poem is about Troilus and so we might imagine that his death will be its end-point thereby making the text the 'tragedye' it describes itself as being (*Troilus*, V: 1786: this, incidentally, is the first use of the word 'tragedy' in English, see also The Monk's Tale (*Tales*, VII: 1991) **[140]**). While we may be prepared to accept a reference to his ghost's final resting place and even a retrospective summary of the whole poem as a way of rounding things off, we are not prepared for the extended coda which moves out from this plot to other tales of Troy (*Troilus*, V: 1765–71) and attitudes to Criseyde (*Troilus*, V: 1772–8) into suggestions of how the text could be interpreted: as an instance of general human betrayal (*Troilus*, V: 1779–85) or as a moral tale on the fortunes of love which should lead us to think of the greater merits of Divine Love (*Troilus*, V: 1828–55). Imbedded in this are wider considerations of the fortune of texts as a whole, which are evidence of Chaucer's consciousness of the vagaries of scribal error, which he fulminates against humorously in 'Adam Scriveyn' **[60]** and which make *Troilus* so appealing for deconstructionists:

> And for ther is so gret diversite
> In Englissh and in writyng of oure tonge,
> So prey I God that non myswrite the,
> Ne the mysmetre for defaute of tonge;
> And red wherso thow be, or elles songe,
> That thow be understonde, God I biseche!
> But yet to purpos of my rather speche.
> (Troilus, V: 1793–9)

This preoccupation with the fate of the text as a document, which could be mis-transcribed and misconstrued, hints at the difference between rewriting an already existing tale and making free with some of its details (which has been Chaucer's practice throughout this poem) and having the coherence of an individual text spoiled through incompetence. Correction should come only from those qualified – Chaucer names Gower and Strode and by so doing treads the fine line of expected humility while preserving his own standing as an author, ready to take his place with the best.

It is not only Chaucer the poet who is aware of the link between text and reputation in this poem, however. Criseyde looks forward from within the story, envisaging how she will be remembered:

> Allas, of me, unto the worldes ende,
> Shal neyther ben ywriten nor ysonge
> No good word, for thise bokes wol me shende.
> O, rolled shal I ben on may a tonge!
> Thoroughout the world my belle shal be ronge!
> And wommen moost wol haten me of alle.
> Allas, that swich a cas me sholde falle!
> (*Troilus*, V: 1058–64)

Concern for her reputation has been a governing factor throughout the poem, and here, in a move reminiscent of *House* **[72, 77]**, Criseyde looks beyond the bounds of her immediate situation and acknowledges the literary character she will be given by the very books that immortalise her. This is a marvellously literary moment, as Chaucer's Criseyde can only voice these words because they have already been proved true. She, like Troilus, is bound by the narrative of her story: she must abandon the idea of returning to Troilus. By making her aware of this, Chaucer perhaps offers his readers the chance to come to a more sympathetic understanding of her plight than that envisaged here, but his narrator's response is more ambiguous. Even as he refuses to condemn her he reminds us of those others who have by shifting from 'Ne me ne list this sely womman chyde/Forther than the storye wol devyse' (*Troilus*, V: 1093–4) to 'Ye may hire gilt in other bokes se' (*Troilus*, V: 1776). The use of 'sely' is not entirely derogatory. It could mean 'silly' as we understand it now, but it also meant 'wretched' or 'innocent' which could become 'ignorant' and thus 'unwise' or, most surprisingly for modern readers, 'happy, blessed'. Less open to benign interpretation is the use of 'slydynge' (*Troilus*, V: 825) which at best means 'flowing', from the verb 'slyde', but more usually 'wavering' or 'changeable', as it does when Chaucer uses it of Fortune in *Boece* (1.m5.34) **[84]**. The effect in this line is doubly damning since the whole phrase is 'slydynge of courage' and forms part of the description of Criseyde which follows that of Diomede as hero. It is as if Criseyde is being re-described in order to begin again as the romantic heroine of another narrative, this time starring Diomede as her lover, but no sooner is she thus re-established than we are reminded of Troilus and that a particular instance of her 'slydynge' nature is her failure to return to him.

The figure of Criseyde has been the focus of much debate over the years, particularly when the question of Chaucer's treatment of women is discussed **[174]**. Such debate seems to have started immediately, as Chaucer incorporates criticism of his treatment of Criseyde into the Prologue to his *Legend*. Alceste takes him to task: 'And of Criseyde thou hast seyde as the lyste,/That maketh men to wommen lasse triste,/ That ben as trewe as ever was any steel.'(*Legend*, F: 333–5). He must write the stories of good women in recompense. Henryson (*c.*1425–1500) **[179]** also suggests that there might have been another version of Criseyde's story and writes *The Testament of Cresseid* to prove it, taking up Cresseid's tale more or less where Chaucer leaves off. In this version she becomes a leper, which perhaps shows Henryson taking Chaucer's Criseyde at her word, as lepers carried a bell to warn people to keep a safe distance.

Criseyde's relation to text is not all to do with her future. It also directly affects her actions in the poem. After seeing her exchange banter on an equal footing with Pandarus and hearing her reservations about entering into a liaison with Troilus, she seems to fall prey to the coercive effect of the song her niece, Antigone, sings in the garden (*Troilus*, II: 827–75). The exact tenor of this song is ambiguous. On the one hand it is a secular love song, extolling the virtues of loving a man who is (inevitably) 'the welle of wothynesse,/ Of trouthe grownd, mirour of goodlihed' (*Troilus*, II: 841–2). As such it is addressed to the god of Love and accords with the classical and secular medieval aspects of the poem. It is this aspect that influences Criseyde, drawing her into the role of lover and lady of romance and apparently allaying the fears the idea of love had raised when suggested by Pandarus. As a result of this, and her conversation with Antigone (who asserts the bliss of love, *Troilus*, II: 885–96), Criseyde 'wex somwhat able to converte' (*Troilus*, II: 903) so that when Pandarus visits her with a letter from Troilus, which he delivers, significantly, in a garden, she is already more open to the idea of the liaison than she was. Note that although she rebukes Pandarus for bringing Troilus' letter, she does not throw it away, but rather reads it in private.

An alternative reading of Antigone's song suggests another way in which the text influences Criseyde. The god of Love can be taken as the Christian God, whose love surpasses human romantic infatuations, as in Chaucer's *An ABC* **[49]**. The blending of religious and secular language is typical of both religious and secular medieval lyrics. If its lead is followed here, Criseyde's subsequent actions make her into not a type of unfortunate or fickle lover, but a weak mortal soul, falling prey to the fears and temptations of the world. A hint of warning might be perceived in Antigone's enthusiastic support for the lover's state in which she refers to both the saints in heaven and the devils in hell (*Troilus*, II: 894–6), but Criseyde is a secular reader and thus seals her fate. Even the dreams Criseyde has that night do not deter her, although the story of Philomel, the nightingale (told in *Legend*, 2228–393 **[104]**) might warn her against becoming entangled in the affairs of men, and the eagle who tears out her heart could symbolise either her fall in Christian terms or her vulnerability in pagan ones.

Criseyde, then, like Dorigen in The Franklin's Tale **[130]** is at the mercy of romance conventions **[32, 40]**, but, like the Wife of Bath **[121]**, is aware of the power of text to define her. Often regarded by critics as a pragmatist, she thus accepts that she will forever be known for being unfaithful to Troilus, so the best she can do to mitigate her reputation is be faithful to Diomede. As she says: 'And that to late is now for me to rewe,/To Diomede algate I wol be trewe.' (*Troilus*, V: 1070–1).

Chaucer never tells us if she is in fact true to Diomede and we have already seen that his attempt to redeem her reputation was not entirely successful, if, indeed, we believe he made such an attempt. Instead what we have is a text in which character is very strong. We may read Criseyde as a metaphor for the human state, as a representation of fortune, as a type, but the intricacy of the text requires that we also read her as a believable, if not likeable, person. Likewise Troilus and Pandarus have individual as well as representational roles to play, while that shadowy figure of the narrator stalks through the text, part identified with Pandarus, part with Chaucer, part with the tale's tradition. The laugh that Troilus sends up at the end of the story is not only the character mocking the vanity of the world that makes the death of a man mean so much and puts his tragedy into comic as well as cosmic perspective, but may also be the laugh of Chaucer delighting in the difficulty of fixing secure meaning on a text so full of different voices.

It is the number of voices, each with its own relation to the central plot, that is worth noting here as Chaucer's fascination with variety and multi-vocal texts is clearly evident. It is this that he goes on to expand, making it his forte, as he moves away from telling one particular story into composing collections of Tales in which both teller and tale are part of a larger framework.

For those interested in Chaucer's use of his sources there are two invaluable books. Windeatt's edition of *Troilus and Criseyde* (1984) presents parallel editions of Chaucer's text and Boccaccio's *Il Filostrato*, accompanied throughout with detailed textual notes. A detailed study of Chaucer's use of Boccaccio is to be found in Havely's *Chaucer's Boccaccio* (1980). Chaucer's use of the courtly love tradition underpins Kittredge (1915) and Lewis (1936). Aers (1986) takes this a step further, pointing out how Troilus, Pandarus and Diomede all exploit the language of male courtly 'service'. Patterson is central on Chaucer's development of the concept of historical sources and deals explicitly with *Troilus* in chapter 2 (Patterson 1991: 84–164). Lawton (1985) is clear on narrators, as is Donaldson on both Crisseyde and the ending of the poem (1970), while Leicester (1987) offers an interesting and comprehensible deconstructionist reading. Feminist critiques are offered by Mann – particularly good on betrayal (1991: 5–47), Dinshaw, who looks at habits of reading (1989: 28–64) and Hansen who concentrates on masculine control of reading (1992: 141–87). A useful overview of the various ways Criseyde and other characters have been read is given by Anne Rooney (1989: 60–5).

(e) COLLECTIONS OF TALES: *THE LEGEND OF GOOD WOMEN*

In the late 1380s Chaucer, now probably resident in Kent **[22]**, was engaged upon his two great narrative collections: *The Legend of Good Women* and *The Canterbury Tales*. It is likely that there was some overlap of composition, but as Pearsall points out, the fact that *Legend* refers explicitly to *Troilus* (Prologue, F: 332–5; G: 264–7) but makes no mention of the *Tales*, whereas the Man of Law speaks of the *Legend* as a 'large volume' (*Tales*, II: 60–76) before going on to tell the tale of Custance (who could easily have been a candidate for inclusion the *Legend*), indicates that Chaucer abandoned the *Legend* once he hit upon the more ambitious plan of *The Canterbury Tales* (Pearsall 1992: 191). This order also makes sense in terms of metre. The *Legend* is composed in couplets in iambic pentameters (heroic couplets) which predominate in the *Tales*. Arguably the slightly looser structure of ten rather than eight syllables and couplets rather than stanzas makes for more elasticity and ease in writing long narrative. On the other hand it runs the risk of monotony, as the ear bumps along with the rhythm of the line, anticipating the end rhymes. Certainly when it came to the greater enterprise of the *Tales*, Chaucer chose to vary the form of the narratives as well as the tellers and the genres. In all likelihood, then, Chaucer worked on *Legend* from 1386 to 1387 and then shifted his attention entirely to the *Tales*.

The notion of collecting stories together is of course very old: the Bible, the Iliad and the Odyssey, the Mahabharata, could all be described as texts made up of a series of tales, but the term 'collection' tends to suggest a group of stories with distinct protagonists brought together through some common theme. A useful example of this is the thirteenth-century *Golden Legend* (*Legenda Aurea*) composed by Jacobus de Voragine (1230–98) which is a collection of lives of saints and other exemplary figures, and stories of miracles and morals. As a collection of religious stories intended to instruct and inspire, this text needs no further rationale and was widely drawn upon for entertainment, sermons and literary reference throughout the Middle Ages. Chaucer probably used it as one of the sources for his Second Nun's Tale and imitates its structure in The Monk's Tale. The word 'legend' for the collection now known as *The Legend of Good Women* also harks back to Voragine, and is used both by Alceste in the Prologue (*Legend*, F: 483) and by the Man of Law (*Tales*, II: 61).

The word 'legend' perhaps summons up expectations of exceptional behaviour or the intervention of gods, but the idea of using some kind of framework to bring together a variety of popular, secular tales was also current. Boccaccio **[40]** used the fiction of a group of nobles retreating to a country house to avoid the plague as the excuse for the tales brought together in his *Decameron*, while Gower **[39]** likewise creates a group of lovers to serve as narrators for his *Confessio Amantis*, which he finished in around 1387. The important point here is that for the legend-type collection the stories are told directly without an obvious narrator figure, whereas the more diverse collections are apparently recorded by someone listening to a series of story-tellers. There is still unity within diversity, however, as both Boccaccio and Gower link their tales by theme. In the *Decameron* a new topic is chosen each day; for Gower the title of the work, which translates as 'The Lover's Confession' declares its theme. In *Legend* and The Monk's Tale we see Chaucer beginning to tinker with these conventions until he overthrows them entirely in *The Canterbury Tales*.

(i) *The Legend of Good Women*

As has been mentioned above **[81]**, the two versions of the Prologue for *Legend* constitute Chaucer's last foray into the dream vision genre. In them we meet several of the elements familiar from his earlier dream poems: an opening address to his reader; the use of a fictionalised form of himself as narrator; delicate description of the natural world and a typically elusive tone which moves between simple narration and ironic comedy. Several lines also refer back more directly to previous poems, such as the use of the gleaning metaphor (F: 73–7; G: 61–5) recalling *Parliament*'s 'olde feldes' (*Parliament*: 22) and the birds addressing their songs to St. Valentine (F: 144–7; G: 131–3) again similar to *Parliament*, although these later birds defy bird-catchers as they sing. It is precisely this less idealised thread which opens *Legend* to rather more sardonic reading than it at first appears to invite, for the main question surrounding this text is: is it all a sarcastic joke?

(ii) The pretext for writing the *Legend*

According to the text itself, the collection of stories about good women is a penance for spreading the disparagement of Love found in *Le Roman de la Rose* by translating it into English **[62–5]**, and for then further defaming the character of true lovers, and women in particular, by telling the story of Criseyde (*Legend*, F: 320–40; G: 246–66). The accusation is levelled by the god of Love, who in the G Prologue goes on to point out that Chaucer has sixty books full of stories of Roman and Greek women in which good women outnumber bad a hundred to one ('And evere an hundred goode agyen oon badde', G: 277). Defence comes from the unexpected angle of Alceste, who is here Love's consort, but it is a rather barbed defence. Perhaps, she suggests, Chaucer simply wrote what was to hand without really understanding what it said, after all he also composed works in praise of Love (*Legend*, F: 362–72; G: 340–52). She then lists most of Chaucer's works including the stories of Palamoun and Arcite and St. Cecilia which are now best known as The Knight's **[110]** and the Second Nun's Tales **[142]** respectively. It is Alceste, then, who proposes that Chaucer exonerate himself by spending the best part of the rest of his life 'In makynge of a gloryous legende/Of goode women,' (*Legend*, F: 483–4; G: 473–4). The penance is accepted and the prologue ends with Chaucer waking from his dream and settling to the task.

The figure of Alceste is significant for two reasons. She herself is a legendary good woman: she volunteered to die in her husband's stead, thus proving her devotion to him, but was rescued by Hercules who challenged Death to a wrestling match with Alceste as the prize. Her later transformation into a daisy seems to be Chaucer's invention and is a detail which neatly brings together the fictional and real contexts of the poem. In the fictional world, Chaucer ventures out in May to seek out his favourite flower, the daisy, whose virtues he details over several lines (*Legend*, F: 40–67; G: 40–60). There is no hint at this stage of the connection between Alceste and the daisy (which is merely asserted in F: 519 and G: 507), but there is a reference to the historical and literary context of the poem. A cult of the daisy, or marguerite, sprang up in honour of Richard II's queen, Anne, which allows for the suggestion that Alceste is here a figure of Anne. Although evidence of the exact status of such cults is thin on the ground, the allusion indicates that Chaucer expected the work to have a court audience. As such the daisy reference becomes part of the courtly contest between the Flower and the Leaf which Chaucer explicitly invokes in the F prologue 'Whethir ye ben with the leef or with the flour' (F: 72) and then elaborately refuses to join in the G version:

> For trusteth wel, I ne have nat undertake
> As of the lef agayn the flour to make,
> Ne of the flour to make agayn the lef
>
> (G: 71–3)

This contest was primarily a May Day game which entailed courtiers playfully swearing allegiance to either the flower or the leaf and then asserting the merits of their chosen icon. The side which provided the best argument won. Two things are of interest here. First, in portraying himself as a devotee of the daisy, Chaucer is in effect espousing the cult of the flower. It may be no coincidence that, according to Deschamps, Philippa, John of Gaunt's eldest daughter, was the patroness of the Flower faction. Second, it places the *Legend* as a whole in the context of a competition, and while the tales of the good women are told as an act of penitence and to redress the balance of his previous work, this broader literary context might have contributed to the eventual framework of *The Canterbury Tales*.

It could be said then that *Legend* partakes in two contests: the Flower and Leaf debate, and the challenge to produce exemplary tales of women. The question is how seriously did Chaucer take that second challenge? Brewer (1998: 250–1) points out that the allusion to the hundred stories of good women to one bad mentioned at G: 277 is immediately followed by a joke at the God of Love's expense as the rhetorical questions 'What seith Valerye, Titus, or Claudian?/ What seith Jerome agayns Jovynyan?' (*Legend*, G: 280–1) could be answered by one who knew with 'not much good about women', despite the implication here that they speak in women's defence. Once that tone is established the Legends themselves are open to ironic interpretation and attention is drawn to the fact that not only do all these women prove their worth by being victims of male betrayal, rather than through active good work, but also that the more one examines the tales, the more one wonders how far some of these women may be called 'good'.

The stories told are, in order, those of Cleopatra, Thisbe, Dido, Hypsipyle and Medea (who share a legend, as they are abandoned by the same man, Jason) Lucrece, Ariadne, Philomela, Phillis and Hypermnestra. The first six are explicitly termed martyrs in the Latin headings to their tales and seven of the ten die, four through suicide. One begins to suspect that the only good woman is a dead woman. Those wishing to defend Chaucer point out that these women are all held up as loyal in love and for Brewer this is evidence of Chaucer's belief in such steadfast love as the central virtue of mankind (Brewer 1998: 254–5), a virtue which Alceste also epitomises (and for which she also nearly dies). More important for the twentieth-century reader is the fact that the best known source for these women's stories was Ovid's *Heroides*, a series of letter-poems composed as if written by women lamenting their betrayal by men. Nowadays, we are more likely to know versions drawn from Ovid's sources, which tell the overall story, such as the tale of Antony and Cleopatra, or the version of Philomela's story which includes (as Chaucer does not) her revenge of serving Tereus a pie made out of his children.

The legends themselves are brief; the longest, Dido's, is 443 lines long, though the legend of Hypermnestra is unfinished. They are self-contained in that they make perfect sense when read without any prior knowledge of the stories or their context, but there is a cumulative effect, which is most explicit in the story of Phillis, who is abandoned by Demophon, Theseus's son. The text hints that she might have expected such a fate, given Theseus's own reputation, already established in the tale of Ariadne, likewise abandoned. As Phillis herself declares, 'ye ben lyk youre fader as in this' (2544) and the narrative notes that women would be well advised to learn from the examples set before them, although it is somewhat harder to judge the tone of the final line of this tale: 'And trusteth, as in love, no man but me'.

Men in fact do rather well out of *Legend* in one particular way – each legend contains many lines devoted to the men associated with the women. Thus we hear a good deal about Antony, about Hypermnestra's father, Egiste and uncle, Danao, about Tereus Philomela's husband (and raper of her sister) and of course about Aeneas and Theseus, all before the women themselves enter their own stories. Perhaps, then, the joke is that *Legend* is less one of Good Women than of Perfidious Men. It is a very courtly joke, as Antony, Aeneas and Jason are all described at various points as the epitome of courtly, knightly virtues. If we accept that Chaucer was expecting primarily a court audience for this text, it makes reading the *Legend* increasingly interesting, as it raises the possibility that he is offering some gentle, humorous criticism of what were becoming increasingly outdated values. In this light the much-acclaimed, highly sexualised, description of the sea-battle in the story of Cleopatra (*Legend*, 635–53) sets the tone for the tales that follow.

In all *Legend* is an experiment in bringing together a series of stories, united by theme, but offering the chance of variety plot and largely disposing of the need of a narrative persona. Yet, while such structure suited Gower and Boccaccio and was used successfully with explicit didactic purpose by Christine de Pizan, Chaucer evidently found it uninspiring and, whether as intentional joke, or as the result of restricted imagination, did not take full advantage of the opportunity to tell a wide variety of narratives. For all we know, he may have been composing further legends sporadically until the end of his life, as his *Retraction* refers to the book of twenty-five ladies (or in some manuscripts twenty-nine). We do know, however, that he exercised a far greater range of genres and character types in what is now his most famous composition, *The Canterbury Tales*.

Further Reading

For criticism of the Prologue see **[83]**. Of the Legends themselves, those of Dido and Cleopatra have drawn particular attention. Dido is discussed by Mann (1991: esp. 5–18) and N. Rudd (1994: 3–31). Hamel shows how Cleopatra's sea-battle draws on literary conventions for the description of naval engagements in a welcome and accessible essay (R. Edwards (ed.) 1994: 149–62). Delany's book prevents us dismissing *Legend* too easily (Delany 1994) and picks up on Dinshaw's groundbreaking reading (Dinshaw 1989: 65–87).

(f) COLLECTIONS OF TALES:
THE CANTERBURY TALES

(i) The 'whole' collection: manuscripts, texts and dates

For many, Chaucer and *The Canterbury Tales* are synonymous. We refer to the collection as if it was a complete and coherent whole, whereas the truth is rather different. Eighty-four manuscripts survive, no two alike, only fifty-five of which seem to have been 'complete' at any point and even amongst those the sequence of tales varies. This has given rise to much debate about the order and overall idea of the collection: does the Second Nun follow the Nun's Priest or the Franklin? Does the Wife of Bath follow the Man of Law or the Pardoner? Was she originally intended to tell the Tale now given to the Shipman? How many Tales were there to have been: one tale per pilgrim or four? In some ways the early manuscripts do not help. Hengwrt, the earliest manuscript, was probably copied in the year of Chaucer's death and can be called the 'best' in that it arguably preserves the closest text to Chaucer's original, but it is incomplete as the scribe seems to have acquired the Tales haphazardly and the manuscript has been bound and rebound in several orders since 1400, thus further scrambling it. Ellesmere is thought to be by the same scribe and is a beautiful, clear text ('best' in a different sense) which forms the basis of most of the modern editions **[157]**.

It is impossible to determine an exact date for the *Tales*, or even a reliable order of composition. The tendency has been to suggest that work on them started in around 1387 and continued intermittently from then until Chaucer's death in 1400. This would mean he was adding to the *Tales* while also writing *Astrolabe* **[86]**, *The Equatorie of Planetis* **[88]**, several short poems and revising the Prologue to *Legend* **[81]**. Very likely he was also tinkering with earlier Tales as he wrote later ones, and certainly was adding linking passages and perhaps internal references and re-assigning tales to characters. It is also entirely likely that the General Prologue was written after several of the tales existed and was still open to adjustment (several pilgrims who tell tales are not featured in it while tales do not exist for some who are described). The result is a more fluid text than we perhaps are used to imagining, in which individual Tales easily stand alone, even if they also have obvious relations to others.

This less settled view of the text indicates that the current habit of reading one or two of the Tales in rather random fashion is not all that far removed from the kind of reception they received from the first. As with *The Legend of Good Women*, *The Canterbury Tales* may have been conceived of as an ongoing project, to which tales could be added at any time and which also offered a home for already extant pieces which were in danger of being overlooked (Pearsall 1992: 228). The reference in the Prologue to *Legend* to what we now think of as The Knight's Tale as 'the love of Palamoun and Arcite/ Of Thebes, thogh the storye is knowen lite'(*Legend*, F: 420; G: 407) supports this view. Similarly, the life of St. Cecile, mentioned in F: 426 (G: 416) became the Second Nun's tale. Neither of these tales would have required much revision, if any, to become part of the larger body of The *Tales*.

Amongst the chaos there is some order. Groups of Tales tend to have stuck together and are now referred to as 'Fragments' labelled either alphabetically A–I, or in Roman numerals I–X. *The Riverside Chaucer* (the edition used here) uses Roman numerals and follows the Ellesmere order, numbering lines from the start of each fragment accordingly. This sequence suggests particular connections between Tales, but we should bear in mind that other correspondences exist and feel free to pursue them, much as we do, perhaps, when reading a book of short stories today.

Further Reading

The manuscripts and the questions raised by them are presented exhaustively but clearly in Owen (1991). More general treatment can be found in Cooper (1984), which explores the effects of order and links between fragments in the *Tales*. For engaging treatment of the *Tales* as a whole it is hard to beat Howard (1979) and Pearsall (1985) while Brewer discusses them in the general context of Chaucer's life and work (Brewer 1998: 261–397). Cooper's tale-by-tale guide is invaluable (Cooper 1996), while Phillips (2000) is approachable and less detailed. A succinct overview of the question of the chronological order of the Tales may be found in Pearsall (1992: 226–31).

(ii) The General Prologue

Probably the most famous prologue in English Literature, the poem begins with a brief description of English spring weather: April showers penetrate dry March roots, setting new life in motion and making everyone restless. For those particularly enamoured of Chaucer's bawdy, these lines carry obvious sexual overtones, but they also reflect the landscape descriptions which commonly open dream poems while simultaneously placing the action of the Prologue in a particular season, country and indeed attitude, when 'longen folk to goon on pilgrimage' (*Tales*, I: 12). The appeal of pilgrimage is as 'sondry' (varied) as the people who embark upon it: for some it is primarily a holiday, an excuse for a change of scene; for others a genuine religious act (although there is no reference to attendance at Mass or other devotions being obser-ved). By rights the Monk ought not to be travelling at all and we might question what prompts the Miller or Pardoner (to select but two) to go along. Chaucer has used the pilgrimage as a credible pretext to gather a carefully selected collection of characters and create a group which is more varied than any likely to unite voluntarily for other reasons. He then isolates them from interaction with any but themselves. In this the *Tales* has much in common with the road or disaster movies of today, but it is important to remember that we are not in fact dealing with individuals, but with representative types: a Knight, a Reeve, a Wife etc. More than that, the Knight is 'verray, parfit gentil' (*Tales*, I: 72), the epitome of a chivalric ideals, the five-times-married Wife is specifically from Bath, a thriving merchant town, whereas the Parson is just 'of a toun' (*Tales*, I: 478) and his brother, the Plowman, is simply described in terms which draw directly on the tradition of the Plowman as a role model of the pious, humble common man.

The pilgrimage motif is thus exploited to gather together a group of people which would never usually occur. For Benson

> *The Canterbury Tales* has the air of actuality because it is based on actuality. A pilgrimage was one of the few occasions in medieval life when so diverse a group of people might have gathered on a basis of temporary equality and might have told tales to pass the time on their journey.
>
> (*Riverside*: 4)

It is a seductive idea, but those 'might's are important. However realistic we may find the *Tales*, this is neither realist fiction nor a fictionalised account of an actual journey. Like many other literary premises it will not stand up to too rigorous scrutiny, for instance it would be impossible for everyone in a band of twenty-four riders to hear the story told by one of their number while travelling. Nonetheless the pilgrimage motif deserves some attention. The destination is St Thomas à Beckett's shrine, one of the most popular pilgrimage centres of the day. To travel there is to take part in a personality cult: the legend surrounding the individual gives the journey meaning. The practice thus validates the concept of individual identity, which in turn concurs easily with reading the journey as one of self-discovery or religious allegory. It is also essential for an enterprise which plays as extensively with ideas of voice and character as the *Tales* does. The sketches of the pilgrims thus draw on the tradition of social satire, as Mann has demonstrated (Mann 1973), but also suggest personalities, thus creating a fertile tension exploited by Leicester (Leicester 1980 and 1990). So The General Prologue introduces more than just characters who will tell stories, it also sets up a pattern, followed by many of the Tales themselves, of a Prologue which introduces themes later elaborated while simultaneously guiding the audience's reading.

The collection of pilgrims is thus eclectic, but not random, and significantly excludes aristocrats as well as beggars and unskilled peasants (ploughmen performed a skilled job). It is a carefully constructed literary fiction, which allows Chaucer to bring together the dominant and emerging traditions of his time, while also pursuing his own creative interests. We have already seen Chaucer explore the possibilities of narrative voice in *Troilus* **[89]** and *Legend* **[100]**. Here he takes a further step by giving himself a variety of personae to adopt, but he also retains his shadowy presence as an observer, who seems only tangentially involved in the action. It is in this presence that Pearsall detects the influence of Froissart's chronicle style, whose apparent disinterest disguises an actual control of material **[41]** (Pearsall 1992: 69). As narrator, Chaucer does not describe himself, that falls to Harry Bailly, the Host, who gives the briefest of sketches of a timid man when he calls upon him to tell a tale (*Tales*, VII: 695–704). Indeed in the General Prologue it at first seems that Harry will be the governing force of the whole text. It is he who suggests that the assembled pilgrims travel together and proposes the story-telling competition, but it is Chaucer who plants ideas in our heads, as when the drawing of lots is described. Whether 'by aventure, or sort, or cas' the Knight begins (*Tales*, I: 844). All three words could mean 'chance', but 'sort' could mean 'class' as well as 'lot', thus referring to the Knight's social standing. The very fact that we speculate on this shows that we are by now fully engaged in this fictional world, for of course it is by authorial design that this is the first Tale, and that it is one which itself treats of chance, standing and character and destiny.

Further Reading

Bloom (1988) provides a good collection of eleven essays on The General Prologue, including Leicester (1980) and the relevant section of Mann (1973) both mentioned above. More taxing and certainly more idiosyncratic is the chapter 'Re-constructing the "General Prologue"' in Frese (1991). Woolf tackles the subject of Chaucer as satirist with clarity. (Woolf 1986: 77–84, reprinted in Burrow 1969: 206–13).

(iii) The Knight's Tale

The longest of the verse Tales and in four parts (three in Hengwrt) **[106, 157]**, The Knight's Tale stands easily on its own, reflecting its original existence as an autonomous text. Chaucer probably composed the previous version, 'Palamoun and Arcite' in the early 1380s. The deft insertion of three lines (Tales, I: 889–91) incorporates the story into the wider structure of the Tales, while also allowing the Knight to refer to the company as a 'route' – a neutral word which nevertheless hints at 'rabble'. Depending on one's view of the Knight himself (Terry Jones presents an eloquent case for him being viewed as a mercenary, rather than a noble practitioner of a dying art, see Jones 1980) the ensuing romance **[39]** is either a prime example of a chivalric tale appropriate for a courtly figure, or a clever use of a high style to assert social superiority. There is no separate prologue, instead the Tale opens directly with the charming formula 'Whilom, as olden stories tellen us' (Tales, I: 859) which is pretty much the equivalent of 'Once upon a time'. The time is that of classical legend, as Theseus returns from conquering the Amazons in what is Chaucer's adaptation of Boccaccio's Teseida **[52]** and encounters a group of women, bewailing the overthrow of their city, Thebes, and the death of their husbands, including king Cappaneus. The widowed queen begs Theseus to revenge them, which he duly does, laying the city waste (Tales, I: 896–1004).

From here the focus shifts onto two cousins, Palamoun and Arcite, who are rescued from a pile of dying warriors and imprisoned. Their similarity to each other and the fact that they are sworn blood-brothers become central to a story of two knights and a lady. Much can be made of the different courses of action these well-nigh interchangeable heroes follow and how much they come to represent contrasting types. Arcite, freed by a powerful friend, but banished from Athens (Tales, I: 1202–15), bewails his enforced separation from the beautiful and oblivious Emelye (Tales, I: 1223–74). He resorts to subterfuge, disguising himself as a minstrel to gain entry to Emelye's court (Tales, I: 1399–

428). Later, when the two cousins are about to engage in formal combat in order to settle who should win Emelye, Arcite selects Mars, god of war, as his patron (*Tales*, I: 2367–70). Palamoun, who has more ignobly escaped from prison, seeks the help of Venus, goddess of love or desire, at the same point in the action (*Tales*, I: 2209–20). Neither deity is entirely noble or trustworthy, as the descriptions of their respective temples reveal (*Tales*, I: 1914–2050). It thus becomes possible to read Arcite as the embodiment of the warrior knight and Palamoun as the epitome of the lover knight – the two aspects which Troilus tried to unite in *Troilus* **[89]** (written at around the same date). The Tale can then be read as a debate over which aspect of the knightly ideal is preferable, in which case it is crucial to include Theseus in the equation, who is arguably the ideal combination of all knightly attributes.

The symmetry suggested by the likeness between Palamoun and Arcite informs the structure of the tale. Helen Cooper has sketched out the parallels (Cooper 1996: 74) and also highlights how the more philosophical elements of the poem are an integral part of its balance. These elements focus on the distinctions between Fortune, Destiny and Providence and owe much to Boethius, whose *Consolatio* Chaucer was translating **[83]** at the same time. It takes most of the poem to work through the differences, all of which come down to human perception, rather than divine ordinance. Thus the changeability of Fortune is first mentioned by Creon's widow, who significantly reminds Theseus of his current good fortune ('Lord, to whom Fortune hath yiven/Victorie, and as a conqueror to lyven', I: 915–16) before blaming the same fortune for her own downfall ('Thanked be Fortune and hire false wheel', I: 925). When Arcite takes up the theme he articulates our often confused use of 'Fortune'. Newly liberated, we would expect him to be rejoicing, but in fact he bewails his position. Fortune favours Palamoun, he asserts ('Wel hath Fortune yturned thee the dys', I: 1237) declaring that 'syn Fortune is chaungeable' (*Tales*, I: 1241) it is possible that Palamoun will achieve his desire (Emelye) by some unforeseeable means. Incapable of applying the logic of his conclusions to himself, Arcite conflates God's providence and Fortune (*Tales*, I: 1252), while ironically wondering why men complain of their current situation, when it often proves better than the one they desire (*Tales*, I: 1252–74). His speech is immediately followed by Palamoun's, which refers not to a changeable wheel of Fortune, but to a cruel goddess who writes the fate of men in adamantine, the hardest stone (*Tales*, I: 1281–333). The confusion is not clarified until Theseus' speech to Emelye in the final book of the poem, in which he replaces the changeability of Fortune and the unmoving cruelty of Fate with the stability of the

First Mover, who governs all things for the good of all (*Tales*, I: 2987–93).

Ironically, the denouement of the plot has been brought about not by some embodiment of order, but by the chaotic god, Saturn, who presents himself as deeper and less civilised forces than either Venus or Mars (*Tales*, I: 2455–78). It is also worth noting that Emelye, too, has prayed to a deity, Diane (*Tales*, I: 2273–366), but whereas Palamoun and Arcite simply request one thing, Emelye's petition is more complicated: if she cannot remain unmarried, then at least let the one who loves her most win her. Perhaps her equivocation is her downfall. Certainly she is given to understand in no uncertain terms that her fate is that of all ladies of courtly romance – to be the prize awarded to the male. Her role here links her to Criseyde **[90, 98]** and Dorigen of The Franklin's Tale **[130]**, both of whom are likewise at the mercy of their romance plots (arguably the Clerk's Griselde is a counter example **[126]**) although Mann argues that the ideal female role embodied by Emelye is presented as essential, not secondary (Mann 1991: 180–2).

Several distinct codes which govern life thus jostle each other throughout The Knight's Tale: philosophy, courtly conduct, and simple narrative drive. This allows the Tale to be read as an exploration of what governs our actions – the chances that befall us ('aventure'), the kinds of people we are ('sort'), or an overarching destiny ('cas'). Additionally it can be assessed primarily as a paradigm of a good story in a contest of tales: the text from which all the other Tales take their cue. The reaction of the pilgrims is interesting here. It is recorded in the Prologue to the Miller's Tale, but as Cooper points out, the prologues frequently round off the preceding Tale before introducing the next (Cooper 1996: 92).

The Knight ends his tale 'And God save al this faire compaignye!' (*Tales*, I: 3108), this makes his audience into a noble group, a description they reciprocate by calling the tale 'a noble storie', one worth remembering (*Tales*, I: 3111). In the next line, however, divisions reappear in the cohesive company, as the gentry are specifically mentioned, and finally the atmosphere of high seriousness is broken by the Host's laugh (3114). His attempt to have the Knight's noble, secular Tale in the high style followed by an equally prestigious but religious Tale told by the Monk is famously overturned by the Miller.

Further Reading

Leicester (1990) devotes six chapters to The Knight's Tale, covering genre, the gaze and the presentation of the gods in his exploration of

Chaucer's subjectivity. Patterson (1991) concentrates on the concept of chivalry. Jones (1980) is a lively, engaging and idiosyncratic reading which deserves attention, but also caution – it is best read in the light of Patterson. Carruthers's discussion of locational memory is scholarly, demanding and rewarding (Edwards, R. 1994: 93–106).

(iv) The Miller's Tale

The Miller's tale features John, a carpenter, his eighteen-year-old wife Alison, their lodger, the student Nicholas and Absolon, the local parish clerk. Both Nicholas and Absolon desire Alison, but Nicholas, using a more direct approach, succeeds where Absolon fails. In order to consummate the affair, Nicholas devises a plan. He tricks the carpenter into believing the next deluge is due and tells him the only way to survive is to take refuge in a wooden trough suspended from the ceiling. With John safely hidden and asleep, Nicholas and Alison slip off to bed. Then Absolon is heard outside, begging Alison for a kiss. The kiss he is granted is what is politely referred to as 'mis-directed', but Absolon realises and fetches a hot iron to wreak revenge. It is Nicholas, however, who receives the branding and the Tale ends in comic chaos.

The image of Robyn, the Miller, drunkenly overthrowing the authority of the Host and insisting on telling his tale next is a prime example of the relation between high literature (romance) and low literature (fabliau) **[40]** in which the driving forces are those of laughter and inversion. Low language, bawdiness and a cavalier attitude to rules mirror the cultured tone and emphasis on right behaviour of romance; yet, although it is tempting to describe such texts as rebellious, the concept of carnival is more useful here. The social structures are acknowledged, but simply inverted in a show of licensed festival. Thus fabliau agrees that there are external forces which govern our lives, but, broadly speaking, represents those forces as lust, greed and luck, which can be met with sex, covetousness, trickery and laughter: very different from the philosophical resignation which the Knight's Tale advocates. We willingly permit such carnivals, and have the option of non-participation. If we join in we know what we are letting ourselves in for:

> ... Whoso list it nat yheere,
> Turne over the leef and chese another tale
> [...]
> Blameth nat me if that ye chese amys.
> The Miller is a cherl; ye knowe wel this.
> (*Tales*, I: 3176–7; 3181–2)

The Miller is out to 'quit' the Knight, to trump his tale with one which takes the same narrative, twists it, and turns it into a comedy of low-life. The rival lovers are no longer knights and cousins, but a poor scholar (Nicholas) and an affected parish clerk (Absolon). The object of their desire, Alison, is 'wylde', 'yong' (*Tales*, I: 3225) and fair, but hardly noble. Described through animal imagery, she is apparently unattainable not because she is a lady, but because she is already married to a carpenter, John, with whom Nicholas lodges. In fact she is not all that unattainable and is soon in cahoots with Nicholas.

The sense of parody pervades plot and language. Like The Knight's Tale, the story begins 'whilom', but instead of a duke we have a 'gnof', a word whose Anglo-Saxon roots betray the more down-to-earth mood of this tale. Likewise the action takes place in a specific place – Oxford – and at a contemporary time, not removed into the land of legends occupied by Theseus. Epithets also take on a new twist as the 'hende' relentlessly applied to Nicholas comes to mean more than 'courteous' as we are reminded through force of association that it also means 'handy'. Is such trickery and cuckolding really 'courteous': are we being invited to comment sarcastically on actual court behaviour or to scoff at the kind of behaviour we might expect from an impoverished scholar? Where Absolon is evidently a figure of fun, with his curled hair, red hose and penchant for serenading (*Tales*, I: 3313–33; 3371–85), Nicholas is more ambiguous. Our interpretation may depend on whether we regard ourselves as noble or as solid townsfolk. Importantly, Nicholas, although clearly the hero of the tale, insofar as there is one, does not escape unharmed. Absolon's branding of him could be a hint that the Church still has the power to correct such opportunistic behaviour, if it is discovered. Interestingly, Alison, like May in the Merchant's Tale **[128]** gets off scott free.

Like The Knight's Tale much of The Miller's Tale is formulaic – the adultery, the hoodwinking, the mis-directed kiss, the cast of characters all fit the form. The actants have enough personality to engage us, but not enough to worry us, and the whole is a deft comic inversion of the Knight's admirable romance. All this leads Cooper to describe it as 'the best' fabliau – a fitting riposte to the Knight's best romance (Cooper 1996: 95). Its remarkable speed makes it vivacious and brings it to a brilliant conclusion with its triumphant plot summary and sudden end, which again recalls the Knight:

> Thus swyved ws this carpenteris wyf,
> For al his kepying and his jalousye,
> And Absolon hat kist hir nether ye,

And Nicholas is scalded in the towte.
This tale is doon, and God save al the rowte!
(*Tales*, I: 3850–4)

The reaction to the Tale at first seems to be unanimous laughter (*Tales*, I: 3855), reminding us that appreciation of fabliau was not restricted to the bourgeoisie any more than romance was to the nobles. However, discrepancy soon surfaces: two lines later 'Diverse folk diversely they seyde' as individuality is re-asserted and is finally voiced by the insulted and angry Reeve who takes up the challenge.

Further Reading

Birney provides a succinct introduction to structural irony in The Miller's Tale and also offers a useful bibliography (Birney 1985: 77–83, 146–50). Lindhal explores the relations between the Miller, oral traditions and insult (Lindhal 1989:134–42), while Knapp concentrates on the competition between the Miller and the Knight in her book *Chaucer and the Social Contest*: the sections relevant to the Miller are usefully brought together by Ellis (Ellis 1998: 62–77; 238). C.D. Benson's fourth chapter also compares the first two tales (C. Benson 1986), while Richardson includes a section on imagery in her book on Chaucer's fabliaux (Richardson 1970: 18–57).

(v) The Reeve's Tale

Also a fabliau, this plot revolves around a miller, two students, a quantity of flour and desire for revenge. Angry at being cheated out of flour from grain they brought to be ground, the students respond by sleeping with the miller's wife and daughter. A moved cot causes confusion and discovery, but the students manage to make off safely with the bags of flour and a loaf made from the amount the miller purloined.

Rumbustious and direct as the Miller's style is, it is left to the Reeve to introduce a personal note. His Prologue is the first self-portrait in the Tales and is less 'confessional' (Cooper 1996: 108) than defiant. Hurling the stereotype of the dishonest miller in Robyn's face, apparently in riposte for the gullible and cuckolded carpenter who figured in the Miller's tale, Oswald reflects the professional rivalry of reeves and millers. Both are on the take, making their profit from others' labours, as reeves manage their lord's land, while millers cheat customers out of flour, through exorbitant prices or theft. This rivalry underpins the tale, but so does anger, and desire for revenge. Portraying himself as old and beyond frivolity (*Tales*, I: 3867–70) the Reeve is far from serene, asserting that the four incentives to life in age are 'Avauntyng, liying, anger, coveitise' (*Tales*, I: 3884). These recall the picture of him in the General Prologue as a choleric man (*Tales*, I: 587), as Chaucer draws on the idea of the humours to create an expectation of an irascible tale.

The expectation is only partially fufilled. Certainly the driving force is revenge and indeed this fabliau could be seen as a series of ways to get even. It takes the Miller's 'quiting' a step further – all the characters are cheated and avenged in turn, as the Reeve illustrates the theme he pronounces at the end of the tale: 'A gylour shal hymself bigyled be' (*Tales*, I: 4321). Even the setting is part of the rivalry, as rural Cambridge replaces Oxford town and the satire becomes cynical as we learn that the social pretensions of the miller and his wife rest on the fact that she is the illegitimate daughter of the priest. Moreover, as Phillips points out, 'the plot is, of course, about rape' (Phillips 2000: 67). Things and women (little distinction is made between the two) are seized willy-nilly in a battle of wits between rival males of different ages, backgrounds and professions. However, the sheer pace of the plot and the lack of characterisation means that this apparently more violent story is less disconcerting for some than the more personality-based sex-tricks of the Miller's and Merchant's Tales. It is a comedy of types in which the northern clerks (complete with northern dialects) take on the stereotypically slow Norfolk man and intellect is pitted against commerce (it is worth remembering that Chaucer was probably resident in Kent at the time of writing this **[22]**). Every loose end is magnificently tied up; every action balanced with counter-action in a story told in language riddled with double-entendre. Even the ruse of cooking up the stolen flour into a cake is bested when the daughter gives the cake to the escaping students. There is no room for emotional involvement here – sheer amoral cleverness rules this world.

For some this world is a dark one: anger begets action, desire for revenge is presented as a commoner motive than lust and the sheer pace prevents emotional engagement or even moral judgement. Yet exhilaration breaks through: an underlying energy of escape, albeit one stemming from the excitment of getting away with something. Perhaps the best figure of this is the horse, let loose by the miller, heading for the company of the wild mares (*Tales*, I: 4064–6). Significantly, the Reeve mimics the Knight in his final sentence: once again the pilgrims are a 'compaignye' and the final judgement is left to God 'that sitteth heighe in magestee' (*Tales*, I: 4322). However, rather than a general response, Chaucer gives us here one pilgrim's gleeful reaction as the Cook takes over the stage.

Further Reading

Knapp 1990 is invaluable on the rivalry theme, while Lindhal provides much useful material on the historical basis for animosity between social groups and how that is reflected in narrative (Lindhal 1989: 73–158). Richardson's fifth chapter is useful on the Reeve in the light of the Miller (Richardson 1970). Kolve is particularly interesting on the imagery, especially the role of the horse (Kolve 1984: chapter 5). Delany illustrates the use of social class and irony, focusing on the 'clerks' as agents of the 'quiting' (Delany 1990: 104–11).

(vi) The Cook's Tale

This last, unfinished, Tale of Fragment I **[106]** promises to follow in the vein established by the Miller and Reeve of capping the previous story. The Cook calls his tale 'a litel jape that fil in oure citee' (*Tales*, I: 4344), thus bringing the action close to home as London replaces Oxford and Cambridge. He fleetingly suggests that the butt of his story will be the Host, but then defers that particular taunt until another time (perhaps reflecting the original ideas of the *Tales* in which each pilgrim told at least two tales). Instead we begin a story of an apprentice given to gambling, who is ejected by his landlord and takes up lodgings with a man with similar interests, married to a prostitute. We are back with the two men, one woman format of The Knight's and Miller's tales, but in the lowest possible setting, the seediest part of the city.

That begining is all we have, arguably because Chaucer had no source to follow (analogues and possible sources exist for all the three previous tales, see Bryan and Dempster 1941), but possibly because in striving to out-fabliau the fabliau genre, Chaucer comes to an imaginative wall, whether intentionally or not (see Patterson 1991: 278–9). Although it seems to be a fabliau, Cooper suggests it does not fit the genre due to the dominance of proverbial wisdom she detects (Cooper 1996: 120). The exchange between the Cook and Host continues the theme of professional rivalry begun by the Miller and Reeve, while the terms used for the various kinds of debauchery indulged in by Perkin Revelour reflect the themes of riot and festival (uncomfortably closely linked) as well as providing some material for the description of London life.

Further Reading

Little has appeared on the Cook's tale alone, most critical responses form part of a general consideration of Chaucer's fabliaux or discussion of Fragment I **[106]**. Thus Kolve (1984) and Lindahl (1987) give it due space. For most purposes, Cooper (1996) and Phillips (2000) give all the detail required.

(vii) The Man of Law's Tale

This is the story of Custance. The daughter of the Holy Roman Emperor, she is married off to the Sultan of Syria ('Surrye'), who agrees to convert to Christianity in order to wed her. This enrages his mother, who arranges for her son and all the Christians with him to be killed at a banquet and for Custance to be put to sea in a rudderless boat. Custance fetches up in Northumbria, where she is taken in by a man and his wife. But the devil, hating Custance, makes a knight kill the wife and accuse Custance. Custance is brought before the King, Alla, for murder, who is impressed by her manner. Her innocence is proved, Alla marries her and they have a son. Alla's mother is not pleased, however, and plots against Custance, with the result that Custance and her son are put to sea in a rudderless boat. They are rescued by a senator, who takes them to Rome, without knowing who they are. Meanwhile, Alla, having had his mother executed, travels to Rome in penance. The family is reunited and Custance is also reunited with her father, before they return to England. Finally, after Alla's death, Custance returns home.

This Tale constitutes a Fragment of its own, but is generally agreed to follow The Cook's Tale. Cooper discusses its links with other fragments, showing how such themes as destiny and reversals of fortune are picked up from The Knight's Tale, but also pointing out that this tale 'makes a new start' (Cooper 1983: 120–4). The tone is certainly very different from the amoral, if not immoral, fabliaux which have dominated since The Miller's Tale and there are some indications that 'The wordes of the hoost to the compagnye' which preface the Man of Law's Tale might have been intended to start the whole series of Tales at one stage (Cooper 1983: 63–4). If so, and there is dispute about this, Chaucer certainly replaced the idea with the current order, leading into The Knight's Tale, as preserved in all the manuscripts. Nonetheless, the rhyming couplets exchange between Host and Man of Law certainly signals a fresh start and is significantly distinct from the rhyme royal Prologue, which leads directly into the Tale.

This exchange begins with the Host noting the time of day and year using the kind of precise calculations that would normally require instruments. The result is a miscalculation, which could either be a slip on Chaucer's part, or a mistake deliberately inserted for comic effect. The Man of Law's part in the exchange consists of a selective resumé of Chaucer's narrative fictions and a reference to Gower's tale of Canacee. The boundary between fiction and the creators of fiction is thus wittily blurred, as The Man of Law in effect presents himself as a narrator struggling in the shadow of these two literary giants. The implication is that since Chaucer has told every tale worth telling in verse, leaving Gower **[39]** only the more unseemly ones (Canacee revolves around incest), what hope is there for such as the Man of Law? He will therefore speak in prose. Except he does not. While this may be further evidence for Chaucer changing his mind about what he wanted to do with this pilgrim and tale, it is also true that all the rhyme royal prologues are followed by rhyme royal tales.

The plot, with its series of trials undergone without complaint and final reunion, recalls the two closely related genres of romance and Saint's Life **[39, 142]**, which share such motifs as the innocent being put to sea in a ruddlerless boat. Stylistically, the stanzaic form and elevated language recalls the epic tone of *Troilus* **[89]** while Custance herself is the first of the female figures of virtue in the *Tales* (the others being the Griselde, Virginia and Prudence of the Clerk's, Physician's and Chaucer's 'Melibee', respectively). Without doubt it is a religious tale following the fortunes and misfortunes of Custance, whose name Chaucer alters from the more explicit 'Constance' used in the sources. She exemplifies constancy in adversity as well as faith as she is passed from father to husband to second husband, converting nations to Christianity as she goes through simple force of personality, before finally washing up (literally) at home again. This repetitive pattern, in which Custance undergoes every trial three times, extends the theme of doubling developed over the course of Fragment I. The tripartite structure potentially reflects several different aspects of the story: it allows for references to the Holy Trinity of the Christian Church, as Custance passes from the house of her father, significantly in Rome, to that of her first husband, thence to her second, returning as herself a spiritual force at the end of the poem. Alternatively it could reflect the three stages of female life: daughter, wife, mother.

It is also interesting to note that it is Custance's two mother-in-laws who are her enemies, each resenting her influence over their sons. Arguably, as well as upholding the Christian law of God, this Tale may be exemplifying a patriarchal viewpoint, by which good women are protected (or governed) by men, while dominant women are dangerous. Portraying women as rivals is typical of this attitude. Human as well as Divine law pervades the Tale as themes of trade, inheritance and marriage, all closely connected to legal affairs, underpin the story.

There is no audience reaction after this tale and indeed there is some question over the Epilogue (printed in square brackets in *Riverside* to indicate the difficulty). The Ellesmere manuscript **[106, 157]** omits it, perhaps indicating that Chaucer intended to cancel it altogether. The pilgrim who spoils the Host's plan of hearing a tale from the Parson is variously the Shipman, Wife of Bath and Squire, which tells us little, but does illustrate 'the device of using the independent-minded pilgrims to bring about apparently random and unhierarchical sequences of tales' (Phillips 2000: 78).

Further Reading

It is worth reading Gower's version of Custance's story in his *Confessio Amantis* **[101]** or the romance *Emaré*, to see how differently the same basic story can be treated. Dinshaw (1989: 88–112) focuses on the significance of Custance's story being told by the Man of Law – a man made up of law and with a personal stake in the maintainance of both law and the patriarchal status quo. Those intrigued by the Host's calculations will be interested by North (1988).

(viii) The Wife of Bath's Prologue and Tale

In effect the Wife of Bath tells two stories: her life story in her Prologue and the Breton lai **[130]** of her actual tale. Her first words sum up the two opposing sides of a debate Chaucer engaged in in various ways throughout his works: which is the more reliable source of knowledge – experience or the authority of books? As very much a woman of the world, it is inevitable that the Wife aligns herself with experience, and thus with the body rather than the intellect; the sexual, not the spiritual. As such she is the epitome of the types of women warned against in the kind of book her fifth husband, Jankyn, wields (literally and metaphorically). She is thus as much an *exemplum* (example) as Custance or Griselde **[118, 126]**; she simply represents the supposedly negative rather than positive role model. Her clear comic quality (heightened by sharing a name, Alison, with the gleeful heroine of The Miller's Tale) and the exuberance Chaucer has created makes her one of the most popular pilgrims, who in the twentieth century has been held up as a champion for women. Feisty, self-confident and successful, she is cited as proof that Chaucer was, in Douglas's term 'all womanis frend' **[175]**. However, Alisoun's prologue poses some questions for those who seek in her a role model for women.

The Prologue

According to her Prologue, Alisoun was first married at twelve, has had five husbands so far and is currently widowed. The first three husbands were good, rich and old, and are not characterised. The fourth was a 'revelour' and had a mistress – something for which the fun-loving, hard-drinking Alisoun made him pay heartily. The fifth, Jankyn, she describes as her favourite, whom she married for love. In her terms, he treated her the worst, taunting her with descriptions of bad wives taken from books, enraging her so much she tears three pages out of the book and the two come to blows. The upshot is reconciliation, lingering deafness on her part, and continuing devotion until his death.

From her appearance in the General Prologue (*Tales*, I: 445–46), to the end of her Tale, it seems that marriage is what the Wife of Bath is all about. While five husbands is just about a credible number for a fourteenth-century merchant woman **[33]** it is still comically exaggerated, as Chaucer has Alisoun flying in the face of religious treatises on marriage and citing Biblical precedents in a deliberate parody of theological debate (*Tales*, III: 9–162). However, marriage is more than just a game – it is a financial transaction, especially for a trader whose business benefits from profitable links. The beautiful, young woman is a desirable commodity and can more or less name her price; the older woman needs to be rich to be sexy. As the Wife says, 'Winne whoso may, for al is for to selle' (*Tales*, III: 414), which casts a more monitory light on being 'a worthy womman al hir lyve' (*Tales*, I: 459) and marrying ' worthy men in hir degree' (*Tales*, III: 8). This double market is evident in lines 587–92 where the ostentatious use of coverchiefs to cover her lack of tears also serves to display her wares literally as well as figuratively: she is a clothier by trade and here presents herself as a viable proposition on all fronts.

Like any other market, though, marriage is not without its dangers and indeed the Wife has promised to tell of wedded woe, not wedded bliss (*Tales*, III: 3). Her accounts recall the more cynical parts of *The Romance of the Rose* **[62]** which, in common with other misogynist writings, assume a predisposition to masochism in women and must surely undermine any easy assertion that the Wife of Bath is a positive role model for women. The obvious example is the fight she has with Jankyn, her apparently much-loved fifth husband. Significantly the word she uses of his love is 'daungerous' (*Tales*, III: 514), which, in the vocabulary of courtly love, indicates both the danger the suitor must overcome to win his lady and the danger to her honour posed by his advances. In the Wife's case the gender roles have been reversed: she is the supplicant and the danger Jankyn poses is not only emotional but real physical violence. Their fight leaves her half-deaf, a detail often read as the symbolic effect of the tales of subservient wives Jankyn insists on reading. More disturbingly, it leaves her more enamoured of him than before: 'thogh he hadde me bete on every bon,/He koude wynne agayn my love anon' (*Tales*, III: 511–12). In all she is similar to the character of Vieille, the Old Woman, in *The Romance of the Rose* **[62]** but she does come out on top, as the final upshot of the fight with Jankyn has been to get her own way, to achieve the very 'soveraynetee' (*Tales*, III: 818) that her Tale asserts is what every woman wants, and which comes up again as a topic of debate in the Franklin's and Clerk's tales.

Drawn as she is from sources which portray only wicked wives (*Tales*, III: 685), Alisoun arguably takes control of those stereotypes and makes them the basis of personal strength. In so doing she acknowledges the power of stories to mould our expectations and of the importance of taking the teller into account: 'Who peyntede the leoun, tel me, who?' (*Tales*, III: 692). Chaucer's fascination with narrative position and control is evident here, as it is in the Tale the Wife tells.

The Tale

The Wife tells the story of a knight, convicted of rape, who is given a year to discover what it is that every woman most desires and report back to court. If he gets the answer wrong, he will die. The year is nearly up and the knight no closer to finding the answer, when he meets an ugly, old crone, who declares she knows what he seeks and will tell him, on condition that he marry her. The knight agrees and returns to court, where the crone's answer proves correct. Most unwillingly, the knight marries the crone, bewailing her ugliness. She gives him a lecture on inner qualities and then offers him a choice: to have her ugly and definitely faithful, or beautiful and take the consequences. The knight asks her to choose, thereby showing he has learnt his lesson and the crone becomes both beautiful and faithful.

Readers and scholars have expected the Wife to tell a fabliau and indeed there is evidence she was originally given the bawdy marriage tale now given to the Shipman. Instead we get this Breton lai, for which there are several analogues (see Cooper 1996: 157–60). Lai is linked to romance and tends to include magic; as such it fits the idea of 'fantasye' and 'pleye' (*Tales*, III: 190, 192), but raises the questions whose fantasy is it and what kind of game is being played here? This leads to comparisons with the Franklin's Tale **[130]**, another lai which revolves around promises and in which easily overlooked phrases take on significance. Thus the line 'Save on the grene he saugh sittinge a wyf' (*Tales*, 998) becomes prophetic, as the hag will become his literal wife, despite his attempt to call her by the other available honorific 'mooder' (*Tales*, 1005). Likewise the romance formula 'I nam but deed, but if that I can seyn' (*Tales*, 1006) is actually true, as failure to discover the riddle will result in death. Conceivably, then, the hag's assertion 'For by my trouthe, I wol be to yow bothe' (*Tales*, 1240) (i.e. both beautiful and faithful) may indicate that if the knight fully understands her lecture on 'gentillesse', she will become in his eyes both fair and true, even in her hag-like form. The moral must be that 'gentillesse' is to be prized. This noble quality (closely linked to 'fre', explored in The Franklin's Tale) is not dependant on bloodline, but rather on temperament and involves the right treatment of others. It is a fittingly valued quality for an aspirant member of the merchant class, and indeed Chaucer devoted a lyric to it **[58]**, but we must be wary of attributing too much anachronistic liberalism to him: the clincher for happiness in The Wife of Bath's Tale is that 'she obeyed him in every thing' (*Tales*, III: 1255).

Further Reading

Extracts from the texts which make up Jankyn's book may be found, translated, in Blamires 1992. Not surprisingly the Wife of Bath has been the focus for much feminst criticism **[174]**, Diamond's essay 'Chaucer's Women and Women's Chaucer' (Diamond 1977, 1988) takes up the question of Chaucer as 'women's friend'; Carruthers focuses on the issue of experience versus authority (Evans and Johnson (eds) 1994: 22–53) and Dinshaw discusses interpretation (glossing) and its effects (Dinshaw 1989: 113–131). Leicester considers the creation of the subject through text both in the form of books referred to in the Wife's Prologue and in the tale she tells (Leicester 1990: 65–160).

(ix) The Friar's Tale

Although the Friar and Summoner are usually cast as an opposing pair, Chaucer clearly intended both to be also challenged by the Wife of Bath, whom they interrupt (*Tales*, III: 829–56). Indeed her ready appropriation of Biblical examples to support her own views neatly parodies the scholarly debates for which Churchmen were criticised. It is this aspect that the Friar picks up as he prepares to tell a tale directed against the Summoner, setting aside serious philosphical debate as inappropriate for 'game'. His Prologue thus establishes the principle of rivalry which provides immediate structure for the Friar's and Summoner's tales and echoes the similar professional rivalry and stories told against each other of the Miller and the Reeve [116].

Briefly, the plot is this. A summoner meets a yeoman, who introduces himself as a fiend. The summoner proposes they keep each other company, each taking what they are given (or extort) along the way. They encounter a carter, cursing his horse for being stuck, but the fiend does not take it, saying the man doesn't really mean his curses – as proves to be the case. Next they visit a woman, from whom the summoner intends to extract money. She wishes him in hell, at which the fiend whisks the summoner off.

Although couched in the tone of fabliau [40], the Tale is in fact closer to an exemplary sermon, that is, the protagonist (a summoner) epitomises certain vices (here greed and extortion). Summoners were minor church officials (not themselves clerics) who summoned people to ecclesiatic courts for offences which fell into the domain of church rather than civic justice e.g. marital disputes or non-payment of tithes (the tax due to the local church). Inevitably the system was corrupt and summoners were accused of trumping up charges, accepting bribes and lining their own pockets. While there are stories which could be Chaucer's sources, it is more likely that his own knowledge of legal records furnished the details. The kind of satire levelled at summoners was close to that currently directed at lawyers, right down to the comparisons with vultures and allusions to the devil being of their party.

As so often in the *Tales*, the crux is the use of words: here, as in the Wife's Tale, intention and word must match. The summoner is not fooled; he is a clever man who puts personal gain above all else and believes himself beyond the reach of law: civil, church or Divine. That is his error and the audience realises that long before he does. As soon as the identity of the mysterious 'yemen' is revealed (*Tales*, III: 1448) and the summoner's assertion of loyalty uttered (*Tales*, III: 1525–34) we wait for the pattern of words that will consign this summoner to hell. Cooper points out that this adds a level of suspense to the irony (Cooper 1996: 170), which is rare in Chaucer, who usually advertises the end of the plot long before he gets there. However, an alert listener might begin to guess the stranger's identity from the description of the yeoman's green clothing, as the colour was associated with the devil (although also suitable for a woodman). Such symbolism would be expected in this exemplum, or homilitic kind of narrative. Also expected is the moral drawn at the end. Significantly, the Friar gets this wrong. According to him, the point is that even the innocent are at risk, but the story clearly shows that those who sin knowingly and refuse to repent are damned: the widow is saved, after all. Thus the tale, while attacking summoners also satirises friars.

Further Reading

Hahn and Kaeuper (1983) give the historical context for the tale; those interested in learning more about the tradition of criticism against friars and other clerics will find Szittya (1986: 3–11; 231–46) informative. Birney's essay on irony is accessible and likeable (Birney 1985: 85–108).

(x) The Summoner's Tale

Like the Reeve's Tale, this fabliau is a direct riposte to the previous Tale. The central figure is a greedy friar, John, whose unseemly eagerness to acquire a bequest from a merchant, Thomas, is rewarded by the bequest being a fart. With comic meticulousness, the Tale goes on to explore how such a gift can be distributed evenly among all the friars of John's community.

The Summoner's prologue gives ample warning of the kind of Tale to follow. His outrage at being the butt of the Friar's Tale continues the quarrels we have already seen between them (*Tales*, III: 829–49; 1265–300) so, although the Prologue is an anecdote against friars, it is no surprise that the longer Tale is also a story of friars getting their comeuppance. It satirizes scholastic nit-picking, punning on the hot-air expelled in empty speech and in flatulance. Its linguistic base of punning and implication is appropriate here, as friars were widely criticised for their habit of twisting words, whether to gain money, goods, or free lodging, in order to seduce or for the joy of abstruse theological argument. This last is the 'glosynge' in which friar John rejoices (*Tales*, III: 1793) and which is parodied in his speeches, as he wilfuly misinterprets Biblical texts. Significantly his long discourse against anger serves merely to enrage Thomas even more and precipitates the eventual revenge. It is a further attack on friars in general that the tale does not end with friar John's discomfiture at Thomas's bequest, but with another household, the lord's, being entertained by the story. This household then adds insult to injury by focusing on, and solving, the comical problem of how Thomas's gift could be divided equally between the friars of the convent, which was the condition of the bequest.

The fact that the last word is given to those who have no connection with any branch of the Church could be a final dismissive gesture at all clerics. As an employee of the church court, it is wise of the Summoner to avoid overt criticism of all clerics, but it is in keeping with the carnival spirit of fabliaux that the witty solution to dividing the fart is offered by a layman and requires a simple cartwheel.

Further Reading

General discussion of Chaucer's representation of religion in the Summoner's Tale can be found in Aers (1986: 37–45), while more detail on it as antifraternal literature is provided by Szytta (1986: 231–46). Birney's highly readable essay examines the comedy of watching the friar talk himself into increasing trouble with the largely silent Thomas (Birney 1985: 109–25). While Lindahl discusses the insult hurling between summoner and friar (1989: 118–23; 144–7).

(xi) The Clerk's Tale

Fragment IV begins with the Clerk's Prologue, in which the Host seeks to forestall the kind of over-learned discourse he seems to expect from this quiet scholar. Significantly, the themes of holding to the terms of an agreement (here the 'pley' of story-telling) and obedience (*Tales*, IV: 22–24) are introduced, but with the easily over-looked caveat 'as fer as resoun axeth' (*Tales*, IV: 25). The Clerk tells us that the tale comes from Petrarch, who in turn took it from Boccaccio **[40]**, but Chaucer also consulted an anonymous French version of the story (Cooper 1996: 188–91). It has attracted strong reaction since its first appearance, ranging from horror at Walter's treatment of Griselde to impatience at Griselde's passivity. Even reading the tale as an allegory illustrating the soul's duty of absolute obedience to God, does not entirely remove the feelings of discomfort engendered by this story. It is this which raises the question of reasonable obedience, hinted at in the Prologue: is there a point beyond which unquestioning obedience becomes culpable? Arguably, this Tale contains one of Chaucer's rare references to contemporary affairs, as Walter's tyranny can be read as a reflection of Bernabò Visconti's Milan **[16]**.

Griselde is a peasant girl, picked out by the local marquis, Walter, to be his wife, in response to pressure from his nobles to marry. Walter demands a condition of total obedience from Griselde, to which she agrees. The people take to Griselde, who proves to be a skilled governor when deputising in Walter's absence. Soon after their daughter's birth Walter decides to test Griselde and has the child removed, ostensibly to be killed. Years pass and a son is born. Again, Walter commands the removal and apparent death of the child. Finally, Walter summons Griselde before him and in full court informs her that he is casting her off. She obeys, first stripping down to her shift in a refusal to take anything that isn't hers. After a few years Walter summons her back to court to prepare the house for his new bride. Again she obeys. Finally it is revealed that the new bride is in fact her daughter and the page her son. Mother and children are reunited and Griselde reinstated as Walter's wife.

Griselde's acquiescence in giving up her children to be killed (as she believes) often provokes outrage, stemming from the belief that a mother's primary concern ought to be for her offspring. This reflects a shift in social attitude: in the fourteenth century children were more explicitly attached to the father, and a woman's duty as wife came before those as mother. The audience is still expected to be outraged, but the weight of opprobrium falls more fully on Walter. Nonetheless, note that in his conclusion the Clerk specifically states that it would be insupportable ('inportable', *Tales*, IV: 1144) for all wives to be like Griselde. Like Custance, Griselde is a type, not a naturalistic character.

The Tale itself has been the focus of feminist and marxist criticism. The Clerk is regarded as both feminised, with his 'coy' attitude, and as a representative of the educated but not necessarily landed classes. Griselde is thus read as his representative in his own tale, being both female and a peasant, but clearly no fool. Her story is one of the more free-standing tales which seems to have been copied frequently on its own, and has continued to crop up in literature down to the present day (she appears in Caryl Churchill's *Top Girls* **[181]**).

Further Reading

Griselde's appropriation into Walter's household is examined as a metaphor of translation and literary tradition by Dinshaw (1989: 132–55) while Hansen discusses Griselde's use of silence (Hansen 1992: 188–208). Aers provides a thought-provoking reading of the Tale as an exposition on the nature of power, usefully read alongside Hansen (Aers 1986: 32–6). Wallace discusses the Tale in the light of Chaucer's travels in Italy (Patterson 1990: 156–215).

(xii) The Merchant's Tale

The Merchant's response to the Clerk's Tale, bewailing the huge differ-ence between his wife's attitude and that of Griselde prepares us for a story populated by characters we can read as real, if only for the space of the narrative. The insistence on identifying the characters as drawn from secular walks of life (*Tales*, IV: 1251; 1322; 1390) suggests that this Tale may have been originally assigned to a religious pilgrim, probably the Monk, (see Cooper 1996: 203–4). However, the latent anxiety about inheritance, the suggestion that May, as a young wife is the ageing Januarie's most valuable investment (*Tales*, IV: 1270), whom he then keeps under lock and key, make it a reasonable tale for a merchant to tell. Simultaneously the names Januarie and May invite symbolic readings of winter being displaced by spring, although such symbolism is not overtly developed.

The Tale itself is another fabliau, which continues the variations on the theme of two men and a woman, but it is more genteel than the Miller's or Reeve's as characters are deceived, but not physically hurt. January is a jealous old man who marries the young May. Damyan is a squire, who falls in love with May, as she does with him, but they lack opportunity to be together. Meanwhile, January has built a walled garden, for which he alone has the key, and gone blind. Taking advantage of this, Damyan and May tryst in a pear tree. This outrages Pluto, the king of fairies, who restores January's sight, but Proserpina, Pluto's wife, promptly endows May with the ability to create plausible excuses. Thus when January suddenly sees the two lovers in the tree he is talked into believing it is some magic ritual designed to restore his sight.

The relations between the protagonists mirrors one of the major paradigms of courtly love, as the young wife is courted by the accomplished squire of her husband's household, while the active role of classical gods (albeit in the less elevated form of fairies, see IV: 2227–37) harks back to romance. The Tale also includes a good deal of learned dispute on marriage in which Januarie and his friends, Justinus and Placebo, cover most of the sources used by Chaucer. As with many of these tales, it literalises a common saying – here that love is blind, as we are reminded when Januarie makes his choice of bride (*Tales*, IV: 1598) – while also playing on women's proverbial deceit and ability to talk their way out of anything.

Further Reading

The parodic relation between Merchant's and Knight's tales is illustrated by Cooper (1983: 214–30). Aers regards the Tale as a disconcerting representation of masculinist control of marriage (1986: 71–5). Hansen is worth reading for her challenge of over-easy readings of the tale, although she presumes some attitudes to the tale, which we may not hold (Hansen 1992: 245–67). A section of Patterson's chapter on commerce focuses on this tale (Patterson 1991: 333–44).

(xiii) The Squire's Tale

Beginning a new Fragment, the Squire's story harks back to the world of kings, knights and ladies. Cambyuskan is celebrating his birthday when into the feast rides an unknown knight, riding a brass horse, wearing a naked sword and carrying a mirror and a ring. Horse, sword, mirror and ring are gifts, whose magic properies the knight describes, adding that the mirror and ring are for Canacee, Cambyuskan's daughter. She is so excited by them that early next morning, while most of the court sleep off the effects of the feasting, she goes for a walk. Thanks to the ring she is able to understand what the birds are saying and overhears a falcon bemoaning the infidelity of her mate. Here the Squire breaks off, promising to return to that story, but first he will tell us about Cancee's brothers and father. He is interrupted by the Franklin and the Host takes advantage of the break to hasten in the next Tale.

The Squire's romance advertises its narrative and fictional nature in a way that is less assured than, for example, the confident references to Petrach used by the Clerk (*Tales*, IV: 31; 147) **[126]**. Arguably this lack of ease reflects the Squire's own position, still in training, not yet a knight, but accompanying his father, the experienced and confident Knight who begins the series of Tales. Romance, with its tropes of young aspirant men successfully negotiating rites of passage, would be particularly fitting for the squire. The jumble of elements – exotic location; stranger's entrance; flying, brass horse; magic mirror, ring and sword; noble princess; heart-broken falcon – might also be taken as deliberate indications of the Squire's inexperience. Alternatively, this could be the beginning of an intricate interwoven romance in which each magic gift has a separate story which are finally brought together for the conclusion. Such a tale would be highly ambitious and whether by accident or design it breaks off two lines into the third part.

The Tale is not without charm; the falcon's complaint (*Tales*, V: 479–631) recalls the betrayed women of *Legend* **[102]** and introduces the theme of gentillesse **[58, 125]** , a concept developed further by the Franklin **[130]**. It also suggests that the cause of the hawk's infidelity is the lure of 'newefangelnesse' (*Tales*, V: 610) the innate desire to try new things, which inevitably engenders restlessness, a theme first sounded in *Anelida and Arcite* (141) and echoed in The Canon Yeoman's Tale **[144]**. This is the very opposite of 'steadfastness' **[56]**, one of Chaucer's central virtues. 'Newefangelnesse' also neatly recalls the fascination exerted by the brass horse in the first section of the tale, which, after drawing all the people to marvel at it, promptly vanishes. Arguably, the Tale as a whole is thus a satiric rewriting of the courtly romance (see Patterson 1991: 71–3) in which man may be entertained by high culture, but is not saved by it, which would connect this Tale to the more ironic elements of *Troilus* **[89]**.

Further Reading

Cooper (1996: 217–29) is invaluable, as is Cooper (1984: 144–54) which discusses the thematic as well as verbal links between the Squire's and Franklin's tales. Lawton (1985: 106–29) discusses most aspects of the Tale in his exploration of narrators in Chaucer. Brewer provides an accessible discussion of the tale in the manuscripts (Brewer 1998: 328–32).

(xiv) The Franklin's Tale

Like The Wife of Bath's Tale **[122]** this is a lai, a form of romance, which often, as here, includes magic. Once again we have a love triangle. This time the original marriage is apparently happy: Averagus has wooed and won Dorigen and they agree that although it will appear that Averagus controls the marriage, in fact Dorigen will be in control. Averagus then goes abroad. In his absence, Dorigen is courted by Aurelius, whom she rejects, suddenly adding that if he can remove the rocks that threaten Averagus's safe return, she will be his. Aurelius goes to a magician-cum-clerk, who charges a thousand pounds and tells him that at a particular time the rocks will vanish. The clerk is right and Dorigen, appalled, tells all to Averagus, who has returned safely some two years previously. He insists she keep her word, and sends her to Aurelius, who is so impressed by Averagus's 'gentillesse' that he sends Dorigen back, untouched. Aurelius then goes to the clerk, confesses he does not have the thousands pounds due and relates the story. Proving himself as 'gentil' as the other two men, the clerk lets Aurelius off the debt. The Tale ends with the Franklin posing the question, who was the most 'fre'? (*Tales*, V: 1623).

This tale revolves around that concept of 'fre' which, as now, means both unconstrained and liberal. It is a quality associated with being noble and closely connected with 'gentillesse'. Thus the tale forms part of the debate on nobility as quality rather than birthright which is found in the Knight's and Wife's Tales **[110, 122]** as well as in Chaucer's lyrics **[55]**. It also continues the discussion of marriage, although as Mann and Phillips point out, this story explores possible developments after the 'happily ever after' of Dorigen and Averagus's marriage which begins the tale (Mann 1991: 111; Phillips 2000: 138). Aurelius is not addressing an unhappy or bored wife and Dorigen has no intention of being unfaithful. However, in issuing the test to Aurelius, Dorigen casts herself as the lady in a romance, honour bound to give the reward promised once the apparently impossible condition has been met. The crux thus becomes the issue of 'treuthe', another noble quality about which Chaucer composed a lyric **[58]**, and Dorigen comes to represent not only her own fidelity, but also the truth of the men in the tale. The difficulty would not have arisen had her words to Aurelius, spoken 'in pleye' (*Tales*, V:988) not been taken in earnest. The trope is familiar from folk tales, to which the lai is also related, and allows the audience to foresee problems ahead.

The role of magic is interesting: the tale's genre expects actual magic, but whereas the Squire's Tale's magic is clearly just that, here there is room for doubt. The magician who knows how to make rocks disappear and resolve conundrums, is also a 'clerk', a scholar, and arguably reminds society (both within and beyond the Canterbury pilgrimage) to treat such people with respect. They are the ones who truly understand the concepts others assume they embody. His magic may be simply advanced learning: certainly he knows his astrology (a science which fascinated Chaucer, as his *Astrolabe* proves **[86]**) and therefore probably knows about tides as well. We could question whether or not those rocks are removed, or just vanish from sight.

Further Reading

The kind of calculations the clerk might have used are explained by North (1988: 422–42). Mann reads the tale as prefering patience and trust to domination ('maistrye') in marriage (Mann 1991: 111–20), while Riddy explores the uses of romance and social conventions (Evans and Johnson 1994: 54–71). More challengingly, Hansen explores the danger the figure of Dorigen poses to the males within and outside the tale (Hansen: 1992: 267–83). A wide range of readings can be found in Morgan (1980).

(xv) The Physician's Tale

Fragment IV begins abruptly with the opening of this Tale. Drawn from *The Romance of the Rose* [62], it is a short tale here, rather in the style of the stories in *Legend* [102], which has led to some unsubstantiated speculation about an early date of composition. Above all it is disconcerting. Less because of its content, than because of the lack of pointers to how to read it. The plot is straightforward. Apius, a lecherous, corrupt judge lusts after a pure young woman, Virginia, the daughter of Virginius. In order to gain the girl, Apius colludes with a churl who trumps up charges against Virginius, designed to result in Virginia being handed over to Apius. Virginius's response is to kill Virginia and send her head to Apius. Apius orders Virginius to be hanged, but the mob rise up against the judge and save him.

All the elements here seem clear enough, but the focus is strangely uncertain. Is the judge, Apius, the central figure, in which case the moral of the tale seems to fit: 'Heere may men seen how synne hath his merite', *Tales*, VI: 277), or is it Virginia, in which case lines 278–9 are severely unnerving: 'Beth war, for no man woot whom God wold smyte/ In no degree, ne in which manere wyse'. Virginia's death fits this description as much as Apius's. Both virtue and corruption can kill us, it seems. The 'worm of conscience' (280) which is then invoked has hardly been seen to act, unless we surmise that it was the reason for the churl telling all, as apparently he did (264–5). Rather than a private worm there is a very public mob.

In comparison with his sources, Chaucer reduces the role of the people. Delany argues that this takes him into 'creative stalemate' (Delany 1990: 136). Yet Chaucer may be invoking the forms of both history (the first line correctly cites Livy, the Roman historian, as the source for the story) and what the Host calls 'piteous tale' (*Tales*, VI: 298), in which case the lack of explanation allows events to speak for themselves, while the exchange between father and daughter creates the pathos. Significantly, it is during that exchange that the daughter is named: 'Virginia' indicates her place as attached to her father (Virginius) and her status as a virgin. Both these attributes, and therefore in textual terms her very existence, are threatened by Apius. Paradoxically the only way she can remain Virginia is through death, fittingly, thus, at the hands of her father and in private. This combination of the actual and the symbolic occurs frequently in our reaction to news as one way of registering the significance of events. The disconcerting nature of this Tale probably springs from the way it fairly accurately represents the way life is: as Brewer points out, it comes close to closure (Brewer 1998: 350).

The hundred lines which intervene before the Physician gets to the matter of his tale are frequently overlooked. Much is said in them about Nature as creator and painter, but there is also much about counterfeits. This links nicely with the portrait of the Physician in the General Prologue and the character of the Pardoner, who tells the next tale, but it also alerts us to the way things are not quite what they seem even in the tale itself. Questions remain unanswered: how did Virginius know that the motive behind Claudius' false accusation was Apius's lust? Does he in fact know, or is he reacting against the idea that his noble daughter will be handed over to a 'churl'? Why are guardians warned to keep a close eye on their charges? For a short and straightforward story this Tale raises a lot of questions; a fact which goes far to contradict the notion that it is one of the weaker of the *Tales*.

Further Reading

Mann reads the tale alongside The Man of Law's Tale, as an exploration of suffering and 'thraldom' (Mann 1991: 142–6), while Brewer emphasises that it reflects fourteenth-century sensibilities (Brewer 1998: 341–50). Delany is interesting on why the tale fails (Delany 1990: 130–40).

(xvi) The Pardoner's Tale

The Host's request that the Pardoner tell a tale as a cure for the effects of the Physician's tale is double edged in that while it is complimentary and appropriate to ask a religious man for solace, the Host actually demands 'som myrthe or japes' (*Tales*, VI: 319), perhaps in parody of the theory of fiction's role as a tonic (Cooper 1996: 259). The Pardoner provides it all: the amusement and trickery strike us first, but his Tale also contains some solace, if we care to extract it.

The Prologue is part self-presentation, part description of his profession and fully in keeping with the criticism levelled at pardoners at the time. Pardoners were so called because they were employed by religious houses, or directly licensed by senior churchmen to raise funds by selling pardons. These were documents, worded in a precise manner, which certified that the person named (usually the buyer) had fulfilled correct penance to be pardoned for specific sins. Theoretically the person pardoned had been duly confessed and had performed appropriate penance, but the system was easily abused and simple payment often took the place of any spiritual endeavour. The status of pardoners was ambiguous. They were usually ordained to the level which licensed them to say mass, preach and perform some of the offices of the church, but not all. Moreover, they were required to gain the permission of the bishop before preaching in his diocese, but frequently they flouted this requirement. The opportunities for malpractice are obvious and Chaucer's Pardoner outlines most of them for us.

He gleefully describes selecting texts which can be worked up into harangues on the evils of wealth and the virtues of donations. He depicts his own presence in the pulpit, from which he lowers down on the congregation and declares that those who have committed some terrible sin and not confessed it will be incapable of walking up to give alms. He talks about the sheep's bones he passes off as relics and ends laughing at people's gullibilty. Then he tells a tale about three revellers who see a friend's body carried past while they are in a tavern and declare they will go and seek Death, and kill him. On their travels they encounter an old man, to whom they are rude, but who tells them they will find what they seek over a style and down a path. What they find is money. They then plot to kill each other in order to have all the gold to themselves and, inevitably, they all die as a result.

Duplicity is the hallmark of Chaucer's Pardoner, as his double-dealings extend from his fraudulent relics into the creative premiss of his Tale. Almost everything is two things at once. He addresses two audiences: the envisaged one of 'the lewed peple' (*Tales*, VI: 392) and the pilgrims, whom he flatteringly terms 'lordynges' (329). His Tale is both pseudo-homily and entry in a story-telling contest. His chosen text both asserts the evil that springs from the love of money and enriches the Pardoner. The tavern in which his Tale begins echoes the 'alestake' (*Tales*, VI: 321) mentioned by the Host (a tavern-owner) just before the Pardoner begins his narrative. The story itself is both the 'ribaudrye' the gentils don't want and the 'moral thing' they do (*Tales*, VI: 324–5) and its plot relies on the 'japes' (trickery) requested by the Host (*Tales*, VI: 319). The old man in the Tale is likewise double as he seems to be a figure both of Death and of one who cannot die, but who shows the three revellers where to find death themselves. More-over, although we are presented with 'Prologue' and 'Tale', the placing of the Latin tag before the Prologue indicates that the two are part and parcel of the same piece. This is a contrast to The Wife of Bath whose Prologue can be regarded as a story of its own, but is distinct from the tale she tells [120]. Finally, in the context of the *Tales* as a whole, the

Pardoner and his Tale should also be read in comparison with the Parson **[148]**, who offers a true sermon and true repentance.

Further Reading

The richness of this Tale means it has received much critical attention. Bloom (188c) is a useful collection of essays on various topics. Minnis (Boitani and Torti 1986: 88–119) provides the best discussion of the Pardoner as sinful preacher, while Patterson (1991: 367–421) explores the motif of confession at length and Howard draws the comparison with the Parson (1976: 333–79). Critics interested in narrative and subjectivity have been particularly drawn to the Pardoner: Lawton (1985: 17–35) and Leicester (1990: 35–64; 161–220) cover this ground. Patterson pairs the Tale with the Physician's Tale and, drawing on Lacan, discusses the theme of confession (1991: 367–423). The suggestion that the Pardoner is a eunuch is most fully exploited by Dinshaw in her chapter 'Eunuch Hermeneutics' (1989: 156–84).

(xvii) The Shipman's Tale

The Shipman's Tale, which lacks preamble of any kind, begins fragment VII, the one containing the most tales and the one subject to the most speculation about its place in the general running order of the *Tales*. The Tale itself was almost certainly originally intended for the Wife of Bath and echoes the views on husbands she expresses in her Prologue (*Tales*, III: 136) **[120]**. The use of the female voice for the Tale (*Tales*, VII: 12; 14; 18; 19) thus reflects incomplete revision rather than a deliberate rhetorical ploy on the part of the Shipman. Nonetheless, this fabliau **[40]** with monetary references is reasonably appropriate for a sea merchant and 'good felawe', as he is called in the General Prologue (*Tales*, I: 395). However, as Cooper points out, there is less connection between teller and tale here than at any other point in the *Tales* (Cooper 1996: 278).

The story concerns a monk, his friend, a rich merchant, and the merchant's wife who is also related to the monk. She complains to the monk that her husband is miserly and that she is in debt. The monk promises to help her, in return for sex. He then goes to the merchant, who is about to go away on business, and begs a loan, which is granted. The monk then gives the wife the money and receives payment in kind. When the merchant returns and asks for the money, the monk says he has given it to the wife. She declares she has spent it, but, now a debtor to her husband, will repay it in bed.

Of all the Tales this is the most explicit on the interchangeability of money and sex which underpins many of the other tales and, arguably, much of society. In keeping with the genre, though, this is exploited for comic effect, rather than being a point of concern. The plot is in fact kind to all the participants; the merchant is rich, forebearing and not made a mockery of in the way the miller of the Reeve's Tale or January in the Merchant's Tale are. The monk is corrupt, of course, but he, too, escapes retribution and indeed garners laughing praise from the Host for his cleverness (*Tales*, VII: 439–51). The wife, likewise, is quick-witted enough to talk her way out of trouble. Humorous appreciation is thus substituted for moral judgement in a tale which revolves around exchange and the profit that comes from it.

One effect of the elision of money and sex is the remarkable lack of overt bawdiness in the tale. We are in no doubt about what is going on, but the language is unfailingly decorous – a marked contrast to the other fabliaux, and indeed fabliaux in general. Another disconcerting, but easily overlooked, consequence of the Tale is that the carefully misleading truth of the monk's words and his cheating are placed on a par with the direct speech and honest trading of the merchant. For Cooper this highlights the extent to which Chaucer was fascinated by language development (Cooper 1996: 283–6) and it is certainly an extension of the awareness of the closeness of truth and lies which underpins *House* **[71]** as well as many of the Canterbury Tales.

Further Reading

Money and sex as commerce is discussed by Patterson (1991: 344–66). Cooper discusses its position in the *Tales* sequence and its slippery language, particularly with reference to the monk's abuse of his relation with the merchant (Cooper 1984: 161–5; 1996: 281–5). The probable source for the tale is found in Boccaccio's *Decameron* (Day Eight) and printed in translation in Bryan and Dempster (1958).

(xviii) The Prioress's Tale

The Prioress prefaces her Tale with a prayer to Mary, which readies us for the story of a miracle performed by Mary which follows. A Christian boy has learnt a Marian hymn, whose words he cannot understand, but which he sings every day out of devotion to Mary. His route takes him through the Jewish quarter and, incited by Satan, some Jews kill the boy and fling his body in a sewer. His mother seeks her son and finds him, throat cut, still singing. The Jews are executed and an abbot finally releases the child's soul.

There is no getting away from the anti-Semitism of this Tale. Contextualising it makes it more comprehensible, but not more comfortable. The fact that, following their explusion in 1290, few Jews were resident in England until the later seventeenth century, made it easy for stories demonising the Jews to circulate in the folk imagination. Setting the story in Asia also helps: anything is believable of so foreign a place. As Brewer points out, the Prioress's Jews are 'bogeymen', not people (Brewer 1998: 359) which merely serves to show how ready any society is to demonise another, especially on the basis of ignorance. 'Demonise' is the right word here, as it is explicitly Satan who incites the Jews to murder the boy (*Tales*, VII: 558) thus heightening the standing of the Tale as Christian story. The Tale does not allow us to question this standing by, for example, describing the boy's deliberate singing of a hymn in praise of Mary while walking through the Jewish quarter as an act of provocation. This is a 'miracle', designed to engender piety and wonder, not sceptical interrogation.

As such it is a story of praise, introduced by the Prioress's Prologue hymn, itself 'perhaps Chaucer's finest religious poetry' (Cooper 1996: 292), whose last line introduces the theme of music: 'Gydeth my song that I shal of yow seye' (*Tales*, VII: 487). The role of song is interesting here: it has a more direct connection with faith than learning has. This may reflect its purely musical aspect: music has no need for language in order to have an effect and it is precisely such affective (as opposed to intellectual) piety that the miracle seeks to engender. Thus it is fitting that neither the boy martyr of the story, nor the older lad from whom he learns the Marian hymn, understands the words. Simple, emotional, faith is the point here. The link is emphasised by the use of the miraculous grain placed on the boy's tongue, which makes him sing even after his throat has been cut. The singing continues until the abbot, explicitly 'hooly' (in contrast to the monks who have figured in previous tales, or indeed the Pilgrim) 'conjures' (*Tales*, VII: 644) the boy to explain the miracle. The role of the Church and learning is thus established as being one of passing on and explaining such stories of exemplary faith to a wider populace.

Direct and essentially uninformed piety thus demands acknowledgement, even if it does not quite command respect. We are left uncertain as to how to read this Tale, an uncertainty reflected in the reaction of the other pilgrims: 'every man/ As sobre was that wonder was to se' (*Tales*, VII: 691–2). Is the solemnity a thoughtful reaction to the story of a miracle and the 'wonder' admiration at its ability to elicit such response? Or is it a wonder that such a diverse group of people actually take such stories seriously? As so often it is the Host who breaks the silence with his customary call for 'a tale of myrthe' (*Tales*, VII: 706).

Further Reading

The best short reading of the tale is Pearsall's (1985: 246–52) which covers the religious nature of the tale and touches on the main issues. It is a good starting place for further reading. The anti-Semitic aspect is best covered by Schoeck (Schoek and Taylor 1960: 1.245–58), who provides the historical context, and Koff, who poses pertinent questions (1988: 204–21). Aers's brief discussion of the tale in the context of Chaucer's general presentation of religion is accessible and useful (1986: 54–7). Robertson draws on French feminist theory and views of female piety as a source of strength (Ellis: 1998: 189–208), while Collette shows how the Prioress, like the Second Nun, carves out her right to speak through invoking worship of Mary (R. Edwards (ed.) 1994: 127–47).

(xix) The Tales of *Sir Topas* and *Melibee*

With a piece of authorial cheek, Chaucer awards himself two Tales: Sir Thopas, a parody romance and The Tale of Melibee, a moral tale in prose that turns into a treatise. Phillips sees the two as going 'beyond the expected definition of story-telling' (Phillips 2000: 171); certainly they can be regarded as occupying opposite ends of a story-telling continuum.

Sir Thopas is a romance **[40]** which assembles all the ingredients required for a tale of an ideal knight errant, but in which nothing actually happens. Adventures are promised, but deferred, as the story-line meanders away from chaste knight falling inexplicably in love with unknown love-object (unknown because unseen, even by Sir Thopas) past chance encounter with giant, to description of Thopas being just like all the other pure knights of romance – at which point the Host cuts 'Chaucer' short. Readers familiar with the nonsense verse of Edward Lear will be familiar with Sir Thopas's world. This is a tale in which both narrator and protagonist literally lose the plot.

The technical form of the poem assists the rambling. Termed 'rym dogerel' by the Host (*Tales*, VII: 925), it is a burlesque of popular romances and ballades composed in simple verse forms, heavy on rhyme, rhythm and formulaic phrases, which keep the momentum of the verse going without necessarily adding much to the poetry. Sir

Thopas takes on a fairly usual stanza form for this genre, rhyming aabaab or aabccb, with occasional variations and additional rhyming two-syllable phrases ('bobs') tacked on to the end of a line. The layout of this verse-form was thus surprisingly complicated and is reproduced in most of the manuscripts of Sir Thopas but not in modern printed editions. Cooper provides an example of how it looks on the page, illustrating how much room there was for confusion (Cooper 1996: 300). Added to the masterly parody of subject and form is a further joke. Sir Thopas is divided into three parts decreasing in length from eighteen, to nine, to four and a half lines: the law of diminishing returns enacted on the page.

In contrast, Melibee has a great deal to say about returns, about the difference between just deserts and the kind of return that a just man should make for injustice done. The tale begins as a parable: Melibee is married to the allegorically named Prudence, their daughter is Sophie, Greek for wisdom. The women are attacked while Melibee is away, significantly at 'pleye' 'for his disport' (*Tales*, VII: 971; 970). Distraught to discover what has happened, Melibee follows Prudence's advise and calls his friends together to tell them about it and ask them what to do. Opinion is divided between those who advocate peace and reconciliation (professional men, beginning with surgeons and doctors) and those who are for vengeance (false friends). It seems that retribution will prevail, but Prudence again intervenes to dissuade Melibee and eventually wins the day. In the course of the discussion the narrative drive lessens, taking this tale away from story towards treatise, thus very like *Boece* **[83]** in tone.

Melibee is a fairly faithful translation of the French version of a Latin 'Book of Consolation and Advice' (*Liber consolationis et consilii*) written by Albertanus in 1246 (Chaucer does not seem to have known the Latin original). It is a treatise of political advice against war which Chaucer may have translated before including it in the *Tales*, possibly for Richard II, though, if so, whether for the young king of the 1370s or the older one of the 1390s is a matter of debate (see Cooper 1996: 311–12). It is also long, overlong in the context of the *Tales* as a whole, which has led most critics to view it as deliberately tedious, as Chaucer sending himself up in prose as well as in verse. Perhaps so, but Mann asserts the centrality of this Tale, and of Prudence in particular (Mann 1991: 120–7). Prudence is also kin to the Clerk's Griselde and, like her, causes the Host to reflect on his own wife and how different she is from these ideal wives. Such reaction diffuses the philosophical atmosphere, but the themes of learning from literary example and drawing on literary sources are continued as the Monk takes up the role of storyteller.

Further Reading

Pearsall places Sir Thopas in the context of romances (1985: 160–5), while Brewer highlights the mocking self-portrait Chaucer offers here (1998: 361–4). Details of the structure and terms in Sir Thopas are discussed by Burrow (1984: 54–8; 60–78). Rigby discusses Melibee in the context of Chaucer's feminism (1996: 153–63), though see also Mann (1991: 120–7). Brewer takes issue with the notion of Melibee's centrality, but also with categorising it as parody (1998: 364–9).

(xx) The Monk's Tale

The similarities between this tale and *Legend* have already been established **[101]**: both are collections of short stories, ostensibly united by theme, but our understanding of that theme alters as we read. Here the Monk promises a selection of tragedies, from which we are supposed to learn that our good fortune may not last. He immediately undermines his ostensible purpose by starting with Lucifer who fulfils the criteria only in the most tenuous fashion – neither man nor victim of Fortune, since he fell through wilful disobedience – his downfall is his only qualificiation for inclusion here. Normally we would expect him to be an example of the fatal folly of pride or insubordination, but the Monk comments on neither; instead he moves on swiftly after giving Lucifer a mere stanza. This departure from the strict definition of tragedy, reprised at the end of the tale of Cresus (*Tales*, VII: 2761–6), is particularly interesting since it was not commonly recognised as a genre at the time. Chaucer first uses the term 'tragedye' at the end of *Troilus* (*Tales*, V: 1786) **[96]** and his description probably has its roots in Boethius, which he was translating at the time **[83]**, but it is the definition of it here in the Monk's Tale which fixed the genre as dealing with the fall of great men for English literary tradition.

The theme of reversals of Fortune was common and features in both The Knight's Tale **[110]** and *Troilus* (e.g. I: 138–40). Interestingly, a wall-painting in Rochester Cathedral depicts the Wheel of Fortune. This allows for the Monk's reference to Rochester (*Tales*, VII: 1926) to be a hint of things to come in his Tale, rather than an indication of the Pilgrims' progress, as has been often assumed.

The structure of The Monk's Tale, with its succession of short stories, imitates that of the *Tales* as a whole. It could go on indefinitely and there is no set order to it, as (purportedly) the stories are set down as they come to mind (*Tales*, VII: 1985–90). This Tale contains explicit references to important, contemporary, political figures, something Chaucer rarely did. A case in point is the stanza devoted to Barnabò Visconti (*Tales*, VII: 2399–406), whom Chaucer met in 1378 **[16]** and who may lie behind Walter in The Clerk's Tale **[126]**. The powerful men featured in the Monk's collection are a mixture of biblical, historical and contemporary figures and the seemingly endless list has an almost hypnotic quality about it, as few of the examples are expanded into full stories.

Further Reading

The Rochester reference is explained by Olson (1986–87). Discussion of medieval tragedy is best found in Kelly (1986). Koff explores the kind of reading the Monk elicits in the context of the way other Tales are received (1988: 84–8). Godman argues that the stories in The Monk's Tale are directed specifically at the Host (Boitani (ed.) 1983: 278–91).

(xxi) The Nun's Priest's Tale

The framework for the Nun's Priest's Tale is the familiar fable of the Cock and the Fox, in which a conceited rooster is first caught by a flattering fox and then escapes by persuading the fox to speak, thus making him open his mouth, enabling the bird to fly free. However Chaucer expands this fable almost out of all recognition by including an old woman who owns the coop, a bossy hen-wife and a discussion of the role of dreams (*Tales*, VII: 2882–3171) which compares with the opening of *House* **[71]**. Here, as there, there is an analogy between how we interpret dreams and how we read literature. This Tale has been read as an allegory on the Church, a metaphorical description of this priest's particular position as attached to a convent, a *tour de force* of the moral beast fable and as 'the wittiest and most original dramatisation ... of the distribution of roles in a conventional marriage' (Mann 1991: 187).

The Tale takes up the theme of the downfall of the affluent as Chaunticleer, the cock, literally rules the roost until he falls prey to a smooth-talking fox. The theme is then reiterated when the fox is about to lose his catch: 'Lo, how Fortune turneth sodeynly' (*Tales*, VII: 3403). Such exclamations link the Tale to the epic romance of The Knight's Tale and *Troilus*, whose high rhetoric is imitated in the mock-lament for Chaunticleer's impending doom (*Tales*, VII: 3338–74) as well as in the previous debate on dreams and philosophy between Chaunticleer and his wife, Pertelote (*Tales*, VII: 2882–3171). The irony is that, having proved to his own satisfaction that dreams are portents and having dismissed Pertelote's opposite view, Chaunticleer then ignores his own advice. Arguably this habit of solemnly agreeing on the worthiness of a text and then ignoring it is hinted at in the Priest's final exhortation 'taketh the fruyt, and lat the chaff be stille' (*Tales*, VII: 3443).

The Tale contains one of Chaucer's rare allusions to contemporary events in England in the reference to the noise of the hunt being like the uproar caused by the Peasants' Revolt (*Tales*, VII: 3394–6) **[21]**. It is impossible to know if the detail is there simply to add local colour or if it reflects some deep-seated response to the uprisings, hounding of foreign workers, damage done to property and threat of revolt.

Further Reading

Mann's reading is one of the most engaging and original (Mann 1991: 186–94); Delany offers a lively reading of the tale including consideration of its popular appeal, but her conclusions about Chaucer's personal life must be treated with caution (Delany 1990: 141–50). A complex and interesting reading focusing on language as reality is provided by Harwood (Ellis 1998: 209–24). Donaldson debunks reliance on allegorical readings of the tale (1970: 146–50) which are recapitulated succinctly in Pearsall's general discussion of the tale (1985: 228–38). Cooper gives an excellent guide to the Tale's variants and critical reception (1996: 338–56) and Brewer gives a concise and useful account of its relation to other cock and fox tales (1998: 371–6).

(xxii) The Second Nuns' Tale

There is no preamble to this Prologue and Tale; Fragment VIII goes straight into the Life of St. Cecilia, which probably pre-dates the *Tales* as a whole, as it is mentioned in the Prologue to *Legend* (F: 424; G: 416) **[81, 100]**. Beyond the title indentifying it as the Second Nun's Tale and the sentence referring back to the story, which begins the link into the Canon Yeoman's Tale, nothing has been done to integrate this tale into the wider structure of the *Tales*. Nor is there any trace of the character of the Second Nun. In all, this Tale can easily be read as Chaucer's foray into the genre of the Saint's Life **[39]**.

Cecile's story is a simple one. On the night of her marriage she tells her husband, Valerian, that her chastity is preserved by an angel, who will slay Valerian if he touches her. Valerian demands proof and is sent to a holy man to be cleansed of sin, after which an angel does indeed appear, corroborating Cecile's words. Valerian is converted and returns home to discover an angel awaiting him with coronets for both him and Cecile. Tiburces, Valerian's brother, comes in, is told all, and is likewise converted. News of Valerian and Tiburces reaches Almache, the ruler of the country, who promptly orders them to sacrifice to Jupiter, as he has commanded. They refuse and as a result are killed, thus becoming martyrs. One of their converts, Maximus, witnesses to their souls' ascent to heaven, and is martyred himself as a result. Finally Cecile is summoned by Almache and they engage in debate. Because Cecile holds to her belief, Almache orders her to be burnt in a bath, but she is miraculously preserved and even survives three blows to her neck for three days, preaching all the while. She finally dies, requesting a church be built in her honour.

Reading a Saint's Life was in itself an act of devotion, which was considered particularly appropriate for women and others who had limited access (or none) to books and education. Saints naturally inspire by their example, but within this Tale there is also the suggestion that books are an equally good, if not more authoritative, source of religious knowledge. Valerian has his readiness to believe and his fitness for conversion proved by the vision of a man holding out a book, written on in gold (*Tales*, VIII: 202–17). There are traces in this image of the Chaucer of the Dream poems **[61]**, while the motif of revelation through vision balances the discussion of dreams found in The Nun's Priest's Tale **[141]**.

Despite the visionary element, the main effect of the story is intellectual. Readiness to believe is tested in both Valerian and Tiburces, but once established, arguments are offered and intellectual debate opened. This is a marked contrast to the affective piety of the Prioress's Tale, which rests on blind faith alone **[137]**. Whereas the Prioress's Tale left the pilgrims in stunned (or moved) silence, there is no recorded reaction to this story of St. Cecile. Arguably martyrdom is so far removed from the experience or aspirations of the pilgrims that no response could be found, except to supplant the tale of transformation from mortal to saint through martyrdom with one of attempted transformation of base metal to gold in the Canon's Yeoman's Tale.

Critically, the Tale has been rather overlooked, perhaps because the lack of intervening pilgrim character leaves readers uncomfortable with the idea that the same man wrote this as the other Tales. Yet the Chaucer of this Tale is the same as that of the Parson's Tale **[148]**, *An ABC* **[49]** and the lyric 'Truth' **[58]**.

Further Reading

An excellent introduction to the Saint's Life genre is provided by Wogan-Browne and Burgass, whose introduction gives some background on the genre and its expected readership (1996). Aers discusses the Tale in the context of Chaucer's presentation of religion and makes illuminating comparisons with the Prioress's Tale (1986: 51–4). Pearsall's rather dismissive treatment of the tale is nonetheless useful (1985: 252–6) although Cooper provides both greater detail and greater engagement (1996: 358–67).

(xxiii) The Canon's Yeoman's Tale

The sudden arrival of the Canon and his Yeoman and the equally sudden departure of the Canon led some critics to suggest these figures were afterthoughts, perhaps reflecting a possible encounter on Chaucer's own part with a fraudulent alchemist (as opposed to a misguided one) in the 1390s. The detail must remain speculation, but a Canon of the King's Chapel at Windsor (for which Chaucer was responsible during his term as Clerk of Works [23]) was cited as an alchemist in 1374. It is possible that he provided the inspiration for the cast of conman Canon and his Yeoman side-kick. It is also possible that their haste is part of their characterisation: they may be escaping some particularly irate victim – but that also is speculation. Their arrival increases the level of drama, however, as Chaucer breaks out of his closed group of original Pilgrims, perhaps an indication that the necessarily repetitive pattern of story, followed by reaction and introduction of next story, was beginning to pale.

Not having featured in the General Prologue, all the description of both Canon and Yeoman must take place in the Prologue to the Tale. The Prologue is therefore similar to the Wife of Bath's and Pardoner's in being a self-portrait, but in the absence of a previous sketch to measure it against, Chaucer uses the Host to draw out details from the voluble Yeoman, prompting him in what is in effect a dramatic monologue. The character that emerges is more complex than the other Pilgrims: it is hard to tell whether the Yeoman still believes there is something to alchemy, despite all the failed attempts, or whether he is irrationally hooked on the process, although rationally aware that it is a delusion. His self-portrait spills over into the first part of his Tale, which is a description of the Canon's tricks of the trade, but the detailed enumeration of all the regalia of alchemy is reminiscent of an addict's obsession.

To an extent this fascination reflects the standing of alchemy itself in fourteenth-century England. The 'science' came from the East, as had astrology and mathematics, and was careful to preserve its mystique. From what we know of Chaucer's interest in all aspects of science and culture, it is more than likely that he was curious about it, and while the Canon's Yeoman's Tale bears witness to his awareness of the trickery that attended alchemy, it also retains a suggestion that there might be a true science lurking behind the fakery. This element of trickery links the Tale with the Pardoner's Tale **[133]**, which likewise revolves around people being taken in through their own greed. The consequences here are scarcely less dire, for the final question of the Tale is not whether or not alchemy is true, but whether or not it is permitted to delve into the secrets of God's universe to this extent. The association of the alchemist with the devil, which runs throughout the Prologue and Tale, reinforces the unease about what exactly alchemy is and links the alchemist with the false summoner of the Friar's Tale **[124]**.

The tale proper really begins in the second part (*Tales*, VIII: 972). A canon gets the trust of a poor chantry priest, whom he tricks into believing that the canon knows the process for turning base metal into pure silver. The canon practises three sleights of hand on the priest, who is so convinced he pays forty pounds for the recipe. The canon then disappears and the priest never understands why he cannot get the process to work.

Humour and anxiety together pervade this text, as Chaucer has a field-day with references to heat, sweating and change in colour, all integral to the alchemical process and all also echoing elements from the Second Nun's life of St. Cecile. Even red and white as symbolic of purification are shared ground: compare Valerian and Cecile's divine coronets (*Tales*, VIII: 253–5) with the red and white elixirs which purify base metals to gold and silver respectively (*Tales*, VIII: 797 and 805). This clever literary linking also raises the question of alchemy as blasphemy; on which note the Tale ends with the rather double-edged tag: 'God send every trewe man boote of his bale' (*Tales*, VIII: 1481). We may no longer be sure what constitutes a true man, nor how we are supposed to test truth, and proverbially it is not always good to be sent a cure for one's ills.

Further Reading

Muscatine links the Tale's interest in experimentation with Chaucer's own literary experiments (1957: 213–21) and Howard explores the themes of idealism, delusion and hope (1976: 292–8). Blake (1985) has argued against this Tale being by Chaucer, but the argument has been generally rejected.

(xxiv) The Manciple's Tale

Fragment IX contains just the Manciple's Prologue and Tale and seems to be incompletely absorbed into the general structure of the *Tales*. The Host's request that the Cook tell a tale ignores the Cook's earlier, unsuccessful attempt and is probably evidence of incomplete revision. The intervention of the Manciple makes sense, however, as an instance of professional rivalry, akin to that between Miller and Reeve, since manciples were in charge of provisions for an institution or household (in this case one of the Inns of Court, I: 567). The Host's hint that the Manciple should be careful of what he says to the Cook (for fear of the Cook revealing the Manciple's sharp practice) works dramatically and also introduces the theme of the Tale: unwary speech.

The Prologue's opening geographical references place the pilgrims close to Canterbury and suggests that several of them have yet to tell stories. However, the Parson's Prologue, the next and last in the series as it stands, indicates that the Pilgrims are closer still to Canterbury, and also declares that only the Parson remains to tell a tale (*Tales*, X: 16). Despite such discrepancies, the weight of evidence is that the Manciple was designed to precede the Parson and thus be the penultimate Tale of the collection.

The Tale itself stands out in the context of the *Tales* as a whole in having a fairly short story and relatively long and repetitive epilogue. The story itself harks back to Chaucer's early use of *The Romance of the Rose* **[62]** and also draws on Ovid. It is a fable of explanation, telling us why all crows are black. Once the crow was white and could sing beautifully and also speak. Phebus kept one, which saw his wife committing adultery. The crow told Phebus, who kills his wife in rage and then in grief curses the crow: henceforth it shall be black and capable only of cawing.

As with all such fables, there is an added moral, but this is where the complexity creeps in. We are expected to take the crow's place in the narrative and to learn that there are times when it is better to keep quiet, particularly in matters of adultery: 'Ne telleth no man in youre lif/How that another man hath dight his wyf' (*Tales*, IX: 311–12). However, if we focus on Phebus another moral emerges, that there are times when it is better to be ignorant or deceived. Phebus kills his wife without stopping to ask questions and then bewails her death. His conclusion is a warning against acting in haste: 'Smite nat to soone, er that ye witen why' (*Tales*, IX: 285). He is of course wrong in asserting her innocence, but we are left with the possibility that in some cases deception is the happier resolution – as the Merchant's Tale suggests **[128]**.

The sixty-two lines of conclusion form a comic epilogue as the moral not to speak unnecessarily is parodied by the constant repetition of the point. Proverbial wisdom gets the bit between its teeth here, but it may also be setting such homespun lore against the more elevated learning gathered from ancient books – authorities. When it comes to it, the advice is much the same, regardless of its source. This theme of the way similar things are awarded different terms depending on their social status, not their intrinsic worth, is dealt with explicitly in lines 212–34 where the pairs 'wenche'/'lady', 'capitayn'/'outlawe' and 'triaunt'/'theef' are held up as examples. The theme recalls the chaotic awarding of renown or notoriety and the fusion of truth and lies in *House* **[71]**. This focus on language tends to be what attracts the most critical attention as it echoes the relation between tales, such as the Knight's and the Miller's **[113]** and also links with the Parson's rejection of frivolous speech in favour of 'vertuous sentence' (*Tales*, X: 63). There are other, more specific, echoes: the caged bird longing for freedom (*Tales*, IX: 172–4) recapitulates the falcon's lament in the Squire's Tale (*Tales*, V: 610–20). In each case the bird is not blamed for acting according to nature, but the desire for freedom is blameworthy because the cage represents fidelity. Reading this Tale at the end of the sequence thus allows resonances with previous Tales to be heard, but there is also a fine irony in a Tale which rejects the value of speech taking part in a story-telling competition.

Further Reading

Cooper considers the Tale in terms of its position in the sequence and its thematic relation to other tales (1985: 195–200). Howard's analysis is engaging and covers most of the ground (1976: 298–306), while Cooper's *Guide* clearly and usefully summarises the main areas of debate (1996: 383–94). Mann focuses on the reversal of the expected trope of female infidelity (1991: 18–22) and Birney considers the relation between the character of the Manciple suggested in the General Prologue and his Tale (1985: 125–33).

(xxv) The Parson's Tale

With the Parson's Tale the idea of a literal pilgrimage, which has held the *Tales* loosely together, is transmuted into a metaphor. Dusk is drawing in and the end of the trip is in sight, but there is no mention of Canterbury. Instead they enter the outskirts of a village (*Tales*, X: 12), at which point the Host declares that they have nearly completed the plan he suggested: there is only one more tale to hear. The atmosphere of conclusion and leave-taking is strong and the Parson effects the final shift into allegory as he explicitly makes their pilgrimage life's journey to the heavenly Jerusalem and 'this viage' becomes 'thilke parfit glorious pilgrymage' (*Tales*, X: 49–50).

Linked with this shift is a refusal to tell a fable, even a moral or religious one, and a rejection of poetry. The cut at '"rum, ram, ruf" by lettre' (*Tales*, X: 43) is a jibe at alliterative verse forms which survived in the north and midlands **[31]** and which, as a 'Southern man' the Parson seems to despise. He is similarly dismissive of rhyme (*Tales*, X: 44), which may refer to the heavily rhymed forms of popular ballad parodied in the Tale of Sir Thopas **[138]**. Both these prejudices reflect Chaucer's own literary preferences and add to an inclination to read the Parson's Tale as Chaucer's own views (an inclination increased by the Retraction which follows the Tale, see below) but, as ever, caution is wise here. It is possible that the treatise which makes up the Tale was written as a free-standing piece and then absorbed into the Tales, but, unlike the Knight's and Second Nun's Tales **[110, 142]**, there is no reference to its autonomous existence. What we have is a Tale told to 'knytte up al this feeste and make an ende' (*Tales*, X: 47) and arguably all the themes of the previous Tales are caught up one way or another in its discussion of penance and description of the seven deadly sins.

The Parson is careful to say that all that follows is 'under correccioun /Of clerkes' (*Tales*, X: 56–7), thus wisely avoiding any charge of heresy and pre-empting scholastic quibbling. However his treatise reveals the love of definition and division that riddled academic debate and gave rise to the huge encyclopedic volumes (*summae*) that were the mark of scholarly endeavour throughout the thirteenth and fourteenth centuries. The habit of breaking down concepts into parts and discussing each division is still a pattern for philosophical discourse; in the fourteenth century it was the common form of any kind of intellectual debate. A good comparison would be Julian of Norwich's *Revelations of Divine Love* **[38]**, which likewise uses this habit as a mark of the logic of her explanations. The Parson's treatise thus follows the expected pattern as it divides penitence into three parts: contrition, confession and satisfaction, and further subdivides those parts so that there are six points of contrition, and confession can be divided into venial and deadly sins. This last allows for the digression into a description of the Seven Deadly sins, each followed with a remedy, which takes up roughly a third of the piece before we are returned to the overall structure with an explanation of the importance of satisfaction, or making amends.

Rhetorically the piece is masterful. It dictates its own pace, but once caught by it, it is easy to be carried by its cadences and the exact logic of its tone makes it almost impossible to question what is being said. This is exactly what such works require, of course, so that even the similes and asides that vary the rhythm and atmosphere work to keep us within the mindset of the piece as a whole. Chaucer was clearly good at and interested in this kind of writing: he translated Boethius [83] and at least one work by Pope Innocent, now lost [25]. He also composed the Astrolabe [86], which uses similar literary effects. It is a mistake to think poetry demands more crafting than prose: the final paragraph of the Parson's Tale demonstrates one aspect of Chaucer's writing at its finest.

(xxvi) The Retraction

Printed at the end of *The Canterbury Tales*, this is the point where Chaucer's voice most clearly blends with that of one of his Pilgrims, the Parson. The opening reference to the 'litel tretys' and the tag '"Al that is writen is writen for oure doctrine"' easily apply to the Parson's Tale, and only possibly to the *Tales* as a whole. Once we get to the list of works, however, we are firmly in the area of Chaucer's own output. Whether the sentiments that follow reflect a deliberate winding-up of a poetical career or the adoption of a literary convention (which could nonetheless be genuinely felt) is a matter of personal conviction. Attempts to render it wholly ironic probably reflect twentieth-century unease with declared piety rather than any approach to truth, but that does not mean we must render it naive. Moreover, Chaucer may not have written it under some approaching apprehension of death, indeed it may not have been the last thing he wrote. The powerful tone of leave-taking, coupled with our habit of reading *The Canterbury Tales* as his last great unfinished work, inclines us to interpret this short piece as Chaucer's final word: we may be wrong on all fronts.

Further Reading

The case for the Parson's Tale as an autonomous composition, added to the *Tales* later is made by Minnis (1984: 207–9). Examples of *Summae* structure are reproduced, with introduction, in Bryan and Dempster (1941: 723–44). Aers focuses on the Parson's treatment of marriage (1986: 66–8). Koff's chapter on 'leave-taking' is an elegant example of the desire to read the Retraction and the Parson's Tale as Chaucer's final words (1988: 222–36). Howard (1976: 376–87) offers an elegiac reading of the Tale, also taking it as Chaucer's final words, a view tactfully countered by Pearsall (1992: 228 and 269–70). Cooper discusses the standing of the Retractions and its thematic links to the *Tales* as a whole (1996: 410–12).

PART III

CRITICISM

In some ways Chaucer started off the criticism of his own works, not least by ensuring we would know that he wrote them by including himself in his texts (e.g. as 'Geffrey' in *House* (729) or as one of the Canterbury Pilgrims (*Tales*, VII: 695) **[109, 138]**) and by listing his works (in the Prologue to *Legend* **[102]** and in the Retraction **[149]**). This self-identification asserts his place in the literary canon as described in The Man of Law's Prologue (*Tales*, II: 46–56) **[118]** and at the end of *Troilus* **[97]**. In this way Chaucer claims authority through a process by which the identity of the creator of a text (author as we think of it today, as distinct from scribe) and the standing awarded to it (authority) enhance each other and are themselves enhanced by the respect accorded to any quotations cited in the text (authorities, in medieval terms) **[72]**. Modern scholarship reflects the way Chaucer presents himself as both author and authority in two major ways. First, the appreciation of his works and the respect accorded to him in 'Lives' and critical biographies have created and maintained a reverence for him as a great literary figure. This reverence is articulated as early as 1412 by Thomas Hoccleve, who describes Chaucer as the 'first fyndere of oure faire langage' (Furnivall (ed.) 1897: 4978). Dryden echoes this praise in the Preface to his *Fables* of 1700 in which Chaucer is the 'Father of English poetry' (Kinsley (ed.) 1962: 528). Such descriptions indicate the importance of Chaucer to linguistic as well as to literary studies; an importance reflected in the sub-sections below. Second, critical analysis and scholarly endeavour have taken up Chaucer's own interest in the origin of stories (evident in *House* **[71]** and The Clerk's Tale **[126]**), the concepts of authority and authorship (reflected throughout *Troilus* **[89]** and in the vexed questions of transmission of manuscripts ('Adam Scriveyn' **[60]** reveals Chaucer's own anxieties on the topic of scribal error). Most recently, the debate surrounding editorial choices and the presentations of text has taken on new life, as electronic editions and hypertexts make their mark. The central question for any kind of edition is: what does one publish and with what effect? There is no such thing as a neutral text, even a hypertext has links created by someone. Thus text and interpretation are closely linked, and perhaps more closely in the case of the *Tales* than in many other texts, where the order in which the tales appear and the character to whom they are given are often germaine to individual readings **[106, 135]**.

Social trends also affect interpretation, not just in critical approaches, but in the popularity of topics or texts studied. For example, describing Chaucer as a master of satire and irony **[165–7]** has given way to emphasis on the ambiguity and uncertainty within his works **[167–9]**, while *Astrolabe*, so highly praised by Dryden, is little read now. As with all authors who have been significant figures in English Studies over a protracted period, fashions in literary criticism are reflected in the kinds of critical approach brought to bear on Chaucer and his works. Three main anthologies of Chaucer criticism through the ages allow readers to gain a general sense of the history of critical reactions to Chaucer: Spurgeon (1925) covers 1357 to 1900; Burrow (1969) provides extracts from 1380 to 1968; Brewer (1978) brings the over-view up to the 1970s. Schoek and Taylor (1960) is still a convenient place to discover critical essays from the first half of the twentieth century, while Ellis (ed. 1998) is one of the best collections for reflecting modern critical views of the *Tales* in general and can be supplemented by Bloom's volumes on individual Tales (ed. 1988a, b, c). For a sense of trends in criticism since 1900, but not extracts from it, Rooney (1989) is useful and concise. Readers seeking an accessible guide to the various forms of Post-Structuralist criticism in general will find it in Young's *Untying The Text* (1995). Regarding individual Chaucer works, The Oxford Guides are invaluable resources for literary study (Minnis 1995 for the shorter poems, Cooper 1996 for the *Tales*), although they do not offer as much social and historical detail as Brewer (1998). For that, Rigby (1996) is useful, if occasionally disappointing, but is a good counter-balance to the eminently readable Howard (1987). The best places to go for speedy updating are the quarterly journal *Chaucer Review* and the annual *Studies in the Age of Chaucer* (now also available on the Internet at http://ncs.rutgers.edu/sac.html). These publications offer not only articles which tend to reflect the current topics of debate, but also book reviews which themselves often provide good starting points for further study or reading of the texts themselves.

There are also many websites now devoted to Chaucer, of these the Chaucer Metapage (http://www.unc.edu/depts/chaucer/index.html) and the homepage of the New Chaucer Society (http://ncs.rutgers.edu) offer excellent places to begin researching both Chaucer and the wider realms of Medieval Studies in general. The CD-ROM *Chaucer: Life and Times* also offers an impressive range of information. Latterly, the history of Chaucer criticism is becoming a topic of critical debate in itself. A recent and important addition to this area is Dane's rather sceptical account of the fortunes of Chaucer criticism and scholarship (Dane 1998) which indicates that a more critical tone may finally begin to creep into our view of Chaucer, although in all likelihood he will retain his pre-eminent position in English Studies.

The sub-sections that follow reflect to some extent the various trends of Chaucer criticism, but such divisions threaten to obscure the interrelated nature of much critical and scholarly endeavour. In order to retain some sense of connection the order of the sub-sections broadly reflects the stages through which Chaucer criticism has gone as it became established as a major literary industry. Thus it begins with Biography, which both creates its subject and comments upon it, thus asserting its importance. That is followed by a discussion of texts and editions, because as nineteenth-century editors proclaimed the importance of Chaucer to English literary tradition, they also began to decide on a canon of Chaucer texts and sought to arrive at definitive and authoritative editions of those texts. The radically different ways of presenting texts offered by modern electronic means has given such debates a new lease of life.

The next section considers Chaucer's role in English language studies, because research into the particular spellings, terms or letterforms used by individual scribes, and investigations into when words or phrases used by Chaucer entered into general use in English, remain central to studies of the development of English language and language use. That in turn links to the next section on source study and literary background, which relates to Chaucer's own interest in language use and in expanding English literary vocabulary by incorporating in his own works words or genres from, for example, French and Italian traditions. From that it is a short step to looking at Chaucer's distinctive use of narrator figures and poetic personae, as it is often through such figures that he introduces comments on the power of literature, as in Cresseyde's complaint in *Troilus*, V: 1058–64, or his self-portrayal in the Prologue to *Legend* (F: 327–40; G: 253–316).

Readings of Chaucer which focus on his irony and cast him as a social satirist concentrate on his narrator figures, in particular on the Pilgrims of the *Tales*, and so discussion of them is to be found in sub-section e. Regarding Chaucer as a satirist inevitably involves placing him within a specific historical moment. This kind of historical approach has been recently revisited with the advent of New Historicism, discussed in sub-section f. This school of criticism owes a great deal to the foregrounding by Marxist and Feminist critics of the ideologies underlying social, scholarly and critical 'givens'. These significant views have made their mark on Chaucer studies and have opened the way to fresh readings, especially those focusing on the portrayal of women and more widely on gender, which are outlined in sub-sections g and h. Finally Chaucer's lasting influence on other authors (as opposed to critics) is considered, since imitation and adaptation are themselves, like biography, forms of critical response.

(a) BIOGRAPHY

Biography and criticism are always closely linked (indeed criticism is a form of autobiography as Jouve (1991) asserts). The earliest biographies of Chaucer are 'Lives' prefaced to editions of his work, a practice still followed, as for instance in the 'Life' which forms the introduction to *The Riverside Chaucer*. This indicates the strength of our inclination to read the works through the author, and vice-versa. Thus Caxton, in the preface to the second, 1484, printed edition of the *Tales*, refers to Chaucer as 'that nobel & grete philosopher' (Crotch 1928: 90). The nobility of work soon transfers onto the man, as Puttenham in 1589 'supposes' him to be a knight on no basis whatsoever beyond his admiration for Chaucer the writer. Speght confirms this habit of creating a socially privileged Chaucer on slender evidence in his 'Life' of 1598, the earliest biography as such **[5]**, and it flourished well into the twentieth century, gathering spurious details such as those quoted in Part I here, from the likes of Godwin (1804) **[5]** and Furnivall (1900) **[8]**.

Things change a little as the social climate changes and critics and biographers alike become more interested in Chaucer's merchant-class origins than his royal connections. Still largely benign (remarkably, Chaucer has attracted no real hostility from his biographers, all having found him to be 'a decent sort of fellow' (Pearsall 1992: 8)) works such as Howard's (1987) present an affable but shrewd person whose works likewise betray astute observation tempered with a generally indulgent view of humanity. It seems that we want Chaucer to be one of us, whoever 'we' may be at the time. Even Strohm's *Social Chaucer* (1987) creates a Chaucer who reaches out down the ages precisely because he was not fully of his own time – a fantasy self-presentation for the perceptive critic as much as the creative artist. Pearsall tackles this habit of drawing up a Chaucer to suit ourselves when he addresses the value of critical biography (Pearsall 1992: 1–8), during which he admits:

> It is not so much the 'real' Chaucer that one can go in search of, though that must be the desire that provides the motive for searching, as the manner in which he constructed his poetic self, or had it constructed for him.
>
> (Pearsall 1992: 5)

This is a particularly interesting reaction in the light of the reasonable amount of independent documentation we have pertaining to Chaucer, almost all of which refers to his jobs, his debts, his social duties and very little indeed to his literary life. Clearly the notion that these documents might represent the 'real' Chaucer does not appeal.

An excellent appraisal of Chaucer biography in these terms is given by Kennedy (Gould and Staley (eds) 1998: 54–67) whose appraisal, with its final plea for more overt acknowledgement of the transcendent Chaucer, may itself reflect the mood of the late 1990s. Nicole Ward Jouve's book considers the symbiotic relation between criticism and biography within a modern sphere of reference (Jouve 1991).

(b) TEXT, MANUSCRIPTS AND EDITING

While speculation about what exactly happened to the end of *The House of Fame* – was it written and then lost or never composed **[71]**? – has fuelled some critical reception of that poem, and although there has been some question over Chaucer's authorship of the fragments of *The Romaunt of the Rose* **[62]** and *The Equatorie of Planetis* **[88]**, the main focus of manuscript debate has been *The Canterbury Tales*. Ever since Caxton there has been dissatisfaction with the printed text of the *Tales*. Indeed, if we are to believe Caxton, the appearance of the second edition in 1484 was entirely due to complaints from 'one gentleman' who 'said that this book was not according in many places vnto the book that Geffrey chaucer had made' (Crotch 1928: 91). The debate has continued since then, moving through the first attempt at a Complete Works in Thynne's 1532 edition (for which Thynne, at Henry VIII's behest, searched libraries and monasteries for Chaucer manuscripts), to Urry in 1721, (who, in common with others before him, included many works not by Chaucer) to Tyrwhitt's *Tales* of 1775 (the first to exclude works and to attempt to recreate an original text through the comparison of manuscripts; Thynne is credited with being Chaucer's first 'modern' editor) to Skeat's Oxford Chaucer of 1894, which still stands as a monument to editorial and textual scholarship. Lately the argument has given rise to *The Variorum Chaucer*. Rather than seeking a single definitive edition which purports to be what Chaucer wrote, based on principles of 'best' text and scholarly reconstruction and correction of sections which are either illegible or incomprehensible, a variorum edition reproduces all the variants and allows readers to draw their own conclusions. The difficulty with the single edited 'ideal' text is that it presents a text which quite probably never existed before. The difficulty with a Variorum, apart from its sheer unwieldiness, is that it is easy to select readings of individual lines which suit one's own inclination, but together result in something that has not existed before:

the integrity of the manuscripts is thus destroyed. Moreover, even a Variorum must decide which text to take as the base, around which the variants cluster, and this in itself gives a particular manuscript or version more canonical standing than the others.

Opinion matters not simply because there are some variant readings, but because overall critical appraisal of the *Tales* assumes a given text, with a given number of Tales and a fairly firm idea of the order of those Tales. The most generally used base text is the Ellesmere Manuscript **[106]**, whose pre-eminent position has most recently been asserted by Frese (1991), who quite remarkably states:

> Chaucer, I claim, devised a final plan for the order and number of the *Canterbury Tales* and inscribed this plan into the poem itself. I am arguing that Chaucer's final authorial intentions can be retrieved, reconstructed, and internally verified by readers whose acquaintance with the work-as-a-whole is long-standing and intertextually informed enough to penetrate the author's ingenious textual systematics.
>
> [...]
>
> Furthermore, and most importantly, I suggest that these instructions to the reader are retrievable only through the hermeneutics of the Ellesmere text.
>
> (Frese 1991: 2)

This assertion, with its premiss that it is not only possible but desirable to retrieve authorial intent, illustrates why questions of textual tradition, transmission and editing can be classified as critical as well as scholarly endeavour. The force of Frese's assertion is due in part to the decision of the *Variorum Chaucer* editors to reproduce the Hengwrt version of the *Tales* as the base text, adding material from Ellesmere as variants.

Hengwrt **[106]** is the earliest manuscript, and as such has the claim of priority, which Blake builds upon both in *The Textual Tradition of the Canterbury Tales* (1985) and for his edition of the Tales (Blake 1980). Taking the fragmentary nature of the poem as a given, Blake dismisses the validity of piecing together an order based on internal references to time or cross-references between Tales. For him 'the question of order is less important than many scholars think' (Blake 1980: 3). Nevertheless, most critics have to come to some kind of conclusion about where they stand regarding this issue.

The fullest treatment of the topic is given by Owen (1991) who discusses the manuscripts in detail. He also takes into account the fact that several of the Tales have autonomous lives, as it were; that is, they were copied and circulated either in smaller groups or independently from the whole Tales series. His work builds on Manly and Rickert (1940) who described all known manuscrips and variants. This area is one that can fascinate, appealing to the detective side of readers who get caught up in the detail of dating, transmission and the truly remarkable ability of some scholars to identify individual scribes from their handwriting and place them in particular regions of the country due to the dialect and spelling conventions they use. Most recently, the topic has been taken up by Dane (1998) who seeks to overthrow the regard in which Tyrwhitt is held, preferring Urry's more inclusive method. Dane needs to be read with caution here, but deserves consideration.

The aim of all this is to produce a reliable text, one whose history is understood and which scholars are happy to call 'Chaucer'. We take for granted the idea that the text we read will be what the writer wrote, but that was a relatively new idea in the fourteenth century, as Chaucer's lyric to Adam **[60]** and his farewell to his text at the end of *Troilus* shows. The plea that 'none myswrite the' (*Troilus* V.1795) indicates the very real possibility that the poem would be changed, cut and circulated in ways totally beyond the author's control. The need for a reliable text was again felt strongly in the late nineteenth century and provided Furnivall with the impetus for not only publishing texts of six manuscripts of *The Tales*, but also founding a Chaucer Society to look after the poet's interest. Particularly interesting here is what Furnivall's *Temporary Preface* reveals about the way Chaucer comes to stand for an ideal of Englishness. Professor Child of Harvard University has been requesting a new edition of Chaucer; Furnivall's response is as follows:

> I am bound to confess that my love for Chaucer – and he comes closer to me than any other poet, except Tennyson – would not by itself have made me give up the time and trouble I can so ill afford to bestow on this task; but when an American, who had done the best bit of his work on Chaucer's works, asked, and kept on asking, for texts of our great English poet, could an Englishman keep on refusing to produce them?
>
> (Furnivall 1868: 3)

The impetus is more than just literary, however, as Child has been active in the cause of the abolition of slavery. Furnivall's Chaucer is to be an act of recognition for this:

... could one who honoured him for it [his anti-slavery stance] ...
fail to desire to sacrifice something that he might help to weave
again one bond between (at least) the Chaucer-lovers of the Old
Country and the New? No.

(Furnivall 1868: 3)

As the current interest in the history of editing expands, and the
debates on the creation of national identity continue, passages such as
this will come under increasing scrutiny.

The influence of editions is not to be underestimated: we tend to
assume that whichever modern text we are using, we are reading
'Chaucer', whereas in fact we are reading a carefully and skillfully recon-
structed Chaucer, in which abbreviated word-forms have been
expanded to make them comprehensible to us and modern punctuation
has been brought in. It is not just modern editors who have thus inter-
vened in the text, of course; the scribes also adjusted spelling and
sometimes metre and words to render them 'right' according to their
own understanding. As Blake points out a 'modern text represents a
version that no medieval reader ever read, for all manuscripts contain
at least a few corruptions. A modern edition is a medieval text seen
through modern eyes' (Blake 1977: 55). Blake here links the areas of
textual and linguistic study in a highly readable consideration of the
interaction between language and literature.

It is clearly a knotty issue, but it is possible to over-emphasise the
pitfalls of correction: copyists made mistakes and sometimes it is very
clear what the word or phrase ought to have been, or that they have
simply missed out a couple of lines through looking between exemplar
(the text being copied) and the page on which they write. The prefaces
to each volume of *The Variorum Chaucer* which discuss this topic and
the questions that affect that volume in particular, make interesting,
if detailed reading.

All these considerations come to bear on the issue of electronic editions and particularly on hyper-text. There the impression is often that
we are somehow more directly connected to the original document,
complete with the opportunity to compare variants for ourselves or
click on aspects we wish to explore further. However, impressive as
these editions are, they are still editions, brought about by a team of
scholars who have made editorial decisions about what appears on
which screen and where links are to be placed.

(c) CHAUCER'S LANGUAGE

When Hoccleve and Dryden eulogised Chaucer [153] they each did so with reference to his influence on the English language. Caxton, too, contributed powerfully to our view of Chaucer as a significant force in the development of English, praising him in particular for having 'enbelyssheyd, ornated and made faire our englisshe' which, according to him, was previously 'rude' as in unpolished, unsophisticated (Crotch 1928: 90). Chaucer is thus regarded as not merely reflecting English in a time of considerable linguistic change, but as directly instrumental in those changes. His visibility, the fact that a corpus of work can be attributed to him with confidence, and his decision to write primarily in English, make him a pre-eminent source of examples of language use and expansion in the fourteenth century: pick up almost any study of the English language and Chaucer features in it.

One recent study serves to illustrate the point. Blake's *A History of the English Language* (1996) deliberately rejects a strict chronological study of the language, which divides it into periods (Old, Middle, Early Modern and Modern) but nonetheless awards Chaucer extended consideration. Here Chaucer is taken to illustrate not only the emerging Standard English, which drew on French and to a lesser degree Latin, but also to show the acute awareness of the range of dialects in fourteenth-century England and the beginnings of social snobbery connected to how people speak. Blake's analysis of the opening of The General Prologue is an excellent example of the first kind of study (Blake 1996: 161–8). The clerks' speech of The Reeve's Tale, perhaps the earliest example of dialect being used for comic effect, is also discussed by Blake (142–4), while the Parson is careful to distinguish himself, a southern man, from the rough northern alliterative poetry of 'rum, ram ruf' (*Tales*, X: 42–3) [39, 148].

An effect of such studies is that Chaucer can come across as creating the language, or at least of suddenly giving it capablities it did not have before. This view is largely upheld by Robinson in his two studies of 1971 and 1972. Robinson deserves consideration, particularly his 1971 study of Chaucer's verse form (prosody) which tackles the problem that if we follow to the letter the instructions of how to pronounce Chaucer, as given in most editions, the result is dry and frequently cumbersome. Chaucer is here discussed in the context of poetry and metre in general, with some space given to his immediate inheritors and imitators, Hoccleve and Lydgate. For Robinson, Chaucer's verse at its best is 'the simulation of speech by a heightening of speech which can yet seem fresh and natural.' Crucially however, verse is not simply imitating speech:

> The metre justifies itself by a concentration of expressiveness, a significance not found so consistently in real conversation. The life of Chaucer's verse is that of the spoken language, but it is a life quite unlike chunks of liveliness.
>
> (Robinson 1971: 172)

This view of Chaucer's language as exceptional or 'new' is counterbalanced by Cannon's recent study which instead asserts its 'traditional' qualities (Cannon 1998: 4–5). Cannon builds on the kind of lexical study offered by Mersand (1937), who focused on Chaucer's use of words from mainly French sources, and seeks to place Chaucer in a precise historical moment of the language, rather than describe all that his language does. Cannon's first chapter, 'The Making of English and the English of Chaucer' (1998: 9–47) is particularly useful to those interested in learning about the ways Chaucer has been regarded over the years or about the various components that make up 'Chaucerian' English. His focus on individual words (lexis), the influence they have and the contexts in which they occur is all the more apposite when we recall Chaucer giving the Manciple some space to muse on exactly this kind of thing in his Tale:

> Ther nys no difference, trewely,
> Bitwixe a wyf that is of heigh degre,
> If of hir body dishonest she bee,
> And a povre wenche, oother than this –
> If it so be they werke bothe amys –
> But that the gentile, in estaat above,
> She shal be cleped his lady, as in love;
> And for that oother is a povre womman,
> She shal be cleped his wenche or his lemman.
> (*Tales*, IX: 212–20)

(d) SOURCES, LITERARY BACKGROUND, RHETORIC AND POETICS

Study of verse form naturally links with the study of Chaucer's ideas about what literary writing should be (poetics) and the kinds of language use appropriate for particular themes, ideas or genre (rhetoric), as well as with questions of which previous writers he was imitating or drawing upon. The work of Bryan and Dempster (1941), Benson and Andersson (1971), Miller (1977), Havely (1980) and Windeatt (1982 and 1984) are fundamental here as they provide extracts or whole texts which are either Chaucer's actual sources or analogues to his works. This allows for a literary contextualising of Chaucer's writing, revealing what he added and altered not just to the stories, but in the genres he drew upon. It is from this basis that works such as the still influential Muscatine (1957) can spring. Muscatine reveals Chaucer's debt to the French forms of debate, dream poetry and fabliau as inspirations for his literary world, not just his language. This emphasises Chaucer's literariness and creates the idea of Chaucer as the writer of allusion and reference that we acknowledge him to be today. Without such work assertions such as Frese's that Chaucer is a fundamentally intertextual writer (Frese 1991: 2 and chapter 2) would not be possible.

The sphere of reference has expanded since Muscatine, with work not just on Italian literature (e.g. Boitani 1977, Havely 1980, Windeatt 1982 and 1984) but also on the Classical inheritance (Minnis 1982) and on scientific texts (Wood 1970 and North 1988). The relations between literature and science and the literature of science is fast becoming an area of critical growth, so one might expect this aspect of Chaucer Studies to expand in the near future. Not all source-based study is quite so specific, however; some of it looks to genres and ideas on how one should write (poetics) rather than at particular authors or texts. One such area is that of rhetoric as it was taught in medieval universities.

The suggestion that Chaucer made use of such forms of writing was first put forward in 1926 by J.M. Manly in an essay now most readily available in Schoeck and Taylor (1960: 268–90). Here Manly points out that many of the features of Chaucer's style are examples of the rhetorical devices favoured in the thirteenth and fourteenth centuries. Thus the use of a proverb or generalisation is an example of *sententia* – Manly takes the opening of *Parliament* as a case in point: 'The lyf so short, the craft so long to lerne'. The love of amplification can be seen in such things as the description of the temples in The Knight's Tale (*Tales*, I: 1881–2094) or in the detailing of the kings who come to fight on Arcite's or Palamoun's behalf (*Tales*, I: 2095–189). These passages between them make up half of part three of the Tale and end with an example of *occupatio* (by which things are described while the narrator protests he will not mention them):

The mynstraclye, the sevice at the feeste,
The grete yiftes to the meeste and leeste,
The riche array of Theseus paleys,
Ne who sat first ne last upon the deys,
What ladyes fairest been or best daunsynge,
Or which of hem kan dauncen best and synge,
Ne who moost felyngly speketh of love;
What haukes sitten on the perche above,
What houndes liggen on the floor adoun –
Of al this make I now no mencioun,
But al th'effect; that thynketh me the beste.

(Tales I: 2196–207)

Manly goes on to argue that Chaucer tired of such rhetorical devices and held them up for ridicule in The Nun's Priest's Tale. Since Manly, much work has been done in this area, not all of it agreeing with his conclusions. Most influential and still enlightening is Payne (1963), who finds Chaucer altogether more creative in his use of rhetorical arts and devices.

Chaucer's use of the recommendations of the rhetoricians was not restricted to linguistic devices alone; he also expanded the practice, citing authorities. References to an actual author or saying were intended to affirm the standing of a work, both in terms of its style and its content. Thus an epic would refer back to the Classical writers, Homer and Virgil, while texts dealing with moral topics would cite the Bible or famous commentators such as St. Jerome. This practice is closely linked with the use of *sententia* (see above), as the words of an authority or author could be deployed to add weight to an argument or a text.

Once deployed, the question is raised of how we are expected to read such references. One way is simply to allow the effect of sententiousness to register, but D.W. Robertson (1962) puts forward the claim that Chaucer and his contemporaries (by which he meant his learned contemporaries) would have automatically read these texts in essentially allegorical terms, translating the symbols and events to give a religious moral to every text. Such reading is called 'exegesis' – which strictly refers to the critical interpretation of any text, but tends to be associated with religious texts. Certainly exegesis flourished, in part reflecting the fact that all philosophical enquiry took place under the heading of theology, in part reflecting a love of categorising and decoding and a habit of intricate and learned discussion. Chaucer clearly parodies this kind of interpretation in the way the Wife of Bath and the Pardoner deal with their texts, and arguably uses it more seriously in the Tales of Melibee and the Parson **[139, 1487]**. Roberston asserts that is the primary tool for understanding all of Chaucer, a view which has faded from popularity, but had important effects at the time. Exegetical readings cannot be dismissed entirely.

However, further research into exactly what Chaucer was doing with his sources has revealed a more creative use of this habit of referring to authorities. Minnis (1988) shows that Chaucer was making use of the role of the compiler (who brought together selections of classical and other influential texts in an anthology) as much as an author, and it is the role, as much as the material, that is of interest:

> ... Chaucer was indebted to the compilers not only for source-material and technical information but also for a literary role and a literary form. Chaucer seems to have exploited the compilers' typical justification of their characteristic role as writers, and to have shared, to some extent, the compilers' sense of *ordinatio partium* [ordering into sections].
>
> (Minnis 1988: 191)

The 'typical justification' Minnis refers to here is the use of phrases such as 'For as myn auctour seyde, so sey I' (*Troilus* II: 18) that Chaucer often uses, in particular throughout *Troilus*, as if to abdicate responsibility for what he is about to say. This is a significant development and affects how we read Chaucer's use of narrators as much as his use of handbooks on poetic style.

(e) NARRATORS, IRONY AND SATIRE

Chaucer's favourite device of imposing between himself and his texts some kind of narrator figure, however shadowy, has naturally attracted a lot of critical attention. Following Minnis, it is possible to regard this as simply a rhetorical device which later centuries have imbued with a presence that would not have occurred to a fourteenth-century audience. That is not to say, however, that Chaucer's contemporaries would have assumed that the narrator was a straightforward representation of Chaucer himself. Then as now, literary artifice makes it naive to believe that the Dream Poems are faithful records of any dream actually dreamt. The standing of Chaucer's narrators has nonetheless created debate. E.T. Donaldson treads a fine line between treating Chaucer's self-presentations as reflections of the real Chaucer and as fictional creations. This treatment extends to the Canterbury Pilgrims, likewise, to the extent that the divide between actual and fictional worlds is often blurred, as here when speaking of the description of the Prioress:

> Undoubtedly Chaucer the man would, like his fictional represen-
> tative, have found her charming and looked on her with affection.
> ... But the third entity, Chaucer the poet, operates in a realm which
> is above and subsumes those in which Chaucer the man and
> Chaucer the pilgrim have their being ... In his poem the poet
> arranges for the moralist to define austerely what ought to be and
> for his fictional representative – who, as the representative of all
> mankind, is not mere fiction, – to go on affirming affectionately
> what is. The two points of view, in strict moral logic diametrically
> opposed, are somehow made harmonious in Chaucer's wonderfully
> comic attitude, that double vision that is his ironical essence.
>
> (Donaldson 1970: 11)

The case here is put in terms of the *Tales*, but it applies also to *Troilus* and attracts degrees of dissent and agreement in either case, as, for instance, from Leicester, who usefully re-evaluates Donaldson, also using this passage (1990: 384–90). Irony in particular is associated with Chaucer, although thankfully no longer quite as synonymously as it once was; the concept can too easily result in reductive readings in which things are labelled as 'ironic' and left at that. Moreover, a tendency to cite Chaucer's personal experiences and position in life as the root cause of his irony leads to such phrases as 'according to his nature, his irony is light rather than dark' (Rowland in Birney 1985: xxvii) which are better avoided. Nonetheless, irony is a useful concept for readers of Chaucer, and Birney's essays are lucid in discussing it.

More nuanced treatment of Chaucer's deployment of poetic personae is to be found in Mehl (1986) and Lawton (1985). Both treat the texts in detail, tracing Chaucer's development of particular aspects of the narrator, according to the material in hand. Lawton argues that not all narrators are fully-fledged personae, and that where there are several such voices, as in the *Tales*, 'the fictional nature of the perfor-mance is ever more forcefully stressed, but the narratorial voice remains fairly constant, subject to rhetorical, not dramatic or psychological [sic for 'psychological'], decisions' (Lawton 1985:13). He goes on to develop this idea of 'performative' texts in which the drama is enacted between audience and text as well as between voices within the text. Mehl also points out the multiple nature of Chaucer's writing, in particular in his chapter on the relation between the story-teller and his material in *Troilus* (Mehl 1986: 65–97). Mehl characterises the third book thus:

> The whole course of the third book, with its continual variation of stylized rhetoric, lyrical interludes and dramatic comedy, suggests that Chaucer is very anxious not to give undue prominence to any one of these divergent elements. However vividly the manipulations of Pandarus are described, his disinterested motives are given equal emphasis.
>
> (Mehl 1986: 83)

When it comes to considering the *Tales*, Mehl makes an important distinction between the thumb-nail sketches of the Pilgrims in the General Prologue, which he terms 'rhetorical portraits' and the impression of character given by the narrative voice of the tales they tell (1986: 145). This is an added level of subtlety, and significantly the only exceptions he makes to this general principle are the Wife of Bath **[120]** and the Pardoner **[133]**, both of whose Prologues are in effect self-portraits. The difficulty for Mehl arises when accounting for their Tales. Here the Wife of Bath's Tale proves intractable and Mehl side-steps the issue.

Satire would seem to offer a resolution to the difficulty in which Mehl finds himself. Certainly this is a point where the adaptation of form noticed by Minnis meets the use of narrative persona advocated by Donaldson. The best exponent of satire as a trope in Chaucer remains Mann. Her book *Chaucer and Medieval Estates Satire* (1973) is a landmark. In it she demonstrates that Chaucer not only imitates, but also revises, the established genre of social satire that depended on dividing society in separate sections (estates) and depicting the particular abuses each typified. The book concentrates on The General Prologue and remains one of the best treatments of it. The main conclusion is that whereas traditional satire leaves the audience in no doubt about where both they and the text stand regarding the object satirised, Chaucer is not so straightforward. We are clear about what Friars, for example, are accused of, but less sure how far the one in front of us as an individual fulfils the stereotype. What are we to make of his twinkling eyes (*Tales*, I: 267–8)? Do they indicate lechery, or humour? Do they predispose us towards this particular friar in spite of the vices he represents?

There is clearly some common ground between Mann and Donaldson here, although Mann's arguments are also a case where an awareness of the connotations of individual words in particular collocations comes into play. Thus 'worthy' comes under scrutiny as applied to several of the Pilgrims:

> The adjective 'worthy' is used as the keyword of the Knight's portrait, where it has a profound and serious significance, indicating not only the Knight's social status, but also the ethical qualities appropriate to it. In the Friar's portrait, the word is ironically used to indicate the Friar's lack of these ethical qualities – but it can also be read non-ironically as a reference to social status ... By the time we reach the Franklin's portrait, the word is used with a vague heartinesss which seems to indicate little beside the narrator's approval.
>
> (Mann 1973: 195–6)

The argument goes beyond discussion of what a putative narrator might think and touches on the way the structure of the General Prologue make us more aware of the tension surrounding the word 'worthy'. Mann regards the sequence in which we encounter the word as crucial to our developing understanding of it in Chaucer's lexis – a view which could be taken to undercut Jones's distinctive reading of the Knight (Jones 1980) **[113]**. However, Mann's reading itself comes under criticism.

The relation of teller to self-portrait is most fully expanded in Leicester's post-structuralist treatment of the Knight, Wife of Bath and Pardoner. *The Disenchanted Self* (Leicester 1990) is a rigorous reading of these three figures from the *Tales*, and a good introduction to post-structural criticism in action (here particularly informed by decon-struction). Leicester highlights the way the portraits of these pilgrims rely on the audience being aware of (or being reminded of) the textual nature of the descriptions and thus open to references not only back and forth within the *Tales*, but also between the *Tales* and other texts. This clearly relates to the intertexuality noted by Frese **[158]**, but Leicester also draws on psychoanalytic readings and on the notion that ideas of the Self are social constructs. In general it is far easier to see this kind of criticism performed than to describe it, but Leicester's own description of the Wife's Prologue may be useful here. He points out that the Wife only really gets going after being interrupted by the Pardoner:

> This shift in tone in reaction to an external stimulus allows us to see the possibility of speaking about the *Wife of Bath's Prologue* less as a preplanned theoretical argument that has to move through a

CRITICISM

certain number of points to a conclusion and more as something practical that happens and alters as it goes along in response to a set of more immediate and unstructured contingencies. ... the most important practical determinant of the poem's unfolding is the vagaries of memory as it doubles and redoubles on itself. We, like the Wife, must concern ourselves less with the plot she remembers than with *the plot of her remembering* in the now of narration.

(Leicester 1990: 83)

The emphasis is on giving the fabric of the text as much attention as the psychology of the invented character.

Just as Leicester re-evaluates Donaldson so he gives some consideration to Mann. The fact that he devotes time to these two critics attests their importance, but his qualifications are also worth considering. His criticism of Donaldson has been mentioned above **[166]**; that of Mann rests on 'her generally distant and unfocused treatment of the speaker: her inattention to sequence is an effect of her relative disinterest (sic) in the poem as performance' (Leicester 1990: 393). According to Leicester, Mann sees the strength of use of an established form but overlooks the power of representation figured by Donaldson. For Leicester, Chaucer not only adapts an authoritative genre, but reveals the act of classification in the person of its narrator.

Of course this last stance assumes a degree of self-awareness with which some may take issue. The next step in this line of criticism comes from those who treat the text as an almost autonomous force which is the product of its time as much as of its writer. The various voices detectable within it thus may not be the conscious creation of the author but an inevitable effect of its historicial moment.

(f) HISTORICISM, OLD AND NEW

The way in which a text can speak simultaneously with several viewpoints has latterly been taken up by critics following the narrative theories of Bakhtin, and those interested in pursuing this particular connection further will find a good starting-point in Rigby, who devotes a sizeable chapter to a discussion of Chaucer in Bakhtinian terms (Rigby 1996: 18–77). A useful introduction to Bakhtin's theories and writings can be found in Dentith (1995), but, put briefly, Bakhtin notes that some institutions, such as the Church, speak with a firm view which they expect their hearers to espouse. Texts which embody such voices are described as monologic: one outlook prevails. Dialogic texts are those which support a dialogue between various viewpoints, without feeling the need to resolve the dialogue into consensus. Crucially, voices which at first seem rebellious are shown to be in fact re-affirming the status of the dominant discourse – if it is rebelled against it must be important – and thus integral to it. Dissent is permitted as a form of safety-valve for discontent: 'carnival' is the term Bakhtin uses here, and the idea of the *Tales* in particular as carnivalesque has proved appealing. The reason is evident if one reflects on the number of discourses potentially vying for dominance within them.

However, such an approach owes a certain amount to simple historical criticism, which puts a great deal of effort into identifying those various voices, noting which terms came from a background of exegesis, social satire, historical fact, legal terminology and so forth. What has been fully supplanted is a simple realist reading of Chaucer, which allowed us to take Caxton's description of the *Tales* at face value as: 'a nobel hystorye of every astate and degre, fyrst rehercyng the condicions and th'arraye of eche of them as properly as possyble is to be sayde, and after theyr tales' (Crotch 1928: 90). It is likely that we ought to revisit that term 'as properly as possyble', but meanwhile reading Chaucer as a realist writer and social satirist who used irony as his central tool has been fully overhauled as New Historicism has come into view.

A primary exponent of New Historicism is Lee Patterson, whose book *Negotiating The Past* (1987) advances its claims, while also pointing out that the term 'designates neither a single methodolgy nor a monolithic critical group' (57). Subtitled 'The Historical Understanding of Medieval Literature', it makes the case for reading Chaucer as a product of his time, but seeing the reception of his texts in the light of fourteenth-century concerns and those of subsequent ages. Critics of this view regard it as ignoring the power of the individual to critique their own times, and certainly it questions the basis upon which certain authors, like Chaucer, are regarded as pre-eminent. Paradoxically, by focusing upon such questions the status of such 'greats' remains largely untouched, even if the basis for their greatness is reassessed.

Patterson devotes a chapter to an overview of the history Chaucer Studies, which is well worth reading (1987: 3–40), before going on to discuss the critical reception of particular texts in detail, amongst them *Troilus* (115–56) which is discussed in terms of recreating how the poem might have been read by a fifteenth-century audience. The central tenet of this view is that 'literary meaning is not an atemporal constant but a historical variable' (Patterson 1987: 115). In this approach the exegetical tools advocated by Robertson are dusted off and reclaimed:

'Exegetics seeks to recuperate less the meaning of the poem per se than the medieval understanding of that meaning' (115). What has gone is the idea that a text has a fixed meaning 'per se' which it is the critic's job to discover. Instead we reconstruct the likely meanings available to a particular audience and realise how much the reaction a poem generates depends upon the concerns of its readership.

This clearly links to questions of audience and theories about what produces a text, concerns which particularly suit medieval texts, with their overt address to audience and faceted notion of author – that is made up of writer, scribe, authorities and other texts. Paul Strohm addresses the concept of audience in Chaucer, moving on from the observation that references to a solely listening audience in the early poems give way to phrases to do with reading (e.g. 'Turne over the leef' (*Tales*, I: 3177) in the Prologue to the Miller's Tale) to discuss the changing circle of Chaucer's actual audience and the ideal audience created by the texts (Strohm 1989: 47–83). Strohm posits a core audience, made up of people who, like Chaucer, were closely involved with the movers and shakers of fourteenth-century England, but were not aristocrats or even large landowners. This educated, 'gentil' group had a literal existence but a shifting membership as friendships grew or lessened and events made direct contact with friends difficult or easy. Although Strohm describes and traces the change in the likely member-ship of this audience, pointing out links with the kinds of readership the texts seem to address, the more important point as far as he is concerned, is the notion of this circle of readers which 'did not cease to exist for him as an inspiration and an animating ideal' (Strohm 1989: 83).

The attitude towards history evinced by New Historicist thus differs from traditional Historicism not only in what is included under the term 'history', but also in the way events, and in particular documents describing events, are regarded. Strohm declares his hand in his Preface:

> I will approach the complex and shifting structure of social relations in Chaucer's lifetime through a variety of contemporary texts, including statutes, poll taxes, and political treatises as well as fictional narratives. Some of these texts look so much like raw data that they have been treated as if they were repositories of unmediated fact. I will, however, treat all these texts as attempts at self-understanding, as imaginary constructions of social reality in their own right. Rather than viewing Chaucer's poetry in relation to a separate body of information, I will place his imaginary depictions of social relations in a larger field of such depictions.
>
> (Strohm 1989: ix)

This is a complete inversion of the view of Chaucer as a realist writer who faithfully presented us with a picture of fourteenth-century life, which could be read almost as a historical document. Where that habit of interpretation (long since refined) placed Chaucer's creative texts on a par with factual documentation, this later one regards historical documents as being as much creative works as poetical fiction. The concept of 'fact' has been unpicked to raise questions of why certain events are recorded in particular ways and regarded as worthy of mention where others are not.

This school of criticism (Strohm is by no means the only critic to advance these views) is clearly indebted to deconstruction, psycho-analytic and perhaps above all to Marxist and feminist criticism as well as to historical study.

(g) POLITICS AND IDEOLOGY

Arguably part of the loose New Historicist collective, and certainly drawn upon by the New Historicists, are the more overtly politically engaged approaches such as Marxism and, to both a lesser and wider degree, feminism. Readings of Chaucer have been reinvigorated by pointing out the dominant ideologies within his work and the places where such dominance is questioned by the text, if not by Chaucer. Areas of tension, unease, lack of resolution and omission are central for this kind of interpretation.

One critic whose reading is informed by Marxism is Aers, whose book *Chaucer* is an accessible and excellent starting point for any critical study of Chaucer. This is not to say that his conclusions must be accepted without question, rather that they must be taken account of in any conclusion one wishes to draw, and may themselves both pose questions and be open to question. Thus his appraisal of The Clerk's Tale explores the creation of power and acquiesence in it exemplified by Walter's despotism and Griselde's passivity: 'the poem is thus a powerful dramatisation of the effects of absolutism on both the ruled and the ruler' (Aers 1986: 34). Aers links this directly with the political position in England in the late 1390s with its growing concern about despotism. For him, although Griselde's ability to rule well offers a radical alternative to monarchical rule, Chaucer does not endorse it:

> here we meet one of the horizons of Chaucer's social imagination, for ... it tends to abandon all ideas of fraternity, social justice and the social embodiment of charity, foreshadowing an ideological

position that would become commonplace with the triumph of bourgois individualism in the later seventeenth and eighteenth centuries.

(Aers 1986: 35–6)

This assertion is endorsed by Tuttle Hansen's persuasive essay 'The Powers of Silence: The Case of the Clerk's Griselda' (reprinted in Hansen 1992: 188–207) which explores the Tale in feminist terms.

Hansen summarizes the Tale thus:

The Tale suggests on one hand that Griselda is not really empowered by her acceptable behavior, because the feminine virtue she embodies in welcoming her subordination is by definition both punitive and self-destructive. On the other hand, the Tale reveals that the perfectly good woman *is* powerful, or at least potentially so, insofar as her suffering and submission are fundamentally insubordinate and deeply threatening to men and to the concepts of power and gender identity upon which patriarchal culture is premised.

(Hansen 1992: 190)

The meeting ground of feminism and Marxism is most clearly seen when Hansen describes the crux of the problem: 'If a peasant woman can so easily rule as well as a noble man – or even better – then Walter's birthright and the whole feudal system on which it depends are seriously threatened' (Hansen 1992: 191). For both Aers and Hansen, the Tale dramatises the dangers of the political system: in order to maintain his own identity Walter must have an Other against which to define himself. Griselde, initially apparently the embodiment of social and gender Otherness, eludes definition through constantly proving her ability to be whatever is required of her. The urge to dominate is thus thwarted even as it is apparently fulfilled. For Griselde, on the other hand, the paradox is that her power resides in the suffering that proves her exceptional quality: when the trials stop she is silenced and her virtue ends. For Hansen, Griselde at the end of the Tale is not returned to a position of power and prestige, but finally forced 'to awaken into the reality of her material, gendered powerlessness' (Hansen 1992: 194).

Delany also shakes her readers out of too complacent a reading of Chaucer. She gives extended consideration to *Legend* in her book *The Naked Text* (Delany 1994), but a more widespread application of her view of medieval literature (which is informed by both Marxisim and feminism) is to be found in *Medieval Literary Politics: Shapes of Ideology* (1990). Over half this book is given over to Chaucer, while the rest usefully provides a way into his literary context. As the title suggests, Delany looks at not only the systems of rules, laws and expectations which create a society (ie. the politics) but also the belief systems and concepts of what it means to be, for example, a woman, or a king, what the moral basis is and how it is created and sustained (ideology). She also pays great attention to individual words and the language of texts in general, relating texts to other texts of a similar kind, highlighting differences in expression, additions or omissions and interpreting their cause. Her discussion of The Physician's Tale **[132]** is a case in point (Delany 1990: 130–40). By comparing the story of Virginia as it is found in Livy (its ultimate Roman source) and in Chaucer's contemporaries, Delany illustrates Chaucer's silent reworking which markedly alters the significance of the story. By making Virginius a knight, not the common soldier of the original, and by removing much of the action from public to private settings, the revolutionary possibilities of the Tale are markedly reduced. The theme becomes one of personal response, not public reaction. Delany's confident explanation for such alteration is that the glorification of popular rebellion, which the original version of the story espouses, 'is utterly alien to Chaucer's world-view: our poet is a prosperous, socially conservative, prudent courtier and civil servant, directly dependent for his living upon the good will of kings and dukes' (Delany 1990: 137). While her confidence and her readings are in many ways persuasive they are also, as the above quotation shows, based on very strong opinions about Chaucer himself. These extend to provocative speculations on artistic development: 'if the project [telling Virginia's story] taught him something as an artist, it was the importance of choosing material more suitable to his own temper. For us it suggests that poetic failure may be as instructive as poetic success, as productive a field for criticism' (140). Delany's comments here illustrate the interaction between biography and criticism.

(h) FEMINISM AND GENDER

As with feminist criticism in general, the earlier feminist readings of Chaucer tend to concentrate on the representation of women in the texts. Thus the Wife of Bath, Alison in The Miller's Tale and Griselde all receive due attention, as does White in *The Book of the Duchess*. The value of such study should not be underestimated, books such as

Power's *Medieval Women* (1975) remain useful and their groundwork is still being built upon, as for instance by Martin's *Chaucer's Women: Nuns, Wives and Amazons* (1990). Also central to any study of Chaucer's women is Blamires' collection of source texts dealing with concepts of and attitudes towards women throughout the Middle Ages (Blamires 1992). Anyone interested in discovering the kinds of literature written for, by and about women will find Barratt's collection *Women's Writing in Middle English* (1992) useful, especially in conjunction with Blamires (1992), while Bynum's *Holy Feast and Holy Fast* (1987) is a detailed discussion of women in relation to religion and food, which can be seen to underpin figures such as Custance, St. Cecile, Alison of the Miller's Tale and the Prioress. For those wishing to discover more about actual women in medieval society to compare with Chaucer's fictional presentations, Goldberg (ed. 1992) is a handy collection of essays, while Erler and Kowaleski (eds 1988) bridges the historical and theoretical study of women and is a good basis for any discussion of women and power.

In general, feminist terminology is marked by references to opposition, hierarchy (in particular patriarchy), determinism and gender divides. However, different branches of feminism have moved on in various ways: to address women's political position in society and hence their position in texts; to draw on psychoanalytic theories, on deconstruction and philosophy; to investigate the construction of gender, male as well as female. While some approaches point out where some or all of these concepts operate in texts, others focus on points where the expected divisions are broken down, or blurred. This broad range means that many prefer to speak of 'feminisms', to avoid implying that all femininst criticism is the same. More importantly, it is not true to say that any study of women in text is necessarily feminist.

Douglas' assertion in his 1513 prologue to Book 1 of his translation of Virgil's *Aeneid* that Chaucer was 'all womanis frend' (Kinghorn 1970: 163) and the Wife of Bath's declaration 'Experience, though noon auctorite' (*Tales*, III: 1) have often been the starting points for feminist investigations of Chaucer's texts. A good example is Diamond's essay 'Chaucer's Women and Women's Chaucer' (Diamond and Edwards 1988: 60–83) which discusses Chaucer's presentation of women, good and ill, finally concluding that, despite reservations, we should endorse Douglas' description.

Chaucer seems no more able to portray a female who is both virtuous and three-dimensional than he is able to portray a cleric who is both good and human. ... He means to be women's friend insofar as he can be, and it is this painfully honest effort, this unwillingness to be satisfied with the fomulas of his age, which we as feminists can honor in him.

(Diamond and Edwards (eds) 1977: 82–3)

The essay plays an important part in later twentieth-century appraisals of Chaucer and is joined in general outlook by Mann's volume in Harvester's Feminist Readings series (Mann 1991). Although not as explicitly feminist as the series title suggests, this is nonetheless a valuable, accessible and reasoned assessment of Chaucer in general feminist tones, which usefully identifies various literary forms and conventions associated with women which Chaucer uses. Central to Mann's reading is detailed exploration of Chaucer's use of passivity and suffering as it moves from the idealised women to the suffering hero. Despite the reservations some more rigorous feminists have about this book, it is nonetheless recommended reading for anyone interested in Chaucer's writing.

Of the more rigorously feminist critics Carolyn Dinshaw is one of the most influential. Her *Chaucer's Sexual Poetics* is a landmark text which thoroughly overhauls our understanding of Chaucer's literary models. Dinshaw focuses on the way specific activities have been gendered or have gender relations built into them. The movement of stories or ideas across texts is a case in point. This is shown to be a form of translation, where the source text is described in terms of a captive woman, who must be cleansed of her connections with her origins, before being absorbed into the new culture (Dinshaw 1989: 22–5). Reading practices are also scrutinised, as Dinshaw develops her case from the common habit of 'reading like a man' in the first chapter (focusing on *Troilus*) to the possibilities of interpreting in a less sexually or gender-determined fashion – the 'eunuch hermeneutics' of her last chapter (focusing on the Pardoner). When criticism returns to the familiar stamping ground of the representation of women in certain texts and genres after the more stringent feminism of critics such as Dinshaw, the effects are immediately apparent. Thus Crane's study, *Gender and Romance in Chaucer's 'Canterbury Tales'* (1994) is a far cry from Muscatine's study of Chaucer's use of romance traditions **[41, 162]**. For Crane, Chaucer's interest in the romance genre led to his interest in the concepts of gender, of how masculinity and feminity are created and sustained.

The world of romance is a basically homosocial one in which the bonds between men are strengthened by placing woman in a position of distant and separate Other. The female role is to be the object of lament and desire, and also to be absent. White in *Duchess* **[68]** quint-essentially fulfils this role by being both loved and dead. In discussing and describing her, the Dreamer and the Man in Black are brought together and the male, homosocial (as distinct from homosexual) bond is cemented. Simultaneously, heterosexual masculinity is confirmed in the desire for the absent woman. Crane takes this understanding of romance genre as her starting point and develops a reading of Chaucer which offers many insights into his texts. For example, the brotherhood between Arcite and Palamoun of The Knight's Tale is seen with fresh eyes when the focus is on the use of the lyrical address (apostrophe) commonly used by lovers to lament their position. The effect of such apostrophes is to isolate the speaker, while also purporting to address the love object, who, crucially, cannot hear the lyric. Crane points out that the two cousins use exactly this form when referring to each other when Arcite is released from prison:

> Although Arcite's lament addresses 'O deere cosyn Palamon' and Palamon's addresses 'Arcita, cosyn myn,' each speaks inconsolably to himself rather than to his brother, as the closing lines of each monologue indicate: Arcite ends his lament with a second apos-trophe not to Palamon but to the similarly absent beloved ('Syn that I may nat seen you, Emelye, / I nam but deed, ther nys no remedye'), and Palamon ends his lament with the third-person notation that he is dying 'For jalousie and fere of hym Arcite' (I: 1234, 1273–4, 1281, 1333). Romantic love has set each young man in lyric isolation from his brother as well as from his beloved.
>
> (Crane 1994: 51–52)

This extract illustrates how feminist criticism moves beyond the simple bounds of the study of female characters into the area of gender identity in general. Palamon and Arcite cast each other in the female, oppositional role to themselves and then confirm that placing through reference to their relation to Emelye.

Masculinity thus becomes a subject for feminist debate, out of which gender criticism is born, which also draws on queer theory. A convenient collection of essays, *Masculinities in Chaucer* (Beidler (ed.) 1998) offers a fair introduction to this relatively new area of literary criticism and its impact on Chaucer studies. In it Ingham's piece on The Knight's Tale builds directly on Crane's work and is a useful place to start. Ingham points out that Emelye is used to define more than just the relation between Palamon and Arcite: her weeping at the end of the Tale, which echoes that of the widows at the beginning, helps to bolster the image of Theseus as wise, moderate, compassionate even sensitive, but above all, manly. This manliness, however, seeks to differentiate itself from the destructive masculinity of Creon. Ingham thus presents a Theseus who strategically borrows feminine attributes in order to create the type of masculinity the situation requires: 'Emily's uncontrollable mourning is useful to Theseus's masculinity because he can again merge gender difference with gender similarity. He is thus marked as both sensitive and manly, neither overrun by the lethal excesses to which mourning women like Emily are subject, nor coldly immune to their pleas' (Beidler (ed.) 1998: 33).

The notion of gender identity being a performance rather than a fixed state, put forward by Judith Butler (1990 and 1993) has been taken up by gay criticism, which is beginning to lead to re-readings of Chaucer's creation of male identities in terms of troubling the boundaries between the sexes. Much of this kind of criticism is also deliberately self-aware, as the critic's own standing is regarded as central to their reading. This, too, is a habit formed by feminists, who sought to debunk the concept of the critic's objectivity. Readers interested in following this line might find Burger's essay a useful example of how such approaches can be adapted for a medieval text (Beidler (ed.) 1998:117–30).

More traditional feminism continues to have its effect, as arguments are reiterated over how positive Chaucer's female characters actually are (although this is naturally dependent on the critic's understanding of 'positive'). The general feminist debate about the uses of male language also continues. A fairly recent addition here comes from Cox, who argues, amongst other things, for a Wife of Bath who enters the competition for authority by using male language and thus is better described as 'quasi-feminist' than feminist (Cox 1997). Also related is the re-evaluation of topics whose interest to Chaucer has already been established. A case in point here would be the study of Chaucer's use of landscape, and in particular the literary theme of gardens, which Lewis began (Lewis 1936). The theme has recently been continued by Howes (1997), whose study is primarily historical, not feminist, as she studies the various uses of the garden topos in Chaucer's work. However, when considering the Knight's, Merchant's and Franklin's Tales she takes up the link between women and nature which has been established by feminist theorists and recently expanded by Ecofeminism.

The best introduction to the various theoretical viewpoints within general feminist criticism remains Moi (1985). There are also several anthologies of feminist readings of medieval literature in general (in addition to the books cited above) of which Evans and Johnson (1994) is especially recommended and contains a very useful further reading section, offering a brief over-view of feminist readings. Diamond and Edwards (1977) collect feminist essays on a variety of topics and usefully place feminist readings of Chaucer in a framework of general feminist critical activity.

(i) IMITATION, MODERNISATION, ALLUSION

Like biography, imitation bestows status on its subject: it says a great deal for Chaucer's standing that there is a group of late-medieval poets known as 'The Scottish Chaucerians'. They include Henryson (?1424–1506), Dunbar (?1456–1513) and Douglas (c.1475–1522), all of whom openly acknowledged their debt to Chaucer. Those interested in exploring them will find Kinghorn (1970) a good starting place. Since then, imitation of and allusion to Chaucer has continued, thus securing Chaucer's standing as 'presiding genius of English poetry', to use Krier's phrase (Krier (ed.) 1998: 1). One use to which imitation was put was to complete Chaucer's texts. The unfinished Tales within the Canterbury sequence, such as The Cook's Tale, were prime candidates for this treatment and indeed the open structure of the *Tales* as a whole invites additions. Cooper gives this area due consideration (Cooper 1996: 413–29), in which she also considers the afterlives of certain of the stories. Most interesting amongst these is the life of Catherine of Aragon by William Forrest, which is closely modelled on The Clerk's Tale to the point of including an explicit comparison between Catherine and Griselde, in which Catherine receives the greater praise as her trials were actual (Cooper 1996: 423).

In additon to conferring prestige, imitation and allusion act as a form of critical as well as creative response to the original text. Henryson's *Testament of Cresseid* is a case in point **[98]**. In it Henryson takes up Cresseyde's story with the provocative question 'Quha wait gif all that Chauceir wrait was trew?' (*Testament* 64 in Kinghorn 1970: 103). By asking who knows if everything that Chaucer wrote was true, Henryson refers directly to the kind of debate about authority and authenticity which pervades Chaucer's works, and also clears the way for his own, rather different, take on Cresseyde's story. His witty, skillful and far shorter poem continues Chaucer's tradition of combining different genres within one work. Cresseid's 'complyent', which is frequently quoted on its own, sits within the narrative in much the same way as the Man in Black's lyric does in Chaucer's *Duchess* (475–86).

Henryson's humour is perhaps a little more sardonic than Chaucer's, but the self-conscious consideration with which he treats Chaucer echoes Chaucer's own treatment of his authors and sources. It is this attitude to poetry and habit of aesthetic self-examination that Chaucer's imitators emulate, rather than simply parroting his verse form, and it is this which makes their imitations a form of criticism. Critical comparison of Chaucer's immediate successors and his own works can be found in the collection *Chaucer and Fifteenth-Century Poetry* (Boffey and Cowen (eds) 1991), elsewhere C. Martin offers an interesting consideration of the effect of Chaucer's poetics in her piece on *The House of Fame* (Krier 1998: 40–65).

Looking over the responses to Chaucer from his immediate inheritors, a noticeable cluster of terms becomes apparent, all describing Chaucer as one who brightened up English poetry with the freshness of his language and verse forms. Hoccleve's phrase 'ornat endytyng ... enlumynyng' (Furnivall 1897: 1973–4) is echoed by Lydgate, in Caxton's 'enbelysshyd, ornated and made faire' and Dunbar's 'fresch anamalit termes celicall'(all cited in Burrow 1969). Things change in 1700 with Dryden's Preface to his *Fables*, where Chaucer's achievements are admired despite the severe handicap of living 'in the dawning of our language', which meant the range of English terms and poetic forms was, in Dryden's view, necessarily restricted: 'the words are given up as a post not to be defended in our poet, because he wanted the modern art of fortifying' (Kinsley (ed.) 1962: 527). For Dryden, poetic skill demands elaborate phrasing, but even here the motif of Chaucer as one who brightens the English poetic scene is evident, albeit that he needs a little help: 'Chaucer, I confess, is a rough diamond, and must first be polished ere he shines'. Dryden proceeds to administer the required polish in his translations of a selection of the *Tales*: 'I have ... added somewhat of my own where I thought my author was deficient' (Kinsey (ed.) 1962: 532–3). The phrase could describe Chaucer's handling of his own sources.

The tradition of translation was notably continued by Pope, whose rendition of the Wife of Bath's Prologue (a section Dryden omitted archly as too coarse) deserves critical attention of its own. Dryden and Pope were not working in isolation, there is a noticeable cluster of modernisations of individual *Tales* in the eighteenth century, some of which have been recently collected together (Bowden 1991). Translation, adaptation and recasting continue in the twentieth century. In 1946 the BBC commissioned for radio broadcast a new verse translation of *The Canterbury Tales* from Neville Coghill, which brought Chaucer popularity. This translation was published by Penguin in 1951 and has not been out of print since. Andrea Newman's 'A Sense of Guilt' is a version of *Troilus* in which the Pandarus figure is a lecturer engaged in a new translation of Chaucer's *Troilus and Criseyde*. Newman is clearly expecting her audience to have some kind of reaction to the idea of Chaucer, even if they do not know his text. The same is true of Margaret Atwood's title for her science-fiction novel, *The Handmaid's Tale*. This text too addresses a listening audience and invites speculation about the ordering of its chapters, as the narrative supposedly comes from a set of unmarked audio cassette tapes. More obviously, Griselda in Caryl Churchill's play *Top Girls* is explicitly introduced as being drawn from Chaucer as well as Boccaccio (Churchill 1982), while Joanna Russ overtly, if somewhat wryly, alludes to Chaucer at the end of her feminist science fiction novel, *The Female Man*:

> Go, little book, trot through Texas and Vermont and Alaska and Mayland and Washington and Florida and Canada and England and France; bob a curtsey at the shrines of Friedan, Miller, Greer, Firestone and all the rest ...
> (Russ 1985: 213)

Churchill, Newman and Russ all take Chaucer as the starting point for their own inspiration in much the same way as Hoccleve did. Spenser, too, developed a new text from the basis of a single phrase: his great poem, *The Fairie Queene*, opens with a direct quotation from Chaucer's Tale of Sir Thopas: 'A gentile knight was pricking on the plain'. However, after that Spenser draws almost entirely on other medieval texts, primarily those relating to the stories of Arthur, thus ensuring that comparisons are rarely drawn between him and Chaucer.

If Frese is right that Chaucer is essentially an intertextual writer **[158]**, it is only fitting that his own works have become integral to latterday intertexuality. Certainly the persistence of Chaucerian allusion is a testament to his standing in our view of English literary heritage. From a critical point of view, research in this area marks a continued interest in the reception of Chaucer across time, rather than an insistence on asserting a single, unchanging, correct interpretation of his works.

A testament to the wide appeal and range of inspiration provided by Chaucer's works is the remarkable and beautiful edition of *The Canterbury Tales* illustrated by Burne-Jones and published by William Morris' Kelmscott Press in 1896. The text itself is carefully presented in a font designed to evoke our latter-day notions of the medieval world. Its clear, thick letters suggest elaborate handwriting and the quality of the paper is likewise thick and expensive. The illustrations are imaginative responses to Chaucer's text, but the decoration is not limited to simple pictures. Taking its cue from medieval illuminated manuscripts, the margins of the text are elaborately and appropriately decorated; for instance, the borders of *The Romance of the Rose* are full of cabbage roses. Both illustration and decoration thus reflect the priorities of the Arts and Crafts movement, in which Morris was a central figure. That movement sought to assert the value of handcrafted skills at a time of increasing mechanisation; hence its interest in things medieval and in particular in suggesting the look of books created before the age of printing. By selecting Chaucer's *Tales* for this luxurious treatment Morris and Burne-Jones were acknowledging the continuing influence this text has on the imagination of writers, designers, artists and readers alike.

CHRONOLOGY

Early 1340s Geoffrey Chaucer born, probably only son of John and Agnes Chaucer, wine merchants.

1346 Battle of Crécy.

1348 Black Death reaches England. Edward III founds Order of the Garter.

1356 English victory against France at Poitiers. King John of France captured, French court begins civilised imprisonment in England.

1357 GC a page in the household of the Countess of Ulster, wife of Lionel, son of Edward III.

1359–60 GC member of Prince Lionel's retinue in France; captured at Reims and ransomed in March 1360. Returns to France later in 1360.

1362 Parliament opened in English for the first time; English established as official language of law courts. GC possibly spending time in Inns of Court or Inns of Chancery.

1365/66 GC marries Philippa.

1366 Father dies; mother remarries. GC travels through Navarre.

Late 1360s GC translates all or some of *Le Roman de la Rose* (*The Romaunt of the Rose*).

1367 GC, now esquire in the royal household, granted 20 marks annuity. Around this time son, Thomas, born.

1368 Abroad on King's service; death of Blanche, wife of John of Gaunt.

1368–72 Somewhere between these dates GC writes *The Book of the Duchess*.

1369–72 In France several times with John of Gaunt and on military campaigns.

1372–73 Travels to Italy (Genoa and Florence) on diplomatic business. Possible first encounter with poetry of Dante, Boccaccio and Petrarch.

1374 Granted a gallon of wine per day for life; rent-free lifelong lease of property in Aldgate; is appointed controller of customs and receives £10 annually from John of Gaunt.

1376 Death of Edward, 'The Black Prince'.

1376–77 In France again on King's business.

1377	Death of Edward III; Richard II becomes King. First Poll Tax.
1378	The Great Schism: two Popes elected. GC in Milan negotiating with Bernabò Visconti. Likely date of *House*. Gower granted power of attorney for GC. GC successfully petitions for 1374 wine grant to be commuted to cash, (20 marks).
1379	Second Poll Tax.
1380	Cecily Champaign accuses GC of rape. Later he is released from any action regarding the accusation. GC's son Lewis, dedicatee of *Astrolabe*, born. Probable date of *Parliament* and *Palamoun and Arcite* (later rewritten as The Knight's Tale). Third Poll Tax.
1381	Death of GC's mother; The Peasants' Revolt. Possible date of *Troilus*, *Boece* and 'Lak of Stedfastnesse'.
1382	GC controller of Petty Custom.
1385	Member of peace commission in Kent, leaves London for Kent about this time.
1386	Gives up lease of Aldgate property; becomes MP for Kent; Testifies in the Scrope-Grosvenor trial, in which describes himself as being more than forty years old; resigns from Customs; around this time composes *Legend*.
1387	Death of wife, Philippa. GC in Calais. Around this time begins *Tales*.
1388	GC's exchequer annuity and wine grant of 1378 transferred to John Scalby.
1389	Appointed Clerk of the King's Works. Summoned for debt six times.
1390	Robbed three times in September.
1390s	Appointed deputy forester for North Petherton. Translates Innocent III's *De Miseria Condicionis Humane*.
1391	Writes *Astrolabe*; resigns as Clerk of Works.
1392	Likely date of *The Equatorie of Planetis*, arguably by GC.
1394	Granted royal annuity of £20.
1396	Probable date for 'Envoy to Bukton'.
1397	Granted tun of wine per year. Probable date for G. Prologue to *Legend*.
1398	Travels through England on King's 'arduous and urgent business'.
1399	Death of John of Gaunt in February; deposition of Richard II in September, accession of Henry IV. GC returns to London.

1400   25 October: death of GC, buried in Westminster Abbey (moved in 1556 to 'Poet's Corner').

BIBLIOGRAPHY

Primary sources and editions

Bennett, D.S. (ed.) (1960, reprinted 1972) *Chaucer, 'The Parlement of Foulys'*, Manchester: Manchester University Press.

Benson, L.D. (ed.) (1988) *The Riverside Chaucer*, Oxford: Oxford University Press.

Benson, L.D. and Andersson, T.M. (eds) (1971) *The Literary Context of Chaucer's Fabliaux: Texts and Translations*, Indianapolis and New York: Bobbs-Merrill.

Blake, N.F. (ed.) (1980) *The Canterbury Tales by Geoffrey Chaucer. Edited from the Hengwrt Manuscript*, London: Edward Arnold.

Brewer, D. (ed.) (1969) *Geoffrey Chaucer The Works 1532: with Supplementary Material from the Editions of 1542, 1561, 1598 and 1602*, London: Scolar Press.

Bryan, W.F. and Dempster, G. (eds) (1941, reprinted 1958) *Sources and Analogues of Chaucer's Canterbury Tales*, Chicago: University of Chicago Press, repr. Humanities Press.

Burne-Jones (illus.) (1989) *The Works of Geoffrey Chaucer Now Newly Imprinted*, London: The Kelmscott Press.

Crow, M.M and Olson, C.C. (eds) (1966) *Chaucer Life-Records,* Oxford: Clarendon Press.

Gordon, R.K. (ed. and trans.) (1934, reprinted 1978) *The Story of Troilus*, London, reprinted Toronto.

Kinghorn, A.M. (ed.) (1970) *The Middle Scots Poets*, London: Edward Arnold.

Kinsley, J. (ed.) (1962) *The Poems and Fables of John Dryden*, London: Oxford University Press.

Miller, R.P. (ed.) (1977) *Chaucer, Sources and Background*, Oxford: Oxford University Press.

Pace, G.B. and David, A. (eds) (1982) *A Variorum Edition of the Works of Geoffrey Chaucer* vol.v: *The Minor Poems*, Norman: University of Oklahoma Press.

Pearsall, D. and Cunnigham, I.C. (1977) *The Auchinleck Manuscript, National Library of Scotland Advocates' MS 19.2.1*, London: Scolar Press.

Phillips, H. and Havely, N. (eds) (1997) *Chaucer's Dream Poetry*, Longman Annotated Texts, London and New York: Longman.

Rand Schmidt, K.A. (1993) *The Authorship of the Equatorie of the Planetis*, Chaucer Studies XIX, Cambridge: Brewer.

Ruggiers, P.G. (general ed.) (1979 ongoing) *The Variorum Edition of the Works of Geoffrey Chaucer*, Oklahoma: Norman.

Windeatt, B. (ed.) (1982) *Chaucer's Dream Poetry: Sources and Analogues*, Cambridge and Totowa New Jersey: Brewer, Rowman and Littlefield.

—— (ed.) (1984) *Geoffrey Chaucer 'Troilus & Criseyde' a new edition of 'The Book of Troilus'*, London and New York: Longman.

Secondary sources

Aers, D. (1980) *Chaucer, Langland and the Creative Imagination*, London: Routledge and Kegan Paul.

—— (1986) *Chaucer*, Harvester New Readings, Brighton: The Harvester Press.

Anderson, J.J. (ed.) (1974, reprinted 1981) *Chaucer: The Canterbury Tales. A Casebook*, London: The Macmillan Press.

Andrew, M. (1991) *Critical Essays on Chaucer's Canterbury Tales*, Milton Keynes: The Open University Press.

Atwood, M. (1987) *The Handmaid's Tale*, London: Virago Press.

Barratt, A. (1992) *Women's Writing in Middle English*, Harlow: Longman.

Beidler, P.G. (ed.) (1998) *Masculinities in Chaucer*, Cambridge: D.S. Brewer.

Benson, C.D. (1986) *Chaucer's Drama of Style: Poetic Variety and Contrast in the Canterbury Tales*, Chapel Hill and London: University of North Carolina Press.

Benson, L.D. (1982) 'The Occasion of *The Parliament of Fowls*' in Benson and Wenzel (eds) (1982) 123–44.

Benson, L.D. and Wenzel, S. (eds) (1982) *The Wisdom of Poetry: Essays in Honor of Morton W. Bloomfield*, Michigan: Medieval Institute Publications.

Birney, E. (1985) *Essays on Chaucerian Irony*, ed. Beryl Rowland, Toronto, Buffalo, London: University of Toronto Press.

Blake, N.F. (1977) *The English Language in Medieval Literature*, London: J.M. Dent and Sons.

—— (1985) *The Textual Tradition of the Canterbury Tales*, London: Edward Arnold.

—— (1998) *A History of the English Language*, London: Macmillan.

Blamires, A. (ed.) (1992) with Pratt, K. and Marx, C.W., *Woman Defamed, Woman Defended*, Oxford: Oxford University Press.

Bloom, H. (ed.) (1988a) *Geoffrey Chaucer's 'The General Prologue to The Canterbury Tales'*, Modern Critical Interpretations, New York and Philadelphia: Chelsea House Press.

—— (1988b) *Geoffrey Chaucer's 'The Knight's Tale'*, Modern Critical Interpretations, New York and Philadelphia: Chelsea House Press.

—— (1988c) *Geoffrey Chaucer's 'The Pardoner's Tale'*, Modern Critical Interpretations, New York and Philadelphia: Chelsea House Press.

Boffey, J. and Cowen, J. (eds) (1991) *Chaucer and Fifteenth-Century Poetry*, London: King's College.

Boitani, P. (1977) *Chaucer and Boccaccio*, Oxford: Medium Aevum Monographs new series 8.

Boitani, P. (1984) *Chaucer and the Imaginary World of Fame*, Cambridge: D.S. Brewer.

—— (ed.) (1985) *Chaucer and the Italian Trecento*, London: Cambridge University Press.

—— and Torti, A. (eds) (1986) *Intellectuals and Writers in Fourteenth-Century Europe: The J.A.W. Bennett Memorial Lectures, 1984*, Tübingen and Cambridge: D.S. Brewer.

Bowden, B. (ed.) (1991) *Eighteenth-Century Modernisations from the Canterbury Tales*, Cambridge: D.S. Brewer.

Brewer, D.S. (1978a) *Chaucer and his World*, London: Eyre Methuen.

—— (1978b) *Chaucer: the Critical Heritage*, 2 vols. London: Routledge and Kegan Paul.

—— (1998) *A New Introduction to Chaucer*, 2nd edn, London and New York: Longman.

Brown, P. (1994) *Chaucer at Work: the Making of the Canterbury Tales*, London and New York: Longman.

Burrow, J.A. (1969) *Geoffrey Chaucer: A Critical Anthology*, Harmondsworth: Penguin.

—— (1971, reprinted 1992) *Ricardian Poetry: Chaucer, Gower, Langland and the 'Gawain' Poet*, London: Routledge and Kegan Paul, reprinted Harmondsworth: Penguin.

—— (1982) *Medieval Writers and Their Work: Middle English Literature and its Background 1100–1500*, Oxford: Oxford University Press.

—— (1984) *Essays on Medieval Literature*, Oxford: Clarendon Press.

Butler, J. (1990) *Gender Trouble: Feminism and the Subversion of Identity*, New York and London: Routledge.

—— (1993) *Bodies That Matter: On the Discursive Limits of Sex*, New York and London: Routledge.

Cannon, C. (1998) *The Making of Chaucer's English: A Study of Words*, Cambridge: Cambridge University Press.

Carruthers, M. (1990) *The Book of Memory. A Study of Memory in Medieval Culture*, Cambridge: Cambridge University Press.

Churchill, C. (1982) *Top Girls*, London: Reed.

Coghill, N. (1951) *Chaucer's 'The Canterbury Tales'*, Harmonsworth: Penguin.

Cooper, H. (1984) *The Structure of the Canterbury Tales*, Georgia: University of Georgia Press.

—— (1996) *The Canterbury Tales*, 2nd edn, Oxford Guides to Chaucer, Oxford: Oxford University Press.

Cottle, B.(1969) *The Triumph of English 1350–1400*, London: Blandford Press.

Courtenay, W.J. (1987) *Schools & Scholars in Fourteenth-Century England*, Princeton: Princeton University Press.

Coulton, G.C. (1908) *Chaucer and his England*, London: Methuen, reprinted 1998, Twickenham: Senate, Tiger Books.

Cox, C. (1997) *Gender and Language in Chaucer*, Gainesville: University of Florida Press.

Crane, S. (1994) *Gender and Romance in Chaucer's 'Canterbury Tales'*, Princeton: Princeton University Press.

Crotch, W.B.J. (1928) *The Prologues and Epilogues of William Caxton*, Early English Text Society, original series 176, London: Oxford University Press.

Dane, J.A. (1998) *Who Is Buried in Chaucer's Tombὲ: Studies in the Reception of Chaucer's Book*, East Lansing: Michigan State University Press.

David, A. (1976) *The Strumpet Muse: Art and Morals in Chaucer's Poetry*, Bloomington: Indiana University Press.

—— (1982) 'An ABC to the Style of the Prioress' in Carruthers, M.J. and Kirk, E.D. *Acts of Interpretation: The Text in its Contexts 700–1600*, London: Pilgrim Books, 147–57.

Delany, S. (1972) *Chaucer's 'House of Fame': The Poetics of Skeptical Fideism*, Chicago and London: University of Chicago Press.

—— (1981) 'Politics and the Paralysis of Poetic Imagination in *The Physician's Tale*', *Studies in the Age of Chaucer*, vol. 3, 47–60.

—— (1990) *Medieval Literary Politics: Shapes of Ideology*, Manchester: Manchester University Press.

—— (1994) *The Naked Text: Chaucer's 'Legend of Good Women'*, Berkeley: University of California Press.

Dentith, S. (1995) *Bakhtinian Thought: An Introductory Reader*, London: Routledge.

Diamond, A. and Edwards, L.R (eds) (1977, reprinted 1988) *The Authority of Experience: Essay in Feminist Criticism*, Amherst: University of Massachusetts Press.

Dinshaw, C. (1989) *Chaucer's Sexual Poetics*, Madison: University of Wisconsin Press.

Dobson, R.B. (1982) 'Remembering the Peasants' Revolt' in W.H. Liddell and R.G.E. Woods (eds) *Essex and the Great Revolt of 1381* Chelmsford: Essex Records Office.

—— (1983) *The Peasants' Revolt of 1381*, 2nd edn, London: Macmillan.

Donaldson, E.T. (1970) *Speaking of Chaucer*, London: Athlone Press.

Doob, P. (1990) *The Idea of the Labyrinth from Classical Antiquity through the Middle Ages*, Ithaca, New York: Cornell University Press.

Dyer, C. (1994) *Everyday Life in Medieval England*, London: The Hambledon Press.

Edwards, A.S.G. (ed.) (1984) *Middle English Prose: A Critical Guide to Major Authors and Genres*, New Jersey: Rutgers University Press.

Edwards, R. (ed.) (1994) *Art and Context in Late Medieval English Narrative: Essays in Honor of Robert Worth Frank, Jr.*, Cambridge: Brewer.

Ellis, S. (ed.) (1998) *Chaucer: The Canterbury Tales*, Longman Critical Readers, London and New York: Longman.

Erler, M. and Kowaleski, K. (eds) (1988) *Women and Power in the Middle Ages*, Athens and London: University of Georgia Press.

Evans, R. and Johnson, L. (eds) (1994) *Feminist Readings in Middle English Literature: The Wife of Bath and All Her Sect*, London: Routledge.

Ford, B. (ed.) (1982) *The New Pelican Guide to English Literature. Part One: Medieval Literature: Chaucer and the Alliterative Tradition*, Harmondsworth: Penguin.

Frese, D.W. (1991) *An 'Ars Legendi' for Chaucer's 'Canterbury Tales'*, Gainesville: University of Florida Press.

Furnivall, F.J. (1868) *A Temporary Preface to the Six-Text Edition of Chaucer's Canterbury Tales*, The Chaucer Society, London: Trübner & Co.

Furnivall, F.J. (ed.) (1897) *Hoccleve's Works: The Regement of Princes and fourteen minor poems*, Early English Text Society, extra series 72, London: Kegan Paul.

Furnivall, F.J. (ed.) (1900) *Life Records of Chaucer*, part 2, London: Chaucer Society.

Gardner, J. (1977) *The Life and Times of Chaucer*, London: Jonathan Cape.

Gellrich, J.M. (1985) *The Idea of the Book in the Middle Ages*, Ithaca and London: Cornell University Press.

Gibson, M.T. (ed.) (1981) *Boethius, His Life, Thought and Influence*, Oxford: Basil Blackwell.

Godwin, W. (1804) *Life of Geoffrey Chaucer, The Early English Poet*, 2nd edn, 4 vols, London: Richard Phillips.

Goldberg, P.J.P. (ed) (1992) *Woman is a Worthy Wight: Women in English Society c.1200–1500*, Stroud: Alan Sutton.

Gordon, I. (1970) *The Double Sorrow of Troilus: A Study of Ambiguities in 'Troilus and Criseyde'*, Oxford: Clarendon.

Hahn, T. and Kaeuper, R.W. (1983) 'Text and Context: Chaucer's *Friar's Tale*', *Studies in the Age of Chaucer*, vol. 5, 67–101.

Hansen, E.T. (1992) *Chaucer and the Fictions of Gender*, Berkeley: University of California Press.

Hardman, P. (1994) '*The Book of the Duchess* as a Memorial Monument', *Chaucer Review* XXVIII, 205–17.

Havely, N. (1980) *Chaucer's Boccaccio: Sources of 'Troilus' and the Knight's and Franklin's Tales*. Chaucer Studies 3, Cambridge and Totowa, NJ: Brewer, Rowman & Littlefield.

Howard, D. (1976) *The Idea of the Canterbury Tales*, Berkeley, Los Angeles and London: University of California Press.

—— (1978) *Chaucer and the Medieval World*, London: Weidenfeld and Nicolson, published in USA as *Chaucer: His Life, His Works, His World*, New York: E.P. Dutton.

Howes, L. (1997) *Chaucer's Gardens and the Language of Convention*, Gainesville: University of Florida Press.

Hussey, M. (1968) *Chaucer's World: A Pictorial Companion*, Cambridge: Cambridge University Press.

Jacobus de Voragine. Graesse, T. (ed.) (1890, reprinted 1969) *Legenda Aurea*, Leipzig 3rd edn, reprinted Osnabrück, 1969.

Jones, T. (1980) *Chaucer's Knight: the Portrait of a Medieval Mercenary*, London: Weidenfeld and Nicholson.

Jouve, N.W. (1991) *White Woman Speaks With Forked Tongue: Criticism as Autobiography*, London: Routledge.

Kaske, R.M. (1979) 'Clericus Adam and Chaucer's Adam Scriveyn' in Vasta, E. and Thundy, Z. (eds) *Chaucerian Problems and Perspectives*, Notre Dame: University of Notre Dame Press, 114–18.

Kean, P.M. (1972) *Chaucer and the Making of English Poetry*, 2 vols, London: Routledge and Kegan Paul.

Keen, M. (1984) *Chivalry*, New Haven: Yale University Press.

Kelley, H.A. (1986) 'The Non-tragedy of Arthur' in Kratzmann, G. and Simpson, J. (eds) *Medieval English Religious And Ethical Literature*, Woodbridge: D.S. Brewer, 92–114.

Kennedy, R. (1998) 'Re-creating Chaucer' in Gould, W. and Staley, T.F. (eds) *Writing the Lives of Writers*, London: Macmillan Press Ltd, 54–67.

Kermode, J. (1999) 'Sentiment and Survival: Family and Friends in Late Medieval English Towns', *Journal of Family History* 24,1: 5–18.

Kittredge, G.L. (1915, reprinted 1970) *Chaucer and His Poetry*, Cambridge: Harvard University Press.

Koff, L.M. (1988) *Chaucer and the Art of Storytelling*, Berkeley and Los Angeles: University of California Press.

Kolve, V.A. (1984) *Chaucer and the Imagery of Narrative: the First Five Canterbury Tales*, Stanford and London: Edward Arnold.

Krier, T.M. (ed.) (1998) *Refiguring Chaucer in the Renaissance*, Gainesville: University of Florida Press.

Lawton, D. (1985) *Chaucer's Narrators*, Chaucer Studies XIII, Cambridge: D.S. Brewer.

Leff, G. (1958, reprinted 1962) *Medieval Thought: St. Augustine to Ockham*, Harmondsworth: Penguin.

Leicester, H.M. (1980) 'The Art of Impersonation: A General Prologue to the *Canterbury Tales*', *PMLA* 95, 46–61, reprinted in Bloom (1988) and Andrew (1991).

—— (1987) 'Oure Tonges *Différance*: Textuality and Deconstruction in Chaucer' in Finke, L.A. and Shichtman, M.B. (eds) *Medieval Texts and Contemporary Readers*, London: Cornell University Press, 15–26.

—— (1990) *The Disenchanted Self: Representing the Subject in the 'Canterbury Tales'*, Berkeley and Los Angeles: University of California Press.

Lewis, C.S. (1936) *The Allegory of Love: A Study in Medieval Tradition*, London: Oxford University Press.

Lindhal, C. (1989) *Earnest Games: Folkloric Patterns in the Canterbury Tales*, Bloomington and Indianapolis: Indiana University Press.

Machan, T.W. (1985) *Techniques of Translation: Chaucer's Boece*, London: Pilgrim Books.

Manly, J.M. (1926) 'Chaucer and the Rhetoricians', *Proceedings of the British Academy* 12: 95–113, reprinted in Schoek and Taylor (1960), 268–90.

—— and Rickert, E. (eds) (1940) *The Text of the Canterbury Tales*, 8 vols, Chicago: University of Chicago Press.

Mann, J. (1991) *Geoffrey Chaucer*, London: Harvester Wheatsheaf.

—— (1973) *Chaucer and Medieval Estates Satire*, Cambridge: Cambridge University Press.

Martin, P. (1990) *Chaucer's Women: Nuns, Wives and Amazons*, London: Macmillan.

Mehl, D. (1986) *Geoffrey Chaucer: An Introduction to His Narrative Poetry*, Cambridge: Cambridge University Press.

Mersand, J. (1937) *Chaucer's Romance Vocabulary*, New York: Comet Press.

Minnis, A.J. (1981) 'Aspects of the Medieval French and English Translations of the *De Consolatione Philosophiae*' in Gibson M.T. (ed.).

—— (1982) *Chaucer and Pagan Antiquity*, Chaucer Studies 8, Cambridge: D.S. Brewer.

—— (1986) 'Chaucer's Pardoner and the Office of Preacher' in Boitani and Torti (eds).

—— (1988) *Medieval Theories of Authorship: Scholastic Literary Attitudes in the Later Middle Ages*, 2nd edn, Aldershot: Wildwood House.

—— (1993) (ed.) *Chaucer's Boece and the Medieval Tradition of Boethius*, Chaucer Studies 18, Cambridge: D.S. Brewer.

—— (1995) *Chaucer's Shorter Poems*, Oxford Guides to Chaucer, Oxford: Clarendon Press.

Moi, T. (1985) *Sexual/Textual Politics*, London: Methuen.

Morgan, G. (ed.) (1980) *Geoffrey Chaucer: The Franklin's Tale from the Canterbury Tales*, London: Hodder and Stoughton.

Morse, D. (1981) 'Understanding the Man in Black', *Chaucer Review* 15: 204–8.

Muscatine, C. (1957) *Chaucer and the French Tradition*, Berkeley and Los Angeles: University of California Press.

Newman, A. (1989) *A Sense of Guilt*, Harmonsdworth: Penguin.

North, J.D. (1988) *Chaucer's Universe*, Oxford: Clarendon Press.

Norton-Smith, J. (1974) *Geoffrey Chaucer*, London: Routledge and Kegan Paul.

Olson, G. (1986–87), 'Chaucer's Monk: The Rochester Connection', *Chaucer Review* 21: 246–56.

Owen, C.A. (1977) *Pilgrimage and Storytelling in 'The Canterbury Tales': the Dialect of 'Ernest' and 'Game'*, Norman: University of Oklahoma Press.

—— (1991) *The Manuscripts of 'The Canterbury Tales'*, Chaucer Studies XVII, Cambridge: D.S. Brewer.

Papka, C.R. (1998) 'Transgression, the End of Troilus and the Ending of Chaucer's *Troilus and Criseyde*', *Chaucer Review* 32, 3: 267–89.

Patterson, L. (1987) *Negotiating the Past: The Historical Understanding of Medieval Literature*, Wisconsin: University of Wisconsin Press.

—— (ed.) (1990) *Literary Practice and Social Change in Britain, 1380–1530*, Berkeley, Los Angeles and Oxford: University of California Press.

—— (1991) *Chaucer and the Subject of History*, London: Routledge.

Payne, R.O. (1963) *The Key of Remembrance: A Study of Chaucer's Poetics*, New Haven: Yale University Press.

Pearsall, D. (1985) *The Canterbury Tales*, London: Allen and Unwin.

—— (1992) *The Life of Geoffrey Chaucer: A Critical Biography*, Oxford: Blackwell.

Peck, R. (1975) 'Public Dreams and Private Myths: Perspective in Middle English Literature', *PMLA* 90: 461–8.

Phillips, H. (2000) *An Introduction to the Canterbury Tales: Reading, Fiction, Context*, London: Macmillan Press.

Power, E. (1975) *Medieval Women*, Cambridge: Cambridge University Press.

Richardson, J. (1970) *Blameth Nat Me: A Study of Imagery in Chaucer's Fabliaux*, Mouton Studies in English Literature 58, The Hague: Mouton.

Rigby, S.H. (1996) *Chaucer in Context*, Manchester: Manchester University Press.

Robertson, D.W. (1962) *A Preface to Chaucer: Studies in Medieval Perspective*, Princeton: Princeton University Press.

Robinson, I. (1971) *Chaucer's Prosody: A Study of the Middle English Verse Tradition*, Cambridge: Cambridge University Press.

—— (1972) *Chaucer and the English Tradition*, London: Cambridge University Press.

Rooney, A. (1989) *Geoffrey Chaucer: A Guide Through The Critical Maze*, Bristol: Bristol University Press.

Ross, D. (1984) 'The Play of Genres in *The Book of the Duchess*', *Chaucer Review* IXX:1-13.

Ruud, J. (1992) *'Many a Song and Many a Lecherous Lay': Tradition and Individuality in Chaucer's Lyric Poetry*, Garland Studies in Medieval Literature 6, New York and London: Garland.

Rudd, G.A. (1994) *Managing Language in 'Piers Plowman'*, Piers Plowman Studies IX, Cambridge: D.S. Brewer.

Rudd, N. (1994) *The Classical Tradition in Operation*, Toronto: University of Toronto Press.

Russ, J. (1985) *The Female Man*, London: The Women's Press.

Salu, M. (ed.) (1979) *Essays on 'Troilus and Criseyde'*, Cambridge: D.S. Brewer.

Scattergood, J. (1987) *'Chaucer a Bukton* and Proverbs', *Nottingham Medieval Studies*, 31: 98–107.

Schoeck, R. and Taylor, J. (1960) *Chaucer Criticism*, 2 vols, Notre Dame and London: University of Notre Dame Press.

Schlauch, M. (1956) *English Medieval Literature and its Social Foundations*, London: Oxford Unversity Press.

Spearing, A.C. (1985) *Medieval to Renaissance in English Poetry*, Cambridge: Cambridge University Press.

Spurgeon, C.F.E. (1925) *Five Hundred Years of Chaucer Criticism and Allusion, 1357– 1900*, 3 vols, Cambridge: Cambridge University Press.

Steadman, J.M. (1972) *Disembodied Laughter: 'Troilus' and the Apotheosis Tradition*, Los Angeles and London: University of California Press.

Stone, B. (1987) *Chaucer*, reprinted 1989 in Penguin Critical Studies series, London: Penguin.

Strohm, P. (1989) *Social Chaucer*, Cambridge, MA: Harvard University Press.

Szittya, P.R. (1986) *The Antifraternal Tradition in Medieval Literature*, Princeton: Princeton University Press.

Thynne, F. (1598) *Chaucer: animaduersions uppon the annotacions and corrections of some imperfections of impressiones of Chaucer's workes*, ed. Kingsley, G.H., Early English Text Society os 9, 1865, London: N. Trübner & Co.

Walsh, P.G. (1999) (ed. and trans.) *Boethius: The Consolation of Philosophy*, Oxford: Clarendon.

Wetherbee, W. (1984) *Chaucer and the Poets: An Essay on 'Troilus and Criseyde'*, Ithaca and London.

Wimsatt, J.I. (1968) *Chaucer and the French Love Poets*, Chapel Hill: University of North Carolina Press.

—— (1991) *Chaucer and his French Contemporaries*, Toronto: University of Toronto Press.

Wogan-Browne, J. and Burgess, G.S. (trans.) (1996) *Virgin Lives and Holy Deaths: Two Exemplary Biographies for Anglo-Norman Women*, London: Dent, Everyman.

Wood, C. (1970) *Chaucer and the Country of the Stars*, Princeton: Princeton University Press.

Woolf, R. (1986) ed. O'Donoghue, H., *Art and Doctrine: Essays on Medieval Literature*, London: The Hambleton Press.

Young, R. (1981) *Untying the Text: A Post-Structuralist Reader*, London: Routledge and Kegan Paul.

Websites

Chaucer Metapage: http://www.unc.edu/dept/chaucer/index.html
Studies in the Age of Chaucer: http://ncs.rutgers.edu/sac.html
New Chaucer Society Homepage: http://ncs.rutgers.edu

INDEX

ABC, An 47, 48, 49–50, 51, 98, 143
'Adam Scriveyn' *see* 'Chaucer's
    Wordes Unto Adam, His Owne
    Scriveyn'
Aers, David 79, 95, 144, 172–3
Aesop 9, 11
Anelida and Arcite 16, 22, 51, 52–3,
    77
Aristotle 39, 72, 83
Augustine 72
Authority 63, 72 153, 164, 178

Benson, Larry 108
Bakhtin, Mikhail 196–70
Bible 38, 39, 63, 72, 121
Black Death (plague) 7, 34, 41
Blanche (wife of John of Gaunt)
    14, 50, 65, 68
Boccaccio 10, 15, 16, 40–1, 48, 52,
    89–91, 100, 101, 105, 110, 111,
    126, 181
Boece 20, 60, 83–5, 97, 111, 139,
    149
Boethius (see also *Boece*) 20, 39, 55,
    57, 58, 76, 81, 83–4, 149
Book of the Duchess, The 14, 16, 22,
    31, 41, 61–2, 65–71, 73, 75, 77,
    85, 94, 174, 177, 179
Brewer, Derek S. 8, 28, 85, 89 92,
    103, 133
Brigham, Nicholas 6, 27

Canterbury Tales, The as a whole 5,
    13, 22, 25, 35, 42, 47, 77, 100–1,
    103, 105, 106–7, 148, 149, 153,
    154, 155, 157, 158, 166, 170,
    176, 179, 180, 181–2; Canon 37,
    144; 'Canon's Yeoman's Tale'
    143, 144–6; 'Clerk's Tale' 16–
    17, 40, 119, 120, 122, 126–7,
    129, 139, 141, 153, 172–3, 174,
    179, 181; Cook 117, 146;
    'Cook's Tale' 117–8, 179;
    Franklin 21, 168; 'Franklin's
    Tale' 31, 47, 87, 94, 99, 106,

112, 122, 123, 129, 130–2, 178;
    Friar 123, 167, 168; 'Friar's Tale'
    123–5; 'General Prologue'
    107–10, 161, 167–8; Host 109,
    117, 118, 129, 132, 133, 134,
    138, 144, 148; Knight 30, 108,
    109, 110, 168; 'Knight's Tale'
    38, 40, 52, 57, 85, 102, 107,
    110–13, 114, 116, 117, 118, 131,
    140, 141, 147, 148, 163–4,
    177–8; 'Manciple's Tale' 146–7,
    162; 'Man of Law's Tale' 13, 25,
    100, 101, 106, 118–20, 153, 175;
    'Melibee, Tale of' 119, 138,
    139–40, 165; Miller 108, 112,
    146; 'Miller's Tale' 47, 80,
    113–15, 116, 117, 118, 120, 124,
    128, 147, 171, 174; Monk 108,
    112, 128; 'Monk's Tale' 16, 96,
    101, 140–1; 'Nun's Priest's Tale'
    21, 34, 63, 81, 106, 141–2, 143,
    164; Pardoner 108, 167, 168;
    'Pardoner's Tale' 25, 106, 133–5,
    144, 145, 164; Parson 108, 149;
    'Parson's Tale' 38, 39, 88, 120,
    135, 143, 146, 147, 148–9, 161,
    165; 'Physician's Tale' 119,
    132–3, 174; Plowman 108;
    'Prioress's Tale' 9, 136–8, 175;
    Reeve 108, 115, 146; 'Reeve's
    Tale' 115–17, 124, 128, 161;
    'Second Nun's Tale' 101, 102,
    106, 107, 142–4, 145, 148, 175;
    Shipman 120; 'Shipman's Tale'
    64, 106, 135–6; *'Sir Thopas'* 64,
    138–9, 148, 181; Squire 30, 120;
    'Squire's Tale' 129–30, 131, 147;
    Summoner 123, 124;
    'Summoner's Tale' 125–6; Wife
    of Bath 60, 99, 108, 120, 121,
    168, 174, 178; 'Wife of Bath's
    Prologue' 34, 94, 120–2, 134,
    144, 164, 167, 175, 180; 'Wife
    of Bath's Tale' 31, 58, 94, 106,
    122–3, 125, 130, 131, 135

Carruthers, Mary 71, 113
Cato 72
Caxton 156, 157, 161, 170, 180
Champaign, Cecily 17–18, 20
Chaucer, Geoffrey birth, 5–6, 12;
   death 6, 26–7; descendants 27;
   education 8–13; father 6, 7, 13,
   18; Grosvenor/Scrope trial 5,
   12, 22; at Inns of Court 13;
   mother 7, 33; sons 18, 27, 86;
   supposed sister 7; travels
   14–17, 22; wife 12, 14–16
Chaucer Society 159–60
'Chaucer's Wordes Unto Adam,
   His Owne Scriveyn' 60, 93, 96,
   153, 159
Clarence, Lionel, Duke of 10–13
Cloud of Unknowyng 38, 39
Classical tradition see Latin
Coghill, Nevil 180–1
'Complaint of Chaucer to His
   Purse, The' 54–5
'Complaint of Mars' 52, 53, 54
'Complaint of Venus' 51–2
'Complaint to His Lady, A' 47, 51
'Complaint Unto Pity' 48, 50, 53
Cooper, Helen 114, 115, 117, 118,
   122, 124, 128, 133, 135, 136,
   137, 139, 144
Conches, William of 84
Coulton, George 31
Courtly love see also romance
   32–3, 42, 67–8, 80, 94–5, 100,
   105
Courtnay, William 10
Crane, Susan 176–7

Dante 10, 11, 15, 16, 28, 40, 48,
   71, 73, 75–6
Deguilleville, Guillaume 50
Delany, Sheila 81, 132, 142, 173–4
Diamond, Arlyn 175–6
Dido 73 104, 105
Dinshaw, Carolyn 120, 135, 176
Donaldson, E. Talbot 91, 92, 142,
   166, 169,
Douglas, Gavin 175, 179
Dream of Scipio 61, 63, 79
Dryden, John 1, 153, 161, 180
Dunbar, William 41, 179, 180

Editing/Editions 153, 155, 157–60
Edward III 29
Edward, Prince of Wales, the Black
   Prince 29–30
Ellesmere manuscript 106, 107,
   120 158
Equatorie of Planetis, The 88–9, 106,
   157

Fabliau 40, 113, 115, 117, 12 8,
   135, 163
'Former Age, The' 55–6
'Fortune' 55, 57
Fortune see also 'Fortune' 57, 69,
   75, 83, 85, 97, 111, 140, 141
French 10, 11, 13, 39, 40, 41–2,
   139, 155, 161, 162, 163, 176
Frese, Dolores 158, 181
Froissart 41–2, 109
Friars 37, 167
Furnivall, F. J. 8, 156, 159

Garden see also 'Romance of the
   Rose' 63–4, 79, 82, 178
Gaunt, John of 12, 13–15, 16, 21,
   25, 27, 33, 66, 68, 103
Gellrich, Jesse, 71
'Gentilesse' 55, 58–9, 131
Godwin, William 5, 156
Golden Legend, The 101
Gower, John 17, 39, 92–3, 97, 101,
   105, 119, 120
Granson, Oton de 41, 51, 52

Hengwrt manuscript 106, 158
Hansen, Elaine Tuttle 173
Henry IV, Bolingbroke 26, 27, 55,
   59
Henryson, Robert 42, 98, 179–80
Hilton, Walter 38
Hoccleve, Thomas 28, 42, 153,
   161, 180, 181
Homer 72, 74, 89, 95, 164
Horace 60
House of Fame, The 13, 22, 40, 53,
   57, 60, 61–2, 71–7, 79, 97, 136,
   141, 147, 153, 157, 180
Howard, David 156
Hundred Years War 5, 12, 29

Italian 10, 11, 91, 163

Kermode, Jenny 33
Kittredge, George 95

Julian of Norwich 38, 148

Lai 40, 120, 122–3, 130
'Lak of Stedfastness' 21, 55, 56
Langland 35, 39
Latin 9, 11, 13, 39, 83, 132, 134,
    139, 161, 163, 164
Leff, Gordon 37
Legend of Good Women, The 22, 24,
    25, 53, 61, 62, 65, 76, 81–2, 98,
    99, 100–5, 106, 107, 109, 132,
    142, 153, 155, 173–4
Leicester, H. Marshall 112, 168–9
'Lenvoy de Chaucer a Bukton'
    59–60
'Lenvoy de Chaucer a Scogan' 59
Lewis, C. S. 95
Lionel *see* Clarence
Lollards 38, 39
London 7–8, 15–16, 18–20, 34, 117
Lucan 89
Lydgate, John 41, 82, 161 180

Machaut, Guillaume de 57, 66, 67
Malory, Thomas 31
Mann, Jill 112, 131, 139, 141, 167–
    9, 176
Maths 9–10, 69, 154, 172–3, 177,
    195
Mehl, Dieter 167
Minnis, Alastair 56, 67, 165

Narrators 63, 73, 79, 82, 91, 92,
    100, 109, 120, 130, 155, 165–9
North, John 87, 120, 131
Norton-Smith, John 59–60

Ockam, William [of] 37
'Of the Wreched Engyndrynge of
    Mankynde' 25, 149
Ovid 9, 11, 53, 55, 61, 65, 66, 67,
    72, 73, 76, 89, 104, 146

Parliament of Fowls, The 22, 61, 62,
    64, 77–81, 102, 163

Patterson, Lee 53, 113, 117, 129,
    130, 170–1
Pearsall, Derek 5, 6, 17, 18, 24, 27,
    28, 82, 89, 100, 144, 156
Peasant's Revolt 5, 20–2, 23, 34,
    79, 142
Petrarch 10, 15, 16, 40, 126, 129
Phillipa, Queen 12, 30
Plague *see* Black Death
Plato 39, 72, 83
Pope 180
Puttenham, George 156

'Retraction' 47, 93, 105, 148,
    149–50, 153
Richard II 15, 16, 21–6; *passim* 30,
    33, 41, 48, 56, 58, 78, 82, 103,
    139
Robertson, D. W. 170–1
Romance 40, 63–65, 69, 89, 94,
    112, 113, 120, 129, 131, 138,
    140, 176–7
Roman de la Rose [*Romance of the
    Rose*] 22, 32, 41, 55, 58, 61, 62,
    69, 79, 84, 102, 121, 122, 132,
    146
Romaunt of the Rose 22, 41, 61,
    62–5, 68, 79, 102, 157, 182
'Rosemounde, To' 48–9, 56
Ross, Diane 69
Russ, Joanne 181

Scattergood, John 56, 69
Sir Gawain and the Green Knight 31
    39
Speght, Thomas 5, 13, 50, 156
Statius 89
Skeat, William Walter 157
Strohm, Paul 156, 171–2
Spenser, Edmund 181

Thynne, William 157
Tragedy *see* 'Monk's Tale' and
    Troilus and Criseyde
Treatise on the Astrolabe, A 18, 25,
    27, 81, 86–8, 106, 131, 149, 153
Trent, Nicholas 84
Troilus and Criseyde 20, 22, 31, 38,
    39, 40, 49, 52, 53, 59, 60, 63, 67,
    77, 79, 81, 85, 87, 88, 89–100,

109, 112, 119, 140, 141, 153,
155, 159, 165, 166, 167, 170,
176, 181
'Truth' 55, 58, 131, 143
Tyrwhitt, Thomas 157, 159

Urry, John 5, 157, 159
Ulster, Elizabeth de Burgh,
Countess of 10–13
Usk, Thomas 84

Virgil 9, 11, 55, 73, 76, 164, 175
Visconti, Bernabò 16, 126, 141

Wood, Chauncy 87
'Womanly Noblesse' 47
Wyclif, 38, 39